# Cutting Edge PowerPoint For Dummies®

**Cheat Sheet**

## Maximum Text Contrast

Dark background:

- Dark text provides the worst contrast.
- Text of a similar color provides a better contrast but is still not legible.
- Light text provides the best contrast.

Light background:

- Light text provides the worst contrast.
- Text of a similar color provides a better contrast but is still not legible.
- Dark text provides the best contrast.

### Safe Background Colors

| Color | Image |
|---|---|
| Blue | Endurance, capability, and vastness |
| White | Peace and blank space |
| Black | Sophistication |
| Violet and purple | Luxury, opulence, spirituality |
| Gray | Balance and stability |

## RGB Color Model

RGB is a *color model* that computers understand. Each color has a numeric value that ranges from 0 to 255.

- When all three RGB values are 0, you get black.
- When all three RGB values are 255, you get white.

You can use different combinations of any three integers between 0 and 255 to create about 16 million shades of color. These are some color values:

- **Blue:** R:0; G:0; B:255
- **Green:** R:0; G:255; B:0
- **Red:** R:255; G:0; B:0
- **Yellow:** R:255; G:255; B:0
- **Orange:** R:255; G:153; B:0

## Audio Formats

PowerPoint can accept and play almost all the standard audio formats including the ones listed here:

- **WAV:** This is the most common sound file format on Microsoft Windows. PowerPoint works well with this type.
- **MP3:** MP3s can be inserted and played inside PowerPoint — but are a no-no for slide transition sounds.
- **WMA, ASF:** The same concepts as MP3 apply to WMA, but since it is a proprietary Microsoft format, stay away from it if your presentations need to be shown on a Mac.
- **MID or MIDI:** These are actual music notations that your computer's sound card interprets and plays in real time. To enjoy this type of sound, you should have a high-fidelity sound card that retails for over a hundred dollars. Anything less than that will still do a good job unless you start comparing the sound outputs!
- **AIFF and AU:** These are the other sound formats that PowerPoint accepts — however, it's best you leave them alone — and they'll probably leave you alone too!

*For Dummies: Bestselling Book Series for Beginners*

# Cutting Edge PowerPoint® For Dummies®

## Video Formats

There is a plethora of video formats that PowerPoint can cope with. Here's a rundown:

- **AVI:** AVI has been around for the longest time and PowerPoint is usually happy with this format unless it has been rendered using a non-standard codec. You'll lean more about codecs later in this chapter.

- **MOV:** These are Apple QuickTime files that can be played easily on Windows based machines using the free QuickTime Player application. Alas, PowerPoint is not so benevolent — it can only play really old QuickTime content rendered using obsolete codecs from a decade ago.

  Newer QuickTime videos use more efficient codecs by default and PowerPoint cannot use any videos rendered using this improved format.

- **MPG, MPEG:** Conventional MPEG movies, also called MPEG 1 movies play well in PowerPoint — and they are the best option if you need to create a presentation that needs to be played on both the Windows and Mac versions of PowerPoint.

- **MPEG 2:** movies are DVD quality and are not too PowerPoint friendly — they are more reliant on both hardware and software and usually may not play in PowerPoint even if they do play well in Windows Media Player.

- **WMV, ASF:** When Microsoft first introduced the Windows Media format, both audio and video files used the ASF extension. Later, Microsoft started using the WMV and WMA extensions for video and audio respectively. For all practical purposes, WMV and ASF are identical.

- **Flash:** Flash is not actually a video format — rather it is a vector format that supports animation. Not surprisingly, PowerPoint, or for that matter Windows itself does not consider Flash as a native video format. However, Flash movies can be successfully played within PowerPoint.

- **VCD:** VCD or Video CD files usually have the DAT extension — for all practical purposes they are MPEG-1 videos and several tools including freeware applications can convert VCD DAT movies to MPEG files without any problem. An online search for VCD to MPEG converter should result in several hits.

- **DVD:** DVD is more of a problem area since it is not too easy to convert (or decrypt) DVD VOB files to MPEG-2. Even if it were easy, there are several copyright issues involved. However, there are third party tools that allow you to play DVD movies right inside PowerPoint.

Copyright © 2006 Wiley Publishing, Inc.
All rights reserved.
Item 9817-1.
For more information about Wiley Publishing,
call 1-800-762-2974

## For Dummies: Bestselling Book Series for Beginners

# Cutting Edge PowerPoint®

## FOR DUMMIES®

by Geetesh Bajaj

WILEY

Wiley Publishing, Inc.

**Cutting Edge PowerPoint® For Dummies®**

Published by
**Wiley Publishing, Inc.**
111 River Street
Hoboken, NJ 07030-5774

www.wiley.com

WILEY

# About the Author

**Geetesh Bajaj** is based in Hyderabad, India, and he got started with his first PowerPoint presentation around a decade ago. He has been working with PowerPoint ever since.

Geetesh believes that any presentation is a sum of its elements. Everything in a presentation can be broken down to this element level, and PowerPoint's real power lies in its ability to act as glue for all such elements.

Geetesh contributes regularly to journals and Web sites, including *Presentations* magazine and the Microsoft.com Web site. He's also a Microsoft PowerPoint MVP (Most Valuable Professional) and a regular on Microsoft's PowerPoint newsgroups. It is from this newsgroup that many of the ideas and thoughts in this book were assimilated.

Geetesh's own Web site at indezine.com has hundreds of pages on PowerPoint usage. It also has a blog, an e-zine, product reviews, free templates and interviews.

Geetesh welcomes comments and suggestions about his books. He can be reached at geetesh@geetesh.com.

# Dedication

This book is dedicated to my family and to my staff at Indezine.com.

# Author's Acknowledgments

I knew I wanted to write a book like this for a long, long time. Yet, when I actually started on this book, it dawned on me that this would not have been possible without the involvement, encouragement, and existence of so many others.

To begin with, I wish to thank God.

And now for the lesser mortals who make miracles happen . . .

Heading this list is my family: my wife Anu, my parents, and my kids.

And thanks to Ellen Finkelstein, who encouraged me to get here.

Thanks to April Dalke, who is my MVP lead at Microsoft. She also helped me go ahead with this whole book concept.

Thanks to acquisitions editor Greg Croy, who probably is the best of his kind on this planet. I couldn't have asked for someone better!

And then this sequence of thanks heads to project editor, Pat O'Brien. Thank you, Pat, for all your patience and confidence levels — I needed them both! You are amazing! And to Andy Hollandbeck, Shannon Jenkins, and Laura Moss.

Thank you to all the wonderful folks at Microsoft. I know I won't be able to put all those names here, but here are some of them, in alphabetical order — Richard Bretschneider, Howard Cooperstein, Abhishek Kant, Shu-Fen Cally Ko, John Langhans, Sean O'Driscoll, Jan Shanahan, and Amber Ushka.

Thanks to so many others, including Rick Altman, Joye Argo, Kurt Dupont, Nicole Ha, Julie Hill, Keith Tromer, Betsy Weber, and Claudyne Wilder.

Thanks also to the PowerPoint MVP team of whom I am privileged to be a part — others include Bill Dilworth, Troy Chollar, Sonia Coleman, Chirag Dalal, Bill Foley, Jim Gordon, Kathy Jacobs, Michael Koerner, Glen Millar, Austin Myers, Shyam Pillai, Brian Reilly, Steve Rindsberg, Glenna Shaw, TAJ Simmons, Mickey Stevens, and Echo Swinford.

Finally, a big thank you to all whose names I have missed here!

## Publisher's Acknowledgments

We're proud of this book; please send us your comments through our online registration form located at `www.dummies.com/register/`.

Some of the people who helped bring this book to market include the following:

### Acquisitions, Editorial, and Media Development

**Project Editor:** Pat O'Brien

**Executive Editor:** Greg Croy

**Copy Editor:** Andy Hollandbeck

**Technical Editor:** James Orr

**Editorial Manager:** Kevin Kirschner

**Media Development Supervisor:** Richard Graves

**Editorial Assistant:** Amanda Foxworth

**Cartoons:** Rich Tennant (`www.the5thwave.com`)

### Composition Services

**Project Coordinator:** Erin Smith

**Layout and Graphics:** Carl Byers, Andrea Dahl, Lauren Goddard, Stephanie D. Jumper, Barbara Moore, Lynsey Osborn, Julie Trippetti

**Proofreaders:** Leeann Harney, Jessica Kramer, Carl Pierce, TECHBOOKS Production Services

**Indexer:** TECHBOOKS Production Services

---

**Publishing and Editorial for Technology Dummies**

**Richard Swadley,** Vice President and Executive Group Publisher

**Andy Cummings,** Vice President and Publisher

**Mary Bednarek,** Executive Acquisitions Director

**Mary C. Corder,** Editorial Director

**Publishing for Consumer Dummies**

**Diane Graves Steele,** Vice President and Publisher

**Joyce Pepple,** Acquisitions Director

**Composition Services**

**Gerry Fahey,** Vice President of Production Services

**Debbie Stailey,** Director of Composition Services

# Contents at a Glance

# Table of Contents

# Introduction

· · · · · · · · · · · · · · · · · · · · · · · · · · · · · · · · · · · · · · · · · · · · · · · · · · · · ·

**W**elcome to *Cutting Edge PowerPoint For Dummies,* a book that will show you how to create PowerPoint presentations that will dance and sing.

Thirty million PowerPoint presentations are created each day. Some of those poor things are never presented! Probably half of those remaining are presented just once. And an average presentation takes almost two hours to create. That brings forth two questions:

- ✔ Why are so many presentations created?
- ✔ Why are so few reused?

This book goes beyond finding the answers. In the process, you'll create presentations that are truly cutting-edge. Even better, these jaw-dropping presentations will take less time to create!

## About This Book

If you use PowerPoint, this book is for you.

*Cutting Edge PowerPoint For Dummies* contains a treasure trove of tips, ideas, and information. Best of all, it is presented in a way that helps you get results immediately. You are truly on your way to PowerPoint *nirvana.*

If you want to be known as the PowerPoint wizard in your office, society, or home, you can't do better than to read this book.

All the information contained within these covers comes from years of experience gained from working with PowerPoint users. This has provided me with an opportunity to realize the type of information that PowerPoint users need.

If you thought this book was going to be fun, you hit the target spot on! I believe nothing can be learned without bringing fun into the experience, and this book is no different.

This book will help you create cutting-edge presentations. And there are tons of goodies on the CD, plus many more you can download from the book's companion site:

www.cuttingedgeppt.com

# How To Use This Book

This book will show you quick ways to create effective design and content — and save you and your audience. Fortunately, you do not need to read this book from cover to cover.

Each chapter can be read individually — in fact, I encourage you to use this as a reference book. Just explore the problem areas that you need to tame:

- ✔ If you have just one day or a few hours to create that critical presentation, explore the areas where you need help. Get ideas to instantly *make over* your presentation. Watch it metamorphose from an ugly duckling into a beautiful swan.

- ✔ Read the chapters on Color and Masters/Templates — that will save you so much time.

- ✔ If you have more time, read this book from cover to cover. Explore all the samples and goodies on the CD.

- ✔ If you have all the time in the world, explore all possibilities. Perform all tutorials. Walk 16 miles each day.

- ✔ If you still have time, send me some feedback. I'll try to send you some pro bono work.

# What You Don't Need To Read

Most of the chapters and sections are self-contained. If there's one thing I value more than my readers, it's their time. This book is designed to save you time — so just read the sections that you need help with. Later, when you need help with something else, read that chapter.

# Foolish Assumptions

I make just one assumption — that you are an existing PowerPoint user.

This means we'll save some trees by not discussing the menus and icons inside PowerPoint. Also, there's no tutorial in this book that shows you everyday PowerPoint tasks, like how to cut and paste, save presentations, and insert a new slide.

✔ If you already know how to do these tasks, this book is for you. I'm so happy you found this book.

✔ If you still want to know about the basics or refresh your skills, there is a bonus chapter on PowerPoint basics on the CD included with this book. I continue to be happy for you.

# How This Book Is Organized

*Cutting Edge PowerPoint For Dummies* is divided into five main parts. Each part is further divided into chapters that contain sections. All chapters are self-contained volumes of inspiration and creativity. At the end of some chapters, "Design Guidelines" explore hidden design facets that will help you make even better PowerPoint presentations.

When required, the book is cross-referenced so that you can move immediately to the topic that interests you. You'll also find references to the CD and companion Web site throughout the book so that all three sources (book, CD, Web site) provide a unified learning experience.

Each part represents a specific area of PowerPoint usage.

## Part I: Powering Up PowerPoint

This part begins by looking at what PowerPoint is and isn't. You'll discover timesaving housekeeping tricks that prevent your presentations from becoming bloated or corrupted. You'll also streamline the PowerPoint interface and learn more about PowerPoint's file formats.

This part also covers color and its relation to contrast and combinations. Use it to your advantage in PowerPoint's amazing Color Schemes feature. And if consistency and time matter to you, you'll love the expert tricks on PowerPoint's masters and templates. Truly powerful stuff.

## Part II: Achieving Visual Appeal

This part looks at adding and enhancing visuals and text. You'll begin the magic with AutoShapes. Using them as individual building blocks, you'll watch, mesmerized, as they create amazing compositions that will blow away effects you thought were possible using only expensive drawing programs. You'll also find out more about PowerPoint's sophisticated fill and line technology.

Discover PowerPoint's drawing abilities with lines and curves — and keep them in control with grids and guides. Discover more about PowerPoint's smart connectors and add pizzazz with shadows and 3-D effects.

This part also has a full chapter that explores the font factor. You'll see how text can be made to look attractive and polished — and how you can convert your Word outlines into instant PowerPoint presentations.

Get ready to parade your photos in slide shows and get the whole skinny on resolution and compression. Learn how to combine Photoshop with PowerPoint and create visuals that evoke *oohs* and *aahs*. And then create fancy charts and graphs that dance to the tune of figures. If that doesn't work for you, get more charts from programs like Visio and SmartDraw right inside PowerPoint.

# Part III: Adding Motion, Sounds, and Effects

This is the part where PowerPoint dances and sings for you and your audience.

Find out everything about sound and video formats and their *codecs*. Add narration to PowerPoint and play back your CD tracks inside a presentation. And then export your presentation to a movie by using Camtasia, which can be used to create a DVD of your presentation! And if you are *geeky,* you can take the movie online.

Animation adds interest to all PowerPoint elements — learn more about PowerPoint's amazing Timeline as well as the entry, exit, and emphasis animations. Get more accolades with trigger and motion path animations and make sure you play with the transitions. Anything for a little fun!

# Part IV: Communicating Beyond the PowerPoint Program

If you think this book is only about PowerPoint, think again — or even better, go straight to this part and learn the cool tricks of working with Flash, Acrobat, Word, and Excel and making them move in concert with PowerPoint.

Take your presentation on the Web and learn awesome distribution and repurposing tricks. Use custom shows and password protect your presentation. Print your handouts and slides.

You'll also see how to do so much more inside PowerPoint — create a quiz, add interactivity between slides, and overcome your linking problems.

And then I tell you about the add-ins and how you can create a standalone EXE from PowerPoint.

## Part V: The Part of Tens

If you thought there was still something left to discover after what you read about the other parts, then you were absolutely right! I saved the absolute pop-their-eyes stuff for this part of the book.

In this part, you'll find my ten favorite PowerPoint tips and tricks, and I'm not even going to give you an inkling about that now. Just turn these pages and discover. I'll teach you how to overcome the ten worst problems and bugs in PowerPointland. You'll also find out about accessibility issues.

## Icons Used in This Book

Throughout this book, I mark certain paragraphs with the following icons to alert you to specific types of information:

This icon is for nerds and geeks. Read this if you want to get to know more about the intricate details or need information that you can use to impress your boss.

Make sure you read these — they contain important information that can help you create the cool, cutting-edge, wow look.

Did you blow a fuse somewhere? Or did lightning strike? Or maybe there are some problem areas in your PowerPoint presentation? The text marked by this icon will tell you how to step gingerly through the technical mine field.

If you ever tied a string on your finger to remember something, this is for you. If you set your morning alarm, this is for you, too — and surprise, this one is also for everyone else too!

If there's something on the CD that works with the example or technique being discussed, this icon tells you that the CD has some goodies or source files that you should take a look at.

# Where to Go from Here

Flip the pages and get into an amazing world where cool presentations help you influence your audiences and get ahead in life.

I wish you all the best with your presentations. Feel free to send me feedback through this book's companion site:

www.cuttingedgeppt.com/feedback

Get ready to go on a fantastic journey into the colorful, musical world of PowerPoint. This book is your ticket. Bon voyage!

# Part I
# Powering Up PowerPoint

The 5th Wave    By Rich Tennant

## In this part . . .

In this part, I show you how you can smooth all the rough edges you might encounter and started you thinking about PowerPoint as a collection of elements. Each element can enrich your overall presentation experience.

# Chapter 1

# PowerPointing with the Best of Them

*U*nlike many other applications, PowerPoint is amazingly easy to learn and to use. Ironically, creating terrible presentations is even easier! Although anyone can create a PowerPoint presentation with a few words and visuals, you can use PowerPoint to its complete potential only if you understand the composition of its *elements*.

All these elements come together to form the *structure* of a presentation — but there's more to a PowerPoint presentation than just structure and the elements. One of the most important ingredients is the *workflow* that makes up the order in which you create and add elements to your presentation.

This chapter discusses PowerPoint's elements, a presentation's structure, your workflow for creating a presentation, and more. Although these topics cover theory more than practical application, if you spend a little time internalizing these concepts, you will go a long way toward making your finished presentations more effective and cutting-edge.

## The Elements of PowerPoint

PowerPoint is just a tool. It presents you with a blank canvas that you color with your ideas and your message. The brushes and paints used for this electronic transformation from a blank canvas to an amazing interactive medium are its elements of composition:

- Text
- Background, images, and info-graphics
- AutoShapes
- Sound and video
- Animations and transitions
- Interactivity, flow, and navigation

In the following sections, I explain more about these individual elements and then follow it up with how they team together to form an entire presentation workflow. Each of these elements is discussed in greater depth in separate chapters throughout this book.

## Text

Text is the soul of a presentation — it relates to content like nothing else.

A barrage of visual content may not be able to achieve what a single effective word can say — sometimes, a word is worth a thousand pictures. Text is significant because it means you have something to say. Without explicit text, what you're trying to say might not come through as strongly as you want.

Too much text is like too much of a good thing — they can both be harmful. For example, a slide with 20 lines of teeny-weeny text that nobody in the audience can read just won't work. The audience can't read it, and the presenter doesn't have time to explain that much content!

## Backgrounds, images, and info-graphics

PowerPoint uses three types of graphical elements:

- **Backgrounds** need to be understated.

  You can create a great presentation with a plain white background. On the other hand, artistic backgrounds are a great way to bring a presentation to life.
- **Pictures** share the stage with text.
- **Info-graphics** combine visuals and text to great advantage.

  These tools can include charts, tables, maps, graphs, diagrams, organization charts, timelines, and flowcharts. Info-graphics can make complex information and statistics easy to understand.

Images and text always work together — collectively, they achieve more than the sum of each other's potential. However, images need to be relevant to the subject and focused; using an unsuitable visual is worse than using no visual at all.

PowerPoint provides many ways to present images — from patterned frames, effects, and outlines to animations and builds.

## AutoShapes

Normal shapes include simple objects such as circles, rectangles, and squares. PowerPoint looks at the entire shape metaphor in a different way through its AutoShapes technology. These AutoShapes seem like regular shapes, but that's where the similarity ends; they are very adaptable in editing and creation. AutoShapes can also function as building blocks and form the basis of complex diagrams and illustrations.

## Sound and video

PowerPoint provides many ways to incorporate sound: *inserted sounds, event sounds, transition sounds, background scores,* and *narrations.*

PowerPoint was perhaps never intended to become a multimedia tool — nor were presentations ever imagined to reach the sophisticated levels they have attained. Microsoft has tried to keep PowerPoint contemporary by adding sound abilities with every release. But that has meant compromises — most sound options are almost inaccessible to the everyday PowerPoint user. They're buried under heaps of dialog boxes and options. In Chapter 10, I show you how to unravel the sound mysteries of PowerPoint.

As computers get more powerful and play smooth full-screen video, viewers expect PowerPoint to work will all sorts of video formats. But that's a far cry from reality. In Chapter 10, I look at workarounds that keep PowerPoint happy with all sorts of video types.

## Animations and transitions

Animations and transitions fulfill an important objective: introducing several elements one at a time in a logical fashion that makes it easier for the audience to understand a concept.

> ✔ Animation is best used for a purpose. An example would be using animation to illustrate a process or a result of an action.

Use animation without a purpose, and your presentation might end up looking like an assortment of objects that appear and exit without any relevance!

✔ Transitions can be either subdued or flashy depending on the flow of ideas being presented. In either case, they need to aid the *flow* of the presentation rather than disrupt it.

## Interactivity, flow, and navigation

Amazingly, interactivity, flow, and navigation are the most neglected parts of many PowerPoint presentations. These concepts are easy to overlook because, unlike an image, they aren't visible.

✔ **Interactivity,** in its basic form, is the use of hyperlinks within a presentation to link to

 • Other slides in a presentation

 • Other documents outside a presentation (such as Word files)

✔ **Flow** is the spread of ideas that evolves from one slide to the other. Flows can be smooth or abrupt.

✔ **Navigation** is the way your presentation is set up to provide one-click access to other slides.

Navigation is mostly taken care of by using PowerPoint's Action Buttons, but you can link from any PowerPoint object.

## Non-PowerPoint Elements

Although you might believe that all the elements of a cutting-edge presentation are accessible from within PowerPoint, that's not entirely true. Professional presentation design houses don't want you to know the secret of using non-PowerPoint elements in your presentation — this knowledge is often the difference between a cutting-edge presentation and an ordinary one!

Examples of non-PowerPoint elements include the following:

✔ **Images retouched and enhanced in an image editor, such as Adobe Photoshop**

✔ **Charts created in a dedicated charting application**

✔ **Music and narration fine-tuned, amplified, and normalized in a sound editor**

> ✔ **Video clips rendered in a custom size and time within a video editing application**
>
> ✔ **Animations created in a separate application, such as Macromedia Flash**

When these non-PowerPoint elements are inserted inside PowerPoint, most of them can be made to behave like normal PowerPoint elements.

# Structure and Workflow

The words *structure* and *workflow* might sound a little intimidating, but they are merely a way of ensuring that your presentation elements are working together.

## Presentation structure

A typical presentation structure combines the six elements mentioned at the beginning of this chapter into something like you see in Figure 1-1.

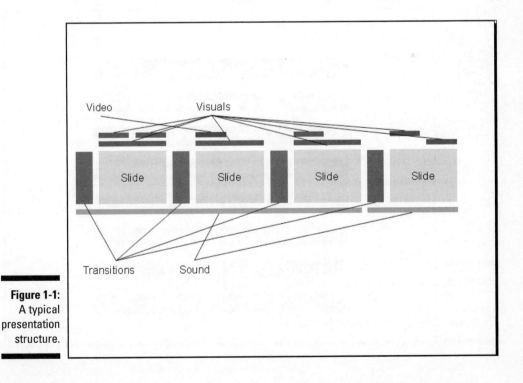

**Figure 1-1:**
A typical presentation structure.

Figure 1-1 is just an example — almost every presentation has a unique structure depending on the content of the presentation and the audience. On the other hand, the presentation *workflow* for most presentations remains unchanged, which is what I explain next.

## Presentation workflow

The presentation workflow decides the sequence of the six elements I explain earlier in this chapter. In addition, it also includes some more abstract elements like *delivery* and *repurposing*. Chapters 14 and 15 discuss these vital concepts.

Figure 1-2 shows a typical presentation workflow.

As you can see, the workflow begins with concept and visualization and ends with delivery and repurposing. But that's not entirely true — repurposing can often be the same as the concept and visualization of another presentation! That's food for thought — and the stimulus for thoughts on another interesting subject. . . .

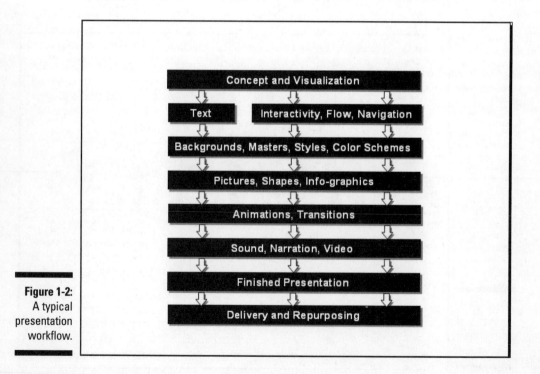

**Figure 1-2:**
A typical
presentation
workflow.

# What Can PowerPoint Be Used For?

PowerPoint can be used to create all sorts of presentations:

✓ **Business presentations:** More than anything else, people use PowerPoint to create presentations intended for the boardrooms and conference halls of the corporate world, where people of all collars come to see and hear content. And as the corporate corridors have discovered, the most important thing is to have a PowerPoint presentation ready for every proposal, product, and prayer — and I should add sale, service, and sin to that list!

✓ **Homework projects:** Don't be flabbergasted if your kid asks you to help create a presentation for school. Or maybe you are a kid reading this and can't understand what's so great about creating a PowerPoint presentation for a project. Schools all over the world are discovering the virtues of PowerPoint — the program lets you assemble all sorts of media, like images, text, and sound, in one document. And think about the amount of paper and ink you save by replacing that project poster with a PowerPoint presentation!

✓ **Educational content:** Colleges and universities commonly have their own banks of presentations for every conceivable subject. Some of these presentations are sold for very high prices as "talks" by specialized vendors — and the high prices are because these talk presentations were created by highly renowned professionals. Even at the high cost, these talk presentations are a steal because they are the next best thing to inviting those professors to speak to your students.

✓ **Kiosks:** Everything is on a kiosk nowadays — from travel information at airports to the play-list at the coffee-shop jukebox. And many of those kiosk displays are actually PowerPoint presentations.

✓ **Religious presentations:** And now for the godly frontiers — that projection of the hymn lyrics in church was likely created in PowerPoint. As was that fancy slide show that showed you pictures from the mission trip to South America.

✓ **Government presentations:** PowerPoint is used everywhere in the administration sphere. Be it presidents or prime ministers — or even organizations like the United Nations and its various agencies all over the world — so much these days happens on a PowerPoint slide. And yes, when something goes wrong, such as space shuttle disasters, PowerPoint gets to share some of that blame!

✓ **Multimedia demos:** This is probably the most controversial use because PowerPoint was never intended to be used as a tool to create multimedia demos that run from CD-ROM. Nevertheless, PowerPoint allows interactivity and navigation between slides — and because so many people already have PowerPoint, all those bosses decided that they might as well ask untrained office staff to put it to good use!

Of course, PowerPoint can be used for so much more — electronic greeting cards, quizzes, posters, and even multiplication tables. You are limited only by your imagination.

# Giving People What They Like to See

The simplest secret of creating great presentations is to give audiences what they like to see. Give them anything else and they are bound to complain and spurt into bouts of loud-mouthed vengeance and stupidity. (Okay — I admit that was an exaggeration. They are more likely to doze off and snore loudly while you are presenting!)

So what do audiences like to see? That's what I discuss next.

## Truth and sincerity

More than anything else, audiences want sincerity and truth. Just because you put that sentence in a 48-point bold font in a contrasting color doesn't mean that your audience will believe what it says. If there's something in common between audiences of any place, age, and sex, it's that they want something they can believe — and if there's even a hint that something mentioned in your presentation is gobbledygook, you can wave goodbye to the remaining 999 slides in that presentation! (And please don't make such long presentations.)

Of course, there are rare exceptions to that rule. A few centuries ago, audiences did not believe that the earth was round — or that airplanes could fly. If what you are presenting is so groundbreaking, I'll let you put that in your next PowerPoint presentation. And I'm so proud that you are reading this book.

## Style and design

To enliven your message, use as many of these style and design guidelines that you can balance on a single PowerPoint slide:

✔ **Choose an uncluttered background for your presentation.**

- Plain color backgrounds get around that clutter problem just by being plain!

- Other background types, such as textures, gradients, and photographs, have to be more carefully chosen.

As a test, insert enough placeholder text in an 18-point font size to fill the entire slide area in two slides. Use black text on one slide and white text on the other.

- If you can read text on both the slides clearly, then your background really works!

- If just one color works, you can use that background if you make sure that you use the right colors for all other slide objects. See Chapter 3 to find out more about picking the "right" colors.

✔ **Make sure your text is large enough that it can be read without squinting by the audience members in the last row.**

✔ **Make sure that you use just the right amount of visual content to get your message across** — not too little and certainly not too much.

- Don't add 16 pictures of something when 2 are enough.

- Use only relevant content; don't waste your audience's time and energy (or yours, for that matter) on images that have nothing to do with the topic of discussion.

✔ **If you're inserting sounds in your presentation, make sure that they all play at the same volume.**

You don't want the sound on one slide to be low and then follow that with a sound that's loud enough to wake up your peacefully sleeping audience.

## Spelling and grammar

Nothing is as embarrassing and shameful as a misspelling on a slide — especially considering that PowerPoint includes an excellent spell checker. But even beyond the spell checker, make sure that the spellings work for the country and audience you are presenting to. Thus, *color* is perfectly fine in the United States, but make that *colour* if you are presenting in the U.K. or in India.

Avoid using the same word twice on a slide. You can use a thesaurus to mix up the text:

✔ PowerPoint 2003 has a thesaurus built in.

✔ If you have an older version of PowerPoint, you can use the thesaurus in Microsoft Word to find new and related words to enrich the text content on a slide.

Don't speak exactly what's on the slide while presenting — slight differences in language and wording can make all the difference. Audiences don't like to hear parrotlike repeated narratives of what's already mentioned on the slide — they want you to take the content further by sharing your experiences, opinions, and ideas on the subject.

## No discrimination

Never use anything that can be thought of as discriminatory toward race or gender. Not only will racist or sexist phrases reflect you in poor light, they will also hijack the entire focus of your presentation.

# Chapter 2

# Empowering Your PowerPoint Program

*In This Chapter*

▶ Getting ready for housekeeping

▶ Keeping PowerPoint updated

▶ Thinking folders, not presentations

▶ Figuring out all those file types

*Y*ou can't learn to swim without getting into the water. That's a good thought if you're jumping into a 3-foot-deep pool, where your chance of drowning is next to negligible. Do the same thing in the middle of the Pacific Ocean and you probably won't come back to read the rest of this book — unless you know how to swim. Even if you know how to swim, you need to be near the coast and be away from sharks.

PowerPoint is more forgiving — you won't drown or be lunch for a fish. Yet, it's a perfectly good idea to take precautions before you step into the deceptive candy floss land (or sea) of PowerPoint. Luckily, you bought this book. I safeguard you with this chapter that contains all the "before-you-begin" tips.

First, I show you how to set up PowerPoint with one-time tweaks that will increase your productivity and also reduce your chances of coming face-to-face with crashes and corrupted presentations.

I also show you how you can keep your PowerPoint program updated with some help from Microsoft — and how the folder metaphor works so much better than a mere presentation.

Finally, I give you an introduction to PowerPoint's file formats, followed by bite-sized chunks about all the bits and pieces that make up a PowerPoint presentation. *Bon appétit!*

# Housekeeping with One-Time Tweaks

How do you tell PowerPoint that you're the boss? If you adapt the application to your working style, PowerPoint realizes that you're the no-nonsense type and works exactly as you want. A few minutes of housekeeping can save you tons of time.

## Turn off Fast Saves

You opened your presentation, deleted a few slides, and saved it. Guess what?! Your file size ballooned instead of going down! No, ghosts and gremlins don't reside inside PowerPoint or your computer. PowerPoint's Fast Saves feature is just working overtime, and nobody is impressed.

Fast Saves is also the culprit for other PowerPoint problems, including corrupted presentations.

By default, the Fast Saves option is turned on in PowerPoint. As the name suggests, Fast Saves lets you save files faster than usual by tagging all changes carried out to the file instead of doing a more substantial save. A few years ago, when processors were slower and memory prices reached for the sky, this was a nice option because the Fast Saves were actually faster!

Times have changed, and PowerPoint doesn't want to move with the times. It's time you make the move:

**1. Choose Tools⇨Options and select the Save tab, as shown in Figure 2-1.**

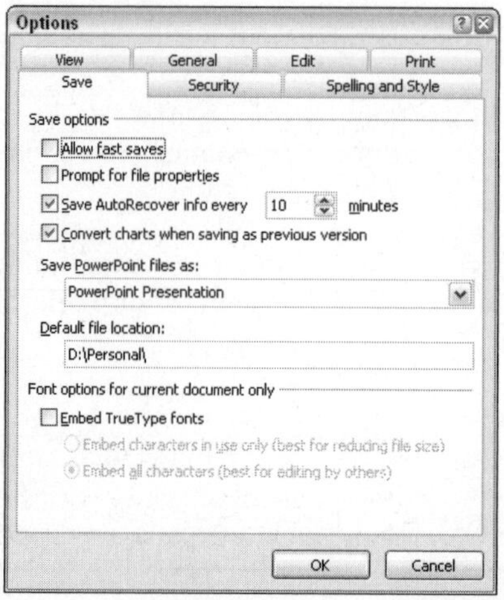

**Figure 2-1:**
Turning off
Fast Saves.

2. **Remove the check mark next to the Allow Fast Saves option.**

3. **Click OK to exit the dialog box.**

Now when you save a file, PowerPoint might take a wee bit longer, but your file size more accurately reflects the size of your presentation.

*Sequential Save* is a free add-in from Shyam Pillai that lets you create a backup of your presentation each time you click the Sequential Save button on the standard toolbar. Download this add-in from

```
www.cuttingedgeppt.com/seqsave
```

## Turn on AutoRecover

AutoRecover is a very useful option that creates a recovery presentation at a preset interval that you decide. This can be a boon if your computer crashes or if the power shuts down without warning.

The next time you launch PowerPoint, it starts with the recovered file open and prompts you to save the file.

Follow these steps to access the AutoRecover options:

1. **Choose Tools⇨Options and click the Save tab to bring up the dialog box shown previously in Figure 2-1.**

2. **If the check box next to the Save AutoRecover Info Every 'xx' Minutes is unchecked, click the check box to turn it on.**

3. **Change the timing (minutes) to something like 10 minutes.**

4. **Click OK to exit the dialog box.**

If you're in the habit of pressing Ctrl+S every other minute, you won't find much benefit with AutoRecover. In that case, consider increasing the 10-minute AutoRecover period to something longer.

The AutoRecover option is not a substitute for the Save command — you still should save your presentation often.

## The save location

By default, PowerPoint saves all your new presentations in your My Documents folder — that's also the default location for opening existing PowerPoint files.

This default location can be changed. This can be helpful if you're working on a particular project and want to choose the project folder as the default save location. After you move on to a new project, you can change the save location to another folder or back to the My Documents folder.

Follow these steps to change the save location:

1. **Choose Tools⇨Options to open the Options dialog box. Click the Save tab to bring up the options you saw last in Figure 2-1.**

2. **Type the path to your folder in the Default File Location text box.**

   You don't get a Browse button to navigate to and select your chosen folder. This means you have to make sure that the path and folder name have been typed correctly!

3. **Click OK to exit the dialog box.**

## Install a local printer driver

If you already have a local printer installed, you can skip this section.

For everyone else, I know it's sort of funny asking you to install a local printer when you have no physical printer attached to your computer. Maybe you use a network printer or perhaps you just don't need a printer. But if you use PowerPoint, a local printer is necessary so that PowerPoint can find all the fonts installed on your system and show you print previews.

You don't need to buy a printer to keep PowerPoint happy. Install a printer driver so that PowerPoint is fooled into believing that you have a printer! If you don't know how to install a local printer driver, follow the steps at

www.cuttingedgeppt.com/localprinter

## Undo levels

PowerPoint's Undo options are great. They let you go back to a previous stage in your presentation. By default, PowerPoint allows 20 undo levels, but you can change it to as high as 150.

 Don't use the maximum number of undo levels. That translates into sluggish performance and a drain on system memory.

Your best bet is to set your undo level to something between 10 and 40, depending on how powerful your system is. Even then, you might want to change the undo levels again per the requirements and needs of each individual presentation.

Follow these steps to change the number of undo levels:

1. **Choose Tools➪Options to summon the Options dialog box.**

2. **Click the Edit tab to bring up the options shown in Figure 2-2.**

3. **In the Undo section, set the Maximum Number of Undos to a number you've chosen.**

4. **Click OK to accept.**

## PowerPoint compatibility features

This option is available only to users of PowerPoint 2002 and 2003.

If you use these more recent versions of PowerPoint and send your presentations to users of older versions, they may complain because they can't view all the latest PowerPoint features, like the new animations and transitions, password protection, and multiple masters.

If required, you can downgrade the capabilities of your PowerPoint version.

To make sure that your presentations remain wholly compatible with earlier versions of PowerPoint, follow these instructions:

1. **Choose Tools➪Options to bring up the Options dialog box.**

2. **Click the Edit tab to face the dialog box shown previously in Figure 2-2.**

3. **In the Disable New Features section, check all three options:**

   - New Animation Effects

   - Multiple Masters

   - Password protection

4. **Click OK to accept.**

Now, when you create a presentation, the new features are unavailable.

You can switch these options back on when required, but your presentation won't run optimally on older versions of PowerPoint.

## Background printing

Background printing doesn't deal with printing PowerPoint slides with fancy backgrounds. It lets you print your presentations while you're working on them.

This feature's usefulness is debatable — especially considering how it can slow down your computer — but PowerPoint installs with this feature active by default. Keeping this option turned on is also known to cause the dreaded ms09.dll error! So, how do you turn off this feature? Just follow these steps:

1. **Choose Tools⇨Options to bring up the familiar Options dialog box and then click the Print tab, as shown in Figure 2-3.**

| Options | ? ☒ |
| --- | --- |

| Save | Security | Spelling and Style |
| --- | --- | --- |
| View | General | Edit | Print |

Printing options

☐ Background printing
☐ Print TrueType fonts as graphics
☐ Print inserted objects at printer resolution

Default print settings for this document

⦿ Use the most recently used print settings
◯ Use the following print settings:

    Print what:    Slides

    Color/grayscale:    Color

    ☐ Scale to fit paper
    ☐ Frame slides
    ☐ Print hidden slides

    OK    Cancel

**Figure 2-3:**
Disable
background
printing.

2. **Remove the check mark in the box next to Background Printing by clicking it.**

3. **Click OK to accept.**

## Automatic layouts

Does your font size keep shrinking as you type text into a placeholder? Worse, does the space between lines of text keep dwindling? This occurs when PowerPoint's AutoFit options are activated. Don't just sit there doing nothing — it's time to act. And you'll act differently depending on which version of PowerPoint you use.

### PowerPoint 2002 and 2003

Follow these steps to turn off (or turn on) the automatic layout options in PowerPoint 2002 and 2003:

1. **Choose Tools➪AutoCorrect Options to summon the AutoCorrect dialog box shown in Figure 2-4.**

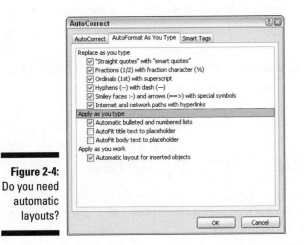

**Figure 2-4:**
Do you need automatic layouts?

2. **Select the AutoFormat as You Type tab.**

3. **Remove (or place) checks next to the boxes for these options:**

   • AutoFit Title Text to Placeholder

   • AutoFit Body Text to Placeholder

4. **Click OK to accept.**

*PowerPoint 2000*

Follow these steps to turn off (or turn on) the automatic layout options in PowerPoint 2000:

1. **Choose Tools⇨Options to bring up the Options dialog box.**

2. **Select the Edit tab to view the dialog box shown in Figure 2-5.**

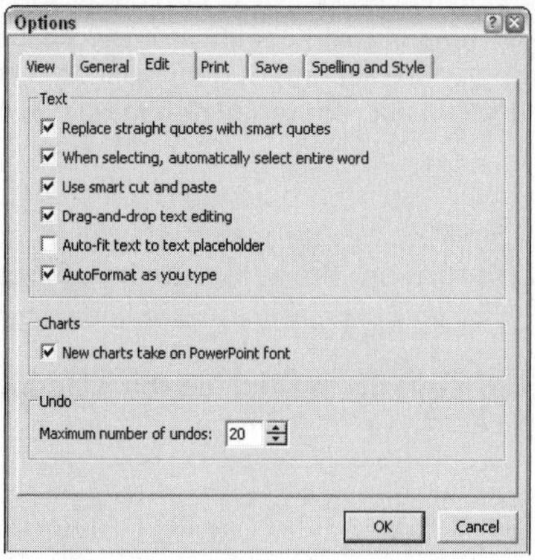

**Figure 2-5:** Turn off automatic layouts in PowerPoint 2000.

3. **Remove (or place) a check mark in the box for the Auto-fit Text to Text Placeholder option.**

4. **Click OK to accept.**

# Keeping Your PowerPoint Updated

If you can do yourself one favor today, download the latest Service Pack for your version of PowerPoint (and Microsoft Office). So what is a Service Pack? And where do you download it?

## Service Packs

Most releases of popular applications are followed by releases of Service Packs that address some bugs and add some new features.

These Service Packs need to be downloaded from the Microsoft site, or, in some cases, they can also be ordered on a CD, which is especially useful if you aren't on a broadband connection.

But wait! You might have some Service Packs already applied. To find this out, choose Help⇨About Microsoft PowerPoint. This brings up a dialog box similar to what you see in Figure 2-6.

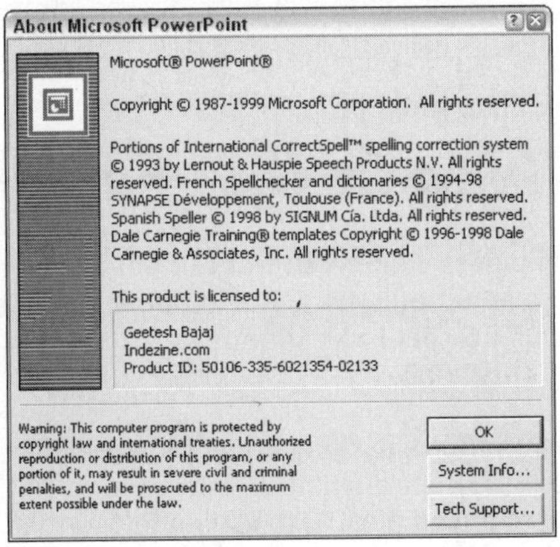

**Figure 2-6:**
Do you have
Service
Packs
installed?

**About Microsoft PowerPoint**

Microsoft® PowerPoint®

Copyright © 1987-1999 Microsoft Corporation. All rights reserved.

Portions of International CorrectSpell™ spelling correction system © 1993 by Lernout & Hauspie Speech Products N.V. All rights reserved. French Spellchecker and dictionaries © 1994-98 SYNAPSE Développement, Toulouse (France). All rights reserved. Spanish Speller © 1998 by SIGNUM Cía. Ltda. All rights reserved. Dale Carnegie Training® templates Copyright © 1996-1998 Dale Carnegie & Associates, Inc. All rights reserved.

This product is licensed to:

Geetesh Bajaj
Indezine.com
Product ID: 50106-335-6021354-02133

Warning: This computer program is protected by copyright law and international treaties. Unauthorized reproduction or distribution of this program, or any portion of it, may result in severe civil and criminal penalties, and will be prosecuted to the maximum extent possible under the law.

OK

System Info...

Tech Support...

The first line of this dialog box identifies the PowerPoint version and the Service Pack number applied. For instance, `PowerPoint 2000 SP-1` signifies that you have PowerPoint 2000 installed with Service Pack 1. The current Service Pack for PowerPoint 2000 is SP-3 — that means this version of PowerPoint is outdated!

To acquire new Service Packs, you need to visit Microsoft's OfficeUpdate site.

## OfficeUpdate

Updating your Service Pack at the OfficeUpdate site is really quite easy, and it works in more or less the same way for PowerPoint 2000, 2002, and 2003:

✔ PowerPoint 2002 and 2003 users can directly access the site from within PowerPoint by choosing Help⇨Check for Updates.

✔ PowerPoint 2000 users need to open the following site in their browsers:

`officeupdate.microsoft.com`

Not surprisingly, this update service works only if you are using Microsoft Internet Explorer as your browser.

Microsoft has the habit of changing Web URLs often — so I created this URL for you:

`www.cuttingedgeppt.com/officeupdate`

If they change the URL, I'll update it on that page!

Keep your original CD (or other installation medium) within reach just in case the Service Pack installation asks for it — you don't want to abandon the installation of the Service Pack midway just because the installation medium isn't handy!

# Assembling Everything in One Folder

PowerPoint is one of the few places where you want to put all your eggs in one basket. Saving all of a presentation's elements in one folder is so important for overcoming link problems that I risk sounding like a parrot by repeating this tip often throughout this book.

You should save all of a presentation's assets in one folder because you don't want PowerPoint to have to remember any paths. PowerPoint isn't too good at remembering the location of linked files, and heaven forbid that you ever have to copy your presentation to a laptop just before an important presentation only to have PowerPoint throw up a message that says your linked file cannot be found! So just put everything in one folder before you link or insert those files from within PowerPoint. Then, when the presentation needs to move, copy that whole folder.

So how do you assemble everything in one folder? Here's how:

1. **Create a new folder and name it after your project.**

2. **Create your basic, bare-bones presentation (probably a one-slide presentation or just an outline) and save it within this folder.**

3. **Copy all the elements that you want to link to this presentation into this folder:**

   • Sounds and videos.

   • All the other documents you want to hyperlink from within the presentation, such as other PowerPoint presentations, Word and PDF documents, and Excel spreadsheets.

4. **After you finish copying these files, work on your presentation again and start inserting or linking the documents, sounds, videos, and other files (all in the same folder) within the presentation.**

5. **If you need to copy your presentation to another computer, just copy the entire folder.**

Making a habit of creating a new folder for every new presentation ensures an almost uninterrupted workflow in which you can concentrate on the creative part of the presentation without having to worry about linking problems later.

# Embracing PowerPoint File Formats

The .ppt file format is the format most commonly associated with PowerPoint, but PowerPoint creates and uses a number of file formats to provide a plethora of PowerPoint presentation possibilities:

✔ PowerPoint's file types:

- **.ppt:** This is the original PowerPoint presentation file type. Unless you tampered with any associations, double-clicking a .ppt file opens it up in PowerPoint. Of course, that's assuming you have PowerPoint installed on your system!

- **.pps:** This is the PowerPoint show format. Again, unless you tampered with any file associations, double-clicking a .pps file results in the presentation playing.

  The only difference between .ppt and .pps files is the last letter of the extension. Yes, it is only the *t* and *s* that make them different file types. Rename those extensions from one to the other a thousand times and you'll still see the same slides! Now that you know this, I wish you happy renaming!

  The default action for double-clicking a .ppt file is opening it in PowerPoint, ready for editing. On the other hand, the default action for double-clicking a .pps file is opening it in Show mode — without the PowerPoint interface.

✔ Other PowerPoint file formats:

- **.pot:** A .pot file is just a PowerPoint template that contains information about the Slide and Title Masters and the Color Schemes. It may or may not include preset font, animation, and transition choices.

  Double-clicking a .pot file results in PowerPoint creating a new, unsaved presentation based on that template.

  Check out Chapter 3 for the lowdown on Color Schemes, and see Chapter 4 for a quick lesson in masters and templates.

- **.ppa:** This lesser-known file type is used mainly to store advanced macro and programming routines. .ppa files are usually PowerPoint add-ins that add new features to PowerPoint.

- **PowerPoint HTML Output:** PowerPoint creates a fairly nice HTML output that looks more or less like the original presentation.

  That's probably not the best virtue of PowerPoint's HTML output. The greatest advantage of this output is round-tripping, which works only in PowerPoint 2002 and 2003. This feature lets you open a PowerPoint HTML presentation in PowerPoint and save it back to the .ppt format — even if you have lost the original .ppt file! I talk about round-tripping in Chapter 13.

# Recognizing All the Pieces and Parts

The following sections orient you to all the terms that you'll hear in the rest of this book.

## Slides and presentations

Every *presentation* comprises one or more *slides*. Slides are individual screens in a presentation — almost like pages in a book.

## Placeholders, layouts, outlines, and text boxes

*Placeholders* are special container frames — you type text in a text placeholder and insert an image into a picture placeholder. Title placeholders contain slide titles.

Special preset arrangements of these placeholders are contained on individual slides. For example, one arrangement might contain a single title placeholder and a single chart placeholder. Or you might have an arrangement with title and text placeholders — or even an arrangement with no placeholders at all. Such preset arrangements are called *slide layouts*.

*Outlines* are the text part of the presentation that's contained within the title and text placeholders. Any other text in the presentation is not part of the outline. Thus if your slide has a title and a text placeholder, all the text within those placeholders is part of the outline for the slide.

In addition to text placeholders, you can add almost any number of *text boxes* to a slide. These text boxes function just like regular text placeholders apart from one important difference: The text contained in text boxes is never a part of the presentation's outline.

## AutoShapes, charts, and diagrams

*AutoShapes* are almost like cookie-cutter shapes that you can insert on a slide with one click — their power lies in their simplicity. They are the real building blocks of PowerPoint.

*Charts* are, well, charts! They are info-graphics that are driven by data and statistics.

*Diagrams* are logical drawings that show relationships.

# Color Schemes

*Color Schemes* are preset color combination values that influence the color of all PowerPoint elements, such as the background, charts, text, diagrams, shadows, and hyperlinks.

Each presentation can contain multiple Color Schemes, and you can change between the Color Schemes to create a new look for your presentation.

# Masters

When you create a preset slide type and choose a slide background, you'll want to save it within the *Slide Master.* Slide Masters can also influence other elements in a presentation, and PowerPoint has three more master types that influence title slides, handouts, and notes. Not surprisingly, those masters are called Title Master, Handout Master, and Notes Master.

# Templates

In its simplest form, a combination of Color Schemes and masters can be saved as a *template* that you can implement across any number of presentations. This very powerful feature can help you create consistency of look across presentations.

# Chapter 3

# Color Is Life

- - - - - - - - - - - - - - - - - - - - - - - - - - - - - - - - - - - - - - - - - - -

- - - - - - - - - - - - - - - - - - - - - - - - - - - - - - - - - - - - - - - - - - -

**A**udiences make lasting opinions when the first slide is projected on-screen. Many times, that's before you speak a single word. Color can either help you win over that opinion or make you lose that first moment.

Color is powerful stuff: Ignore it at your own peril. But don't worry. This chapter shows you how to pick the right color for your presentation.

Color theory is art and science working together. Don't run away — I have no ambitions to convert you into a color scientist. I won't even suggest reading a book about color theory because you probably don't have that sort of time. Instead, through a set of no-brainer guidelines, I mesmerize you as colors come alive in a magic laboratory contained in this book! Don't be skeptical about all these wonderful color things — let your inspiration soar and touch the rainbow. If you want inspiration, this book provides oodles of that rare commodity. If you want the moon . . .

## Why Is Color So Important?

French painter Yves Klein said, "Color is sensibility turned into matter, matter in its primordial state."

Nothing could be truer in the world of PowerPoint. When asked to name just one thing that can make a limp, uninspiring presentation look dazzling and cutting-edge, I answer *color.*

## Background and foreground; contrast and combination

In PowerPointland, color expresses its omnipresence through combinations and contrasts between these two elements:

- The slide background
- The foreground elements (everything else in PowerPoint, such as text, diagrams, charts, and AutoShapes)

*Contrast is king.* The first basic color rule in PowerPoint is to make sure that your background and foreground colors are as different as night and day.

The examples in Figure 3-1 show how contrast makes text more legible.

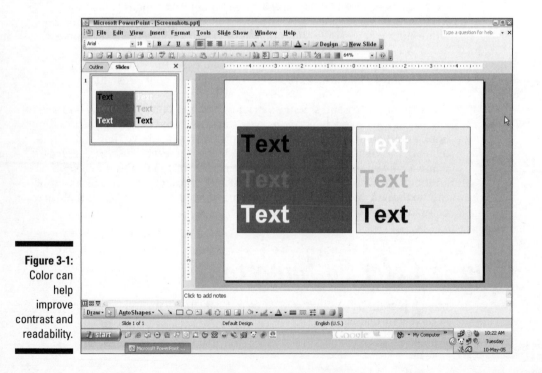

**Figure 3-1:**
Color can help improve contrast and readability.

For the best contrast, use

- ✔ Light text over a dark background
- ✔ Dark text over a light background

For clarity, avoid these:

- ✔ Similar text and background colors
- ✔ Light text on a light background
- ✔ Dark text on a dark background

## *Grayscale and contrast*

Even if your actual presentation is shown in full color, check the contrast in grayscale. Often, color prevents you from judging contrast.

If colors have good contrast in grayscale, they work well together in color.

The steps to use PowerPoint's grayscale preview depend on your PowerPoint version.

### *PowerPoint 2002 and 2003*

Use these steps to control PowerPoint's grayscale preview in PowerPoint 2002 and 2003:

1. **Start the grayscale preview by choosing View➪Color/Grayscale➪ Grayscale. (See Figure 3-2.)**

   If you end up with a Black & White view rather than Grayscale, choose the Automatic option in the Grayscale View toolbar shown in Figure 3-2.

2. **To get back to the normal color view, choose View➪Color/Grayscale➪ Color.**

### *PowerPoint 2000*

Use these steps to control PowerPoint's grayscale preview in PowerPoint 2000:

1. **Start the grayscale preview by choosing View➪Black and White.**

2. **To get back to the normal color view, choose View➪Black and White again.**

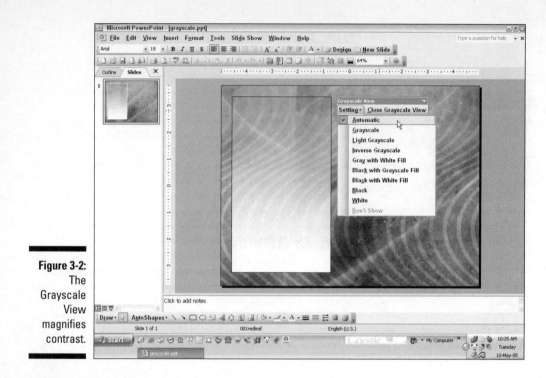

Microsoft PowerPoint - [grayscale.ppt]

**Figure 3-2:**
The
Grayscale
View
magnifies
contrast.

# Background Color

Don't even tell me that you plan to use a chocolate-magenta gradient as the background for your next presentation.

A bad background color choice can ruin a presentation more than anything else. Fortunately, changing the background color is one of the most effective makeovers possible.

## Replicate nature

Why are blue and green the favorite background colors for PowerPoint presentations? You find blue in the skies and the seas; green pervades forests and meadows. It's almost as if nature starts with a blue or green canvas and then paints everything over these colors. No wonder we humans subconsciously re-create the same effect on our PowerPoint slides!

*Imitate nature* if you can. That's the second color rule in PowerPointland.

## Use corporate colors

You might be unable to replicate nature if your company colors are orange and purple. You might also have strict instructions to not change any colors. Luckily, there are lots of ways you can cope with that situation.

- Mix white with the color (*lighten* it) to create a *tint*.

  All pastel colors are tints.

- Mix some black (*darken*) to create a *shade* while retaining your original color value.

Using either tints or shades makes the background color less *saturated* and ensures that either white or black text is easily readable over the background.

If you need to use a bright, saturated color like red or yellow as a background, use a *texture* as the background. Textures let you play with a wide gamut of values and saturations while leaving the color hue unchanged.

Textured backgrounds using difficult colors like red and yellow are in the Chapter Files folder on the *Cutting Edge PowerPoint Presentations For Dummies* CD.

## Colors influence moods

Colors are associated with moods. Although rules are meant to be broken, you should know the essential psychology of color.

Any color family can be used successfully in presentations, but some colors are much easier to use.

---

# Favorite background color

An online survey on my Web site asked visitors to vote for their favorite presentation background colors. The results make very interesting reading:

- If *blue* is your favorite background, you aren't alone. Nearly 42 percent of the respondents polled provided the same answer.

- *Green* fared well with 16 percent of the votes.

- *Black, white, violet,* and *purple* polled between 7 and 9 percent each.

- *Red, brown, yellow,* and *orange* were the least favored colors.

### Safe choices

It is hard to go wrong when you use these colors in your presentations:

- ✔ **Blue** signifies endurance, capability, and vastness.

  The color of tranquil skies and water is reassuring.

- ✔ **White** denotes *peace* and *blank space*.

  White works well for such purposes as research, nonprofit organizations, education, venture capital, funding, and IPOs.

- ✔ **Black** signifies *sophistication*.

  Black works very well in visually rich presentations for fields such as fashion, art, jewelry, space research, and many sciences.

- ✔ **Violet and purple** denote *luxury* and *opulence* and provide a *spiritual fervor*.

  Use in presentations intended for travel, interior design, self-improvement, and alternative medicine.

- ✔ **Gray** denotes *balance* and *stability*. Gray works well with visuals of differing styles.

  Gray is the color to deliver bad news.

### Risky choices

These colors can work in your presentation if you take necessary precautions:

- ✔ **Green** denotes *trust*. It is a great choice for presentations to new audiences. Use it for banking, industry, and government sectors.

  Avoid *fluorescent* greens. Opt for paler tints and shades of the color.

- ✔ **Red** is suitable for internal presentations that *call for action*.

  In its pure saturation, red is a screaming color totally unsuited for presentation backgrounds. Mix red with black or white to create suitable backgrounds.

- ✔ **Orange** denotes *authority* and *influence*. It's a nice choice to neutralize a disadvantage.

  Use a *pale* shade of orange and combine it with *beige* or *dark blue* text.

- ✔ **Brown** is associated with *growth* and *lifestyle*.

  A slide covered entirely with brown could mean either *death by chocolate* or *death by PowerPoint*.

✔ **Yellow** indicates *youth, warmth,* and *optimism.* Use it for education, royalty, travel, and design.

Be wary of using the more saturated values of yellow. If a particular yellow value hits you in the eye, stay away from it.

✔ **Pink** is a controversial color associated with the feminine look a decade ago. Pink in various shades and tints is used for spheres such as haute couture, decorative arts, and even finance.

# Color Schemes

Every PowerPoint slide element (such as background, text, chart, AutoShapes, and lines) is associated with a *default* color. These default colors are stored in palettes called *Color Schemes.*

You can quickly make over a presentation by changing its Color Scheme. To see how Color Schemes can change the look of a presentation, look at Color Plate 3-1 in the color insert in the middle of this book.

The source presentation for Color Plate 3-1 is included in the Chapter Files folder on the *Cutting Edge PowerPoint Presentations For Dummies* CD — it is called colorscheme.ppt.

## Color swatches

Each PowerPoint presentation can contain several Color Schemes. Each Color Scheme contains eight color swatches that are used for particular elements, as explained in the following sections:

### Background

The background swatch is used for the slide background — even if you use a patterned or gradient background, the slide is associated with a solid background color. When choosing a background color, make sure that either *white* or *black* text placed over the color is legible and visible.

If neither white nor black text shows well over the background color, you've made a wrong background choice.

### Text and lines

This swatch dictates the default color of all text and lines, including placeholder text, arrows, table borders, and chart axes.

As much as possible, this color should contrast with the background color.

### Shadows

This swatch is used for all sorts of shadows for slide elements, like text, AutoShapes, 3-D Styles, and so on.

Often, a medium gray is a safe choice for a shadow color. Black works well, too, although you can't use a black shadow for black text. Because the purpose of a shadow is to make the text stand out, the shadow color must be distinctly different from the text color. And it helps if the color is a shade darker than the background color.

### Title text

This swatch is used for the text placeholders in the Title slide.

Because this color is used less often than the regular text color, you can experiment a little (but always make sure that the color provides a good *contrast* with the background color).

### Fills

This swatch is used as

- ✔ The default fill for any AutoShape you draw on a slide, including rectangles and ellipses
- ✔ The first fill color for any charts or diagrams you create in PowerPoint

Sometimes, the fill color is called the *foreground* color.

### Accent

The accent color is the second fill color for any chart or diagram that you create in PowerPoint.

Try to make the accent color something that works well with the fill color.

### Accent and hyperlink

This is another color used for fills in charts and diagrams.

Make sure that this color provides a strong contrast to the background color because this color is also used for *hyperlinked* text.

### Accent and followed hyperlink

This is used as

- ✔ A fill color (like the accent and hyperlink color)
- ✔ A followed (visited) hyperlink color

Make sure that this color contrasts well with the background color.

# Applying Color Schemes

Every presentation and slide already has a Color Scheme applied. You can open a presentation and change the Color Scheme for a whole presentation or for specific slides.

The steps to assign a Color Scheme depend on your PowerPoint version. (Later in this chapter, I show you how to create and customize Color Schemes for your version of PowerPoint.)

You can practice applying different Color Schemes on the `colorscheme change.ppt` presentation in the Chapter Files folder on the *Cutting Edge PowerPoint Presentations For Dummies* CD.

The steps to manage Color Schemes depend on your PowerPoint version.

## PowerPoint 2002 and 2003

PowerPoint 2002 and 2003 provide separate tools for managing Color Schemes in complete presentations and specific slides.

### Complete presentation

In PowerPoint 2002 and 2003, follow these steps to change the Color Scheme in an entire presentation:

1. **Choose Format⇨Slide Design.**

   This activates the Slide Design task pane.

2. **In the Slide Design task pane, click the Color Schemes option.**

3. **Click any preview in the task pane to change the Color Scheme for all the slides (as shown in Figure 3-3).**

   If you inadvertently click a preview icon you don't like, press Ctrl+Z to undo the change.

### Specific slides

If you want to select a Color Scheme for specific slides in a PowerPoint 2002 or 2003 presentation, follow these steps:

1. **Choose View⇨Slide Sorter.**

2. **Select the individual slides you want to change.**

   • To select *consecutive* slides, select the first slide and then Shift-click the *last* slide in the sequence.

- To select slides *out of sequence,* select the first slide and then Ctrl-click *individual* slides.

**3. Click any of the previews in the task pane to change the Color Scheme for the selected slides (as shown in Figure 3-3).**

If you click a preview icon you don't like, press Ctrl+Z to undo the change.

### PowerPoint 2000

In PowerPoint 2000, follow these steps to change Color Schemes for either a complete presentation or for specific slides:

**1. Choose Format⇨Slide Color Schemes.**

This opens the Color Scheme dialog box shown in Figure 3-4.

**2. Select any Color Scheme thumbnail.**

**3. Click the Preview button to instantly see how it affects the active slide.**

Previewing how a slide looks with a new Color Scheme is a great way to experiment. Try all the Color Schemes available to find out which looks the best.

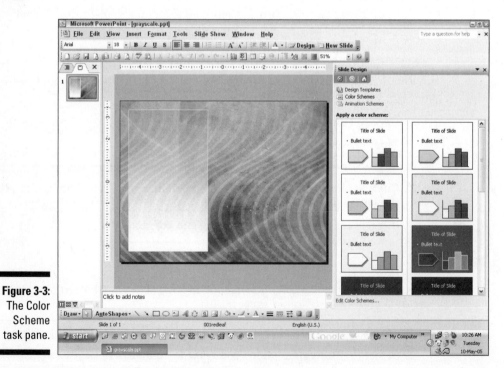

**Figure 3-3:**
The Color
Scheme
task pane.

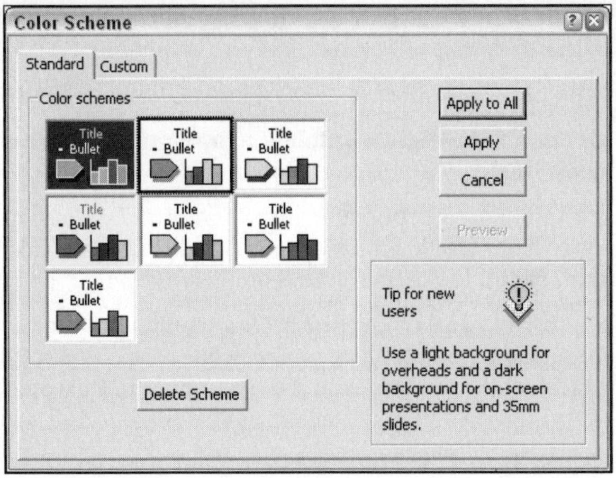

Figure 3-4:
Color
Scheme
dialog box.

4. **If you like the Color Scheme, you can apply it as follows:**

   - To apply the Color Scheme on just the active slide, click the Apply button.
   - To apply a Color Scheme on all slides in a presentation, click the Apply to All button.

# Creating Color Schemes

Seeing a slide metamorphose from one family of colors to another might look like magic. You can be a part of this magic by creating your own Color Scheme.

The steps to create a Color Scheme depend on your version of PowerPoint.

## PowerPoint 2002 and 2003

To create a Color Scheme in PowerPoint 2002 or 2003, follow these steps:

1. **Choose Format⇨Slide Design.**

   This activates the Slide Design task pane.

2. **In the Slide Design task pane, click the Color Schemes option.**

3. **Below the Color Scheme previews, click the Edit Color Schemes hyperlink.**

   This opens the Edit Color Scheme dialog box, shown in Figure 3-5.

4. **Double-click any of the eight swatches to open the Windows Color Chooser dialog box.**

   The Standard tab lets you choose from a hive of 127 colors. In addition, you can choose from black, white, and 15 shades of gray. Take a peek at how the Standard tab looks in Figure 3-6.

   If you prefer more control over your colors, you'll love the Custom tab. This lets you mix your own colors or enter specific color values using the RGB and HSL color models. You can see how the Custom tab looks in Figure 3-7.

   The sidebars, "RGB and the colors of light" and "HSL and the human eye color system," explain more about RGB and HSL.

5. **After you have chosen colors for all eight swatches, you can save the group of them as your own Color Scheme. Click the Add As Standard Scheme button.**

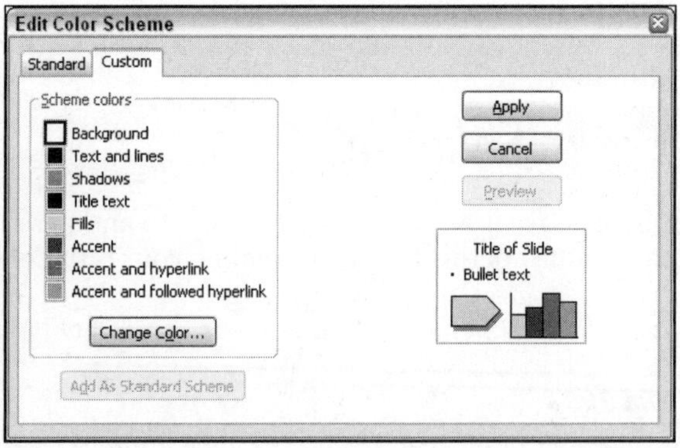

**Figure 3-5:**
The Edit
Color
Scheme
dialog box.

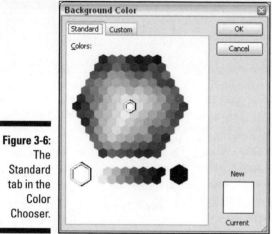

**Figure 3-6:**
The
Standard
tab in the
Color
Chooser.

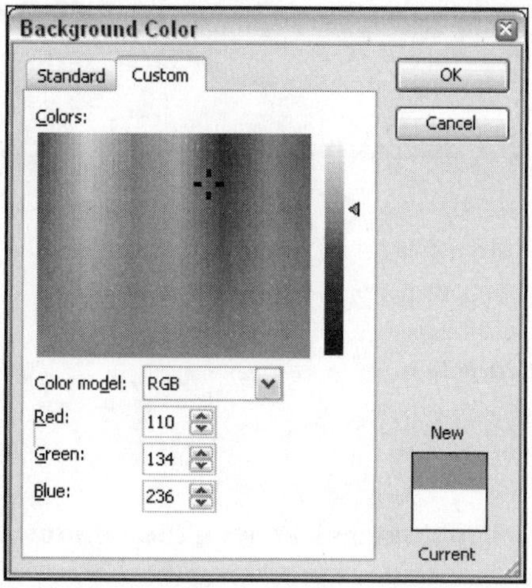

**Figure 3-7:**
The Custom
tab in the
Color
Chooser.

# RGB and the colors of light

Normal people like you and me mix regular paints to create new colors. You probably mixed yellow and red in school to create orange.

Guess what — if you tell your computer or resident geek that red and yellow make orange, you'll be electrocuted through the keyboard! That's because computers mix the colors of light rather than those amazing paints to create new colors. All colors in your computer come from just three pure colors: red, green, and blue.

I'm sure you've guessed that *RGB* stands for Red, Green, and Blue. RGB is a *color model* that computers understand. Each color has a numeric value that ranges from 0 to 255.

✔ When all three RGB values are 0, you get *black.*

✔ When all three RGB values are 255, you get *white.*

You can use different combinations of any three integers between 0 and 255 to create about 16 million shades of color. These are some common color values:

✔ **Blue:** R:0; G:0; B:255

✔ **Green:** R:0; G:255; B:0

✔ **Red:** R:255; G:0; B:0

✔ **Yellow:** R:255; G:255; B:0

✔ **Orange:** R:255; G:153; B:0

Color Table 3-1 (in the color insert in the middle of the book) is an RGB Color Reference chart.

## PowerPoint 2000

To create Color Schemes in PowerPoint 2000, follow these steps:

1. **Choose Format⇨Slide Color Schemes.**

   This opens the Color Schemes dialog box.

2. **Choose the Custom tab.**

3. **Double-click any of the eight swatches to open the Windows Color Chooser dialog box.**

   The Standard tab lets you choose from a hive of 127 colors. In addition, you can choose from black, white, and 15 shades of gray. Take a peek at how the Standard tab looks in Figure 3-6.

   If you prefer more control over your colors, you'll love the Custom tab. This lets you mix your own colors or enter specific color values using the RGB and HSL color models. You can see how the Custom tab looks in Figure 3-7.

   The sidebars, "RGB and the colors of light" and "HSL and the human eye color system," explain more about RGB and HSL.

4. **After you have chosen all eight colors, you can save the group of them as your own Color Scheme. Click the Add As Standard Scheme button.**

# HSL and the human eye color system

The HSL color system stands for *hue, saturation,* and *luminosity.*

✔ **Hue is the *pure color* value.**

This value can be any numeric value between 0 and 255. Changing this value moves the hue in the color spectrum.

✔ **Saturation is the *strength* of the color.**

If a color is too *bright,* just reduce the saturation value.

✔ **Luminosity (or Luminance) denotes light or dark values.**

Colors can be mixed with white to make tints or mixed with black to create shades.

HSL works like the human eye, so most designers and purists prefer using it to RGB.

The figure shows the Custom tab of the Color Chooser with the HSL color model selected. It is easy to manipulate the HSL model:

✔ Changing the *Hue* value moves the crosshair in the color spectrum horizontally.

✔ Changing the *Saturation* value moves the crosshair in the color spectrum vertically.

✔ Changing the *Luminosity* value moves the arrow in the Luminosity bar vertically.

Color Table 3-2, in this book's color insert, is an HSL Color Reference chart.

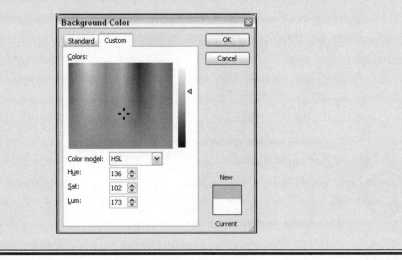

PowerPoint lets you save 16 Color Schemes in a single presentation or template. If you want to create a larger library, download a free copy of Color Schemes Manager from www.cuttingedgeppt.com/color.

# Choosing Colors

Creating a Color Scheme is easy — but then it's almost as easy to create a Color Scheme that has no visual meaning.

✔ **Build on an existing Color Scheme:** Most of PowerPoint's built-in Color Schemes were created using sound color principles. If you find a Color Scheme that suits your presentation and identity, just go ahead and use it. Even if you need to create a new Color Scheme, it's a good idea to use the existing schemes as a foundation to build upon.

✔ **Extend your identity:** Many times, your company already has a visual style manual that's used for stationery, on Web sites, and in advertisements — build a Color Scheme around that identity.

# Design Guidelines

Using color can be fun — and most of the time, it is a good idea to experiment with combinations, layouts, and ideas. However, combine those ideas with some guidelines and you can't go wrong.

✔ The background should stay in the background — don't use any color in the background that tries to come in front.

✔ Use the same Color Scheme for an entire presentation (or a set of presentations). Corporate houses often use a single Color Scheme for all their presentations to maintain consistency.

✔ Limit your color palette.

Use a single color hue and vary the saturation and luminance.

✔ Create a grayscale color scheme that you can apply with one click to an entire presentation.

This provides more control if you need to print to a black-and-white printer.

✔ Use the HSL (instead of RGB) model to mix your colors.

This lets you observe and understand color theory more closely.

✔ Color Schemes are contained both in

• A PowerPoint template

• A presentation that uses the Color Scheme

✔ Be wary of using red and green next to each other. Many people are red-green *colorblind*. These two colors look alike to them.

# Chapter 4

# Streamlining with Masters and Templates

*E*volve a presentation through edits and you might end up with something that has as much consistency as unbaked lasagna — in a presentation, this lack of consistency shows up in many ways:

✔ Differing font sizes and styles

✔ Diverse layouts

✔ Charts and graphs in non-complementing colors

✔ Dissimilar backgrounds across successive slides

It might be good enough to enjoy some inconsistency once in a while, but do the same thing to your slides, and your audience won't be too happy. And you won't be able to blame it on the lunch!

Correcting each individual slide for these problems can be laborious and time-consuming, especially if you need to do it for many slides or for multiple presentations. Your woes can be multiplied if you want to change things very often.

Does this sound familiar?

Thankfully, PowerPoint offers a simple solution to these problems in the form of masters and templates. Change a master, and all slides based on that master change instantly!

# Masters and Templates

Masters and templates act like frameworks that let you create presentations that are consistent in look and layout.

- ✔ **Think of masters as design boilerplates that influence slides.**

  Even if you aren't aware of it, PowerPoint uses a master for every new slide.

- ✔ **Combine masters with Color Schemes and you have a template. If you don't know much about Color Schemes, consult Chapter 3.**

- ✔ **Masters are contained within the presentation.**

- ✔ **Templates are separate files that use a different format than your presentation.**

- ✔ **PowerPoint templates can be identified by their .pot file extension, which is different from PowerPoint's regular .ppt file extension.**

  When you apply a template to a presentation, it's stored within that presentation as distinct masters and Color Schemes. The presentation no longer links to the original template file. Later in this chapter, you find out how to create and apply templates.

# Mastering Masters

To really benefit from using masters, you must start with a presentation from scratch and then fine-tune the masters. This ensures that individual slide edits don't alter the Master Slide links.

Color Plate 4-1 shows a basic presentation — it contains almost no formatting other than titles and bulleted lists that use the Arial typeface for text elements.

Formatting individual slides without using masters may result in a presentation that lacks consistency — Color Plate 4-2 shows a sample presentation formatted without masters. (This is the same presentation shown in Color Plate 4-1.)

The number-one reason that presentations go bad is that masters aren't used.

# Types of masters

PowerPoint can create and store four types of masters:

- ✔ Slide Master
- ✔ Title Master
- ✔ Handout Master
- ✔ Notes Master

## Slide Master

The Slide Master influences the layout of all slides in a presentation except *title slides,* which are based on the Title Master. Any customization in the Slide Master shows up on all slides of your presentation, although you can override this on individual slides. (I show you how later in the chapter.)

Follow these steps to edit a Slide Master:

**1. Choose View⇨Master⇨Slide Master.**

The Slide Master view opens, as shown in Figure 4-1. You find placeholders for title, text, bullets, date, footer, and slide number.

**Figure 4-1:**
The Slide Master shows placeholders for titles and text.

2. **Choose Format⇨Background.**

   Format your slide background and change the slide look.

   Look at the section "Background effects," later in this chapter, to find ways to add some pizzazz to your presentation.

3. **Format the text.**

   Select the text in any of the placeholders and alter the size or style of the font. You might want to use a more interesting font style or make some text bold or italic — whatever you want to do, this is your chance to make PowerPoint realize that you're the boss.

   Chapter 7 offers more information on dressing up all the text.

4. **Add more elements like a picture or a text box — anything inserted in the Slide Master will show up in all slides based on the particular Slide Master.**

5. **After the master is to your liking, get back to normal slide edit mode by choosing View⇨Normal.**

## Title Master

The *title slide,* which is normally the first slide of a presentation (or a section of a presentation), is influenced by the Title Master. All other slides are influenced by the Slide Master.

Usually, you want your Title Master to look similar to (read *coordinated with*) the Slide Master except for a few changes.

To create a Title Master, follow the steps for your version of PowerPoint.

### PowerPoint 2002 and 2003

Follow these steps to create a Title Master with PowerPoint 2002 or 2003:

1. **Get into the Master editing mode by choosing View⇨Master⇨ Slide Master.**

2. **Choose Insert⇨New Title Master to create a new Title Master.**

3. **Format as required.**

   All formatting options are similar to those explained earlier under the "Slide Master" section. Text formatting options are covered in Chapter 7.

4. **Choose View⇨Normal to return to Normal view.**

*PowerPoint 2000*

Follow these steps to create a Title Master with PowerPoint 2000:

1. **To access the Title Master view, choose View➪Master➪Title Master.**

   If the Title Master option is grayed out, it means your presentation has no Title Master that you can edit. To create a new Title Master, follow these steps:

   a. Choose View➪Master➪Slide Master.

      This gets you in the Slide Master view.

   b. Choose Insert➪New Title Master.

2. **Format as required.**

   All formatting options are similar to those explained for the Slide Master.

3. **Choose View➪Normal to return to Normal view.**

## Handout Master

The Handout Master decides the look of presentation handouts that you print and distribute. Handouts are covered in Chapter 14.

Follow these steps to edit the Handout Master:

1. **To go to the Handout Master view, choose View➪Master➪ Handout Master.**

2. **Edit and customize the Handout Master.**

   Within the Handout edit area, you find four editable regions (on the four corners of the page), as shown in Figure 4-2. These are the header, footer, number, and date. All four regions can be edited; because all edits are being done on the Handout Master, you see the results in every printed handout.

3. **Edit the background as required.**

   Choose Format➪Handout Background and choose from any of the background options.

4. **Choose View➪Normal to exit the Handout Master view.**

If PowerPoint doesn't let you customize handouts as much as you want, check out *Handout Wizard,* a PowerPoint add-in that lets you do much more. Download a trial version of Handout Wizard from

www.cuttingedgeppt.com/handoutwizard

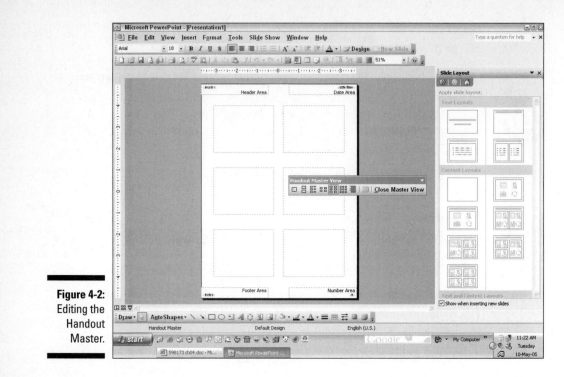

### Notes Master

The Notes Master defines the look of printed notes. Follow these steps to edit
the Notes Master:

1. **Get into Notes Master view by choosing View➪Master➪Notes Master.**

2. **Edit and customize your Notes Master.**

   Within the Notes edit area, you find four editable regions on the four
   corners of the page, as shown in Figure 4-3. These are header, footer,
   number, and date.

3. **Indulge yourself and edit as required.**

   You can also select the text in the Notes area below the slide and change
   the font as required.

4. **Choose View➪Normal to return to Normal view.**

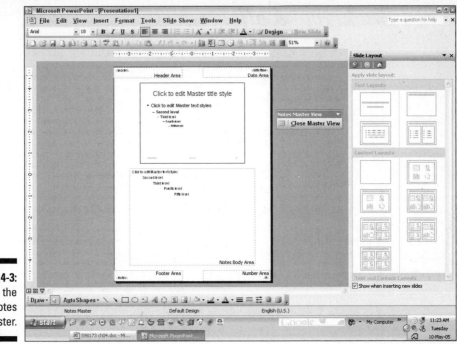

**Figure 4-3:**
Editing the
Notes
Master.

PowerPoint's capacity to store masters depends on the type of master and the PowerPoint version:

- ✔ Slide and Title Masters are stored inside both PowerPoint presentations and templates.

- ✔ PowerPoint 2000 can create and use a single instance each of the Slide and Title Masters.

- ✔ PowerPoint 2002 and 2003 include the capability to create multiple Slide and Title Masters.

    You can find more about using multiple masters later in this chapter.

- ✔ Handout and Notes Masters are stored only inside presentations — templates just ignore them.

    All PowerPoint versions can store only one instance each of the Handout Master and Notes Master.

## Background effects

PowerPoint allows you to use all of the following fill effects options as slide backgrounds:

- ✔ Solid color
- ✔ Gradient
- ✔ Texture
- ✔ Pattern
- ✔ Picture

As far as possible, change the background for the slides in Master editing view rather than in Normal view. PowerPoint uses the background options specified in the master for all slides unless you override the background choice by formatting the background in Normal view.

Follow these steps to alter the backgrounds in Slide Master view:

1. **Choose View➪Master➪Slide Master.**

   - If you're using PowerPoint 2002 or 2003, choose one of the master previews on the left pane (see Figure 4-4).

   - If you're using PowerPoint 2000, your Slide Master will already be selected because this version allows only one Slide Master.

2. **Follow the instructions to change the background fill type as detailed in the sections below.**

### Solid color

To apply a solid-color background to a Slide Master, follow these steps:

1. **Choose Format➪Background.**

   The Background dialog box appears, as shown in Figure 4-5.

Figure 4-4:
Choose a
master to
edit.

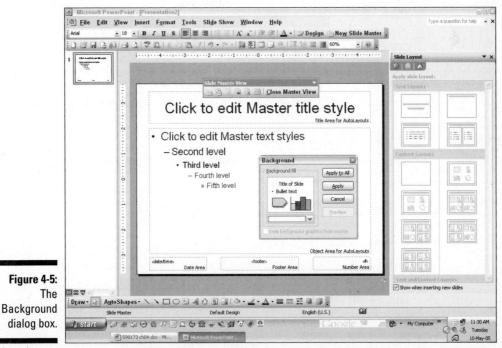

Figure 4-5:
The
Background
dialog box.

2. **Click the downward-pointing arrow below the slide preview.**

3. **Choose More Colors from the resulting drop-down list.**

   This opens the Colors dialog box, shown in Figure 4-6.

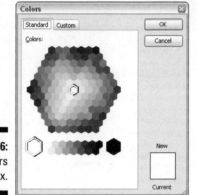

**Figure 4-6:**
The Colors
dialog box.

4. **Choose any of the colors from the color hive in the dialog box.**

   If you want to use a color that isn't available in the hive, select the Custom tab, which lets you choose any color from a spectrum.

5. **Click OK to exit this dialog box.**

6. **Click Apply in the Background dialog box to get back to Master editing view.**

### Gradient

Gradient backgrounds are a quick way to escape the plain look of just one color.

Gradient backgrounds may improve the *performance* of your computer:

   ✔ They aren't as processor-intensive as textured or full-screen backgrounds.

   ✔ They keep file sizes small.

Follow these steps to apply a gradient background:

1. **Choose Format➪Background.**

   The Background dialog box appears, as shown previously in Figure 4-5.

2. **Click the downward-pointing arrow below the slide preview and choose Fill Effects from the resulting drop-down list.**

   This opens the four-tabbed Fill Effects dialog box.

3. **Click the Gradient tab, as shown in Figure 4-7.**

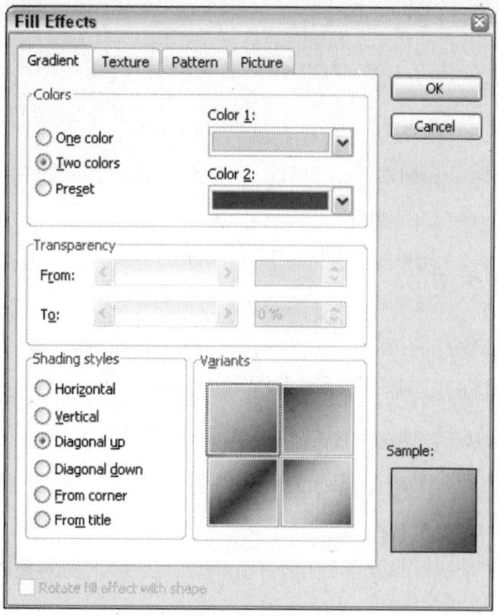

**Figure 4-7:**
The Fill
Effects
dialog box
showing the
Gradients
tab.

**4. Choose a gradient and then click OK.**

You can create gradients from three color systems:

- *One-color gradients* allow you to use a graduated fill that merges one color with either black (dark) or white (light).

- *Two-color gradients* allow you to merge shades between any two colors.

- *Preset gradients* are part of PowerPoint's fill engine — some of these gradients use more than two colors. You can't edit any presets.

In addition to colors, you can choose the direction of the gradient.

**5. In the Background dialog box, click Apply to return to the Master editing view.**

Gradient backgrounds have a couple of drawbacks:

✓ **Gradients are unsuitable for presentations with numerous elements.**

Many slide objects work better with a solid-color background rather than a gradient that uses two colors.

✓ **Gradients don't display similarly across different systems.**

Some machines may display banding. *Banding* is the visibility of distinct lines of colors being mixed between the two gradient colors — this normally happens when you're running your computer in 8-bit color (that's 256-color mode). Almost all computers shipped in the last five years can display millions of colors.

### Texture

Textured backgrounds use seamless tiles to repeat a pattern all over the slide background.

PowerPoint includes a few seamless textures that you can use by following these steps:

1. **Choose Format⇨Background.**

   The Background dialog box appears (refer to Figure 4-5).

2. **Click the downward-pointing arrow below the slide preview.**

3. **Choose Fill Effects from the resulting drop-down menu.**

   This opens the four-tabbed Fill Effects dialog box.

4. **Click the Texture tab, shown in Figure 4-8.**

5. **Choose a background texture and click OK.**

   You can choose any of PowerPoint's default textures. Alternatively, click the Other Texture button to open the Select Texture dialog box, which lets you browse and choose a graphic image to tile in the background.

   The accompanying CD contains more than a hundred seamless textures ready for you to use as fills in your presentations.

6. **In the Background dialog box, click Apply to get back to the Master editing view.**

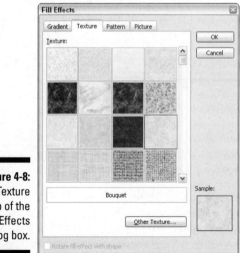

**Figure 4-8:**
The Texture
tab of the
Fill Effects
dialog box.

### Pattern

Patterns are created by using any two colors in combination with a set of default designs. Follow these steps to create patterned backgrounds:

1. **Choose Format⇨Background.**

   The Background dialog box appears (refer to Figure 4-5).

2. **Click the downward-pointing arrow below the slide preview and choose Fill Effects from the resulting drop-down menu.**

   This opens the four-tabbed Fill Effects dialog box.

3. **Click the Pattern tab, as shown in Figure 4-9.**

4. **Choose any of the patterns and then click OK.**

   Choose the twin colors that form a pattern with care — the safest bet is to use light, pastel, or neutral colors so that any text or visuals placed over the background are distinctly visible.

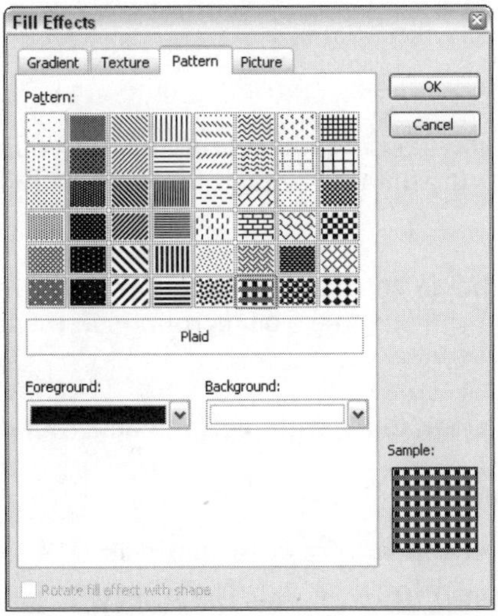

**Figure 4-9:**
The Pattern
tab of the
Fill Effects
dialog box.

5. **Click Apply to get back to the Master editing view.**

Patterns are rarely used as backgrounds because they're distinct and sharp. They have to be handled more carefully than any other background.

It's easy to create a patterned background that can strain the eyes of a viewer. To prevent this, use color combinations that don't contrast too much between each other — for example, light blue and light gray make a more subtle patterned background than the outstandingly contrasting black and white.

### Picture

Picture backgrounds are the most attractive and versatile of all backgrounds.

Avoid picture backgrounds if your presentation consists of a lot of elements, unless the picture you're using is very *neutral, faded,* or *blurred.*

Usually, you have to tweak picture backgrounds in an *image editor* — a separate application that allows you to edit and create images. The most well-known image editor is Adobe Photoshop, but there are plenty of free and low-priced alternatives. You can find many options listed on this book's companion site at

```
www.cuttingedgeppt.com/imageeditors
```

Within your image editor, experiment with adjustments in brightness, contrast, and saturation to attain an image that can be an acceptable background. You might also want to use the image editor to resize the background.

Size dimensions for an ideal presentation picture background are

- ✔ 1024 x 768 pixels
- ✔ 800 x 600 pixels

While designing your backgrounds, try creating variations for your slide and title slides and a coordinated print-suitable background that includes large areas of white.

On the CD accompanying this book, you can find over a hundred ready-to-use presentation backgrounds. You can use these backgrounds in the following tutorial.

Follow these steps to create master slides with picture backgrounds:

1. **Choose Format⇨Background.**

   The Background dialog box appears (refer to Figure 4-5).

2. **Click the downward-pointing arrow below the slide preview and choose Fill Effects from the resulting drop-down menu.**

   This opens the four-tabbed Fill Effects dialog box.

3. **Click the Picture tab, as shown in Figure 4-10.**

4. **Click the Select Picture button.**

   This opens the Select Picture dialog box, which lets you browse and choose an image.

5. **Navigate to and select the background picture that you want and then click Insert.**

6. **Click OK and then Apply in successive dialog boxes to get back to the Master editing view.**

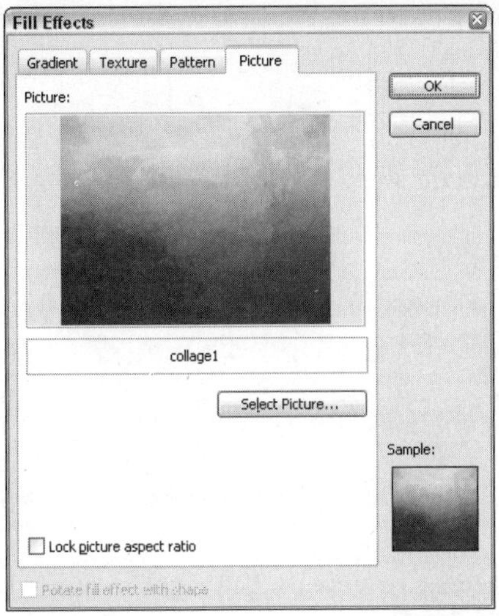

**Fill Effects**

Gradient | Texture | Pattern | Picture

Picture:

OK
Cancel

collage1

Select Picture...

Sample:

☐ Lock picture aspect ratio

☐ Rotate fill effect with shape

**Figure 4-10:**
The Picture
tab of the
Fill Effects
dialog box.

## Multiple masters

PowerPoint 2002 and 2003 support using more than one Slide Master and Title Master within a single presentation.

Follow these steps to add more masters in PowerPoint 2002 and 2003:

1. **Choose View➪Master➪Slide Master to get into the Master editing view.**

2. **Choose Insert➪New Slide Master to add a Slide Master, or choose Insert➪New Title Master to add a Title Master.**

   If the New Title Master option is grayed out, you need to add a new Slide Master before inserting a Title Master.

All Title Masters are linked to a Slide Master. The number of Title Masters in any presentation must be either *equal to* or *less than* the number of Slide Masters.

## Applying masters

Follow these steps to apply masters to individual slides in PowerPoint 2002 and 2003. You needn't manually apply a master in PowerPoint 2000 because that version allows only one master, so it's already applied by default.

First, make sure Multiple Masters hasn't been disabled:

1. **Choose Tools➪Options.**

2. **Click the Edit tab and make sure the Disable New Features check box is unchecked.**

### Complete presentation

Follow these steps to change the master for all slides in a presentation:

1. **Choose Format⇨Slide Design.**

   The Slide Design task pane activates, as shown in Figure 4-11. In the top area of the task pane are several master previews under the heading "Used in This Presentation."

   If you can't see more than one master preview in the Used in This Presentation area, it means that your presentation doesn't have multiple masters. Refer to the "Multiple masters" section, earlier in this chapter, to create more masters.

2. **Click the appropriate master preview on the right to apply the master to all slides in the presentation.**

If you inadvertently click a preview icon that you don't like, press Ctrl+Z to undo the change.

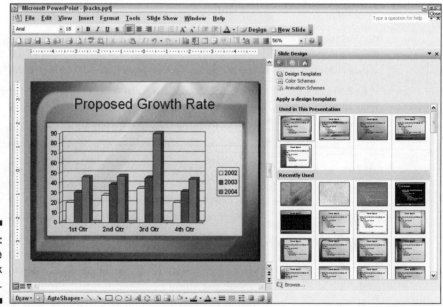

**Figure 4-11:** The Slide Design task pane.

### Specific slides

If you want to apply a master to specific slides in a presentation, follow these steps:

1. **Choose View⇨Slide Sorter.**

2. **Choose the individual slides that you want to change:**

    • To select slides in a sequence, select the first slide and then Shift-click the last slide in the sequence.

    • To select slides out of sequence, select the first slide and then Ctrl-click individual slides.

3. **Choose Format⇨Slide Design.**

    The Slide Design task pane activates (refer to Figure 4-11). In the top area of the task pane are several master previews under the heading Used in This Presentation.

    If you can't see more than one master preview in the Used in This Presentation area, it means that your presentation doesn't have multiple masters. Refer to the "Multiple masters" section, earlier in this chapter, to create more masters.

4. **Click any of the master previews in the task pane to change the master for selected slides.**

If you inadvertently click a preview icon you don't like, press Ctrl+Z to undo the change.

## Masters: Design guidelines

Masters ensure that your presentations remain consistent in design, layout, and form. These guidelines will help you attain that goal:

✔ **Overriding masters:** For a certain slide, you might want to override the master with your own settings. While in slide view, you can use PowerPoint's Format menu options to change the background or color scheme of the active slide. This change at the slide level overrides the master settings — any changes you make to the master aren't reflected on that slide, text box, or placeholder thereafter.

✔ **Company logos in masters:** You can place a company logo within a slide or title master if the logo is available in a picture format that PowerPoint can import. (See Chapter 8 to find out all about pulling pictures into your presentations.)

✔ **Footers in masters:** Editing footers in masters allows you to add the time, date, author name, and/or slide number to all slides that are based on that particular master.

✔ **Renaming masters:** Within the Master view, you can right-click a master thumbnail within the left pane and choose Rename from the context menu to provide meaningful names to all your masters.

# Transforming Masters into Templates

You have created masters and fine-tuned Color Schemes in the presentation. Now you want thousands of PowerPoint users to maintain the same look and identity in their presentations.

This is simple enough: Just evolve your master to become a template. Every master's lifelong dream is to someday become a template!

## Housekeeping

Before you fulfill that dream, you should do some housekeeping so that your template is well organized and not as bloated as a hippopotamus.

1. **Include the Properties information for the template.**

   Choose File⊅Properties and describe your template in the Summary tab of the Properties dialog box. Also, give it a name and add your name as the template creator. You can see the Properties dialog box in Figure 4-12.

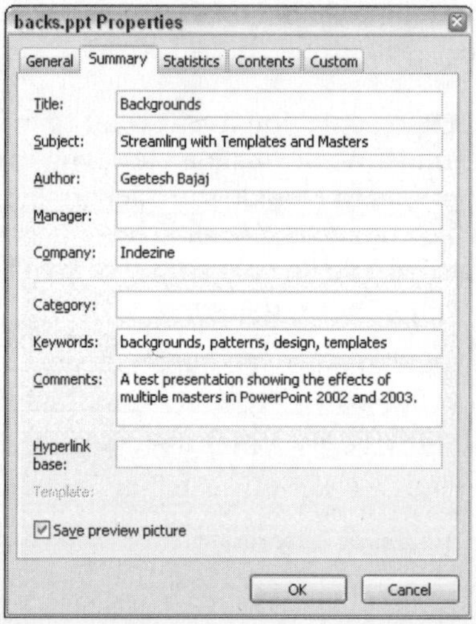

**Figure 4-12:** The Properties dialog box.

**2. Delete all slides in the presentation.**

Even if you delete the slides, the masters and Color Schemes don't get deleted. Removing all slides makes the presentation template more compact.

Don't save the presentation yet — the following steps show you how you can save the presentation as a template.

## Save as template

To save a template, follow these steps:

**1. Choose File⇨Save As.**

This opens the Save As dialog box.

**2. In the Save as Type drop-down list, choose Design Template (*.pot), as shown in Figure 4-13.**

By default, PowerPoint automatically saves templates in a specially designated template folder, though you can opt to save to any other folder instead.

**3. Click Save.**

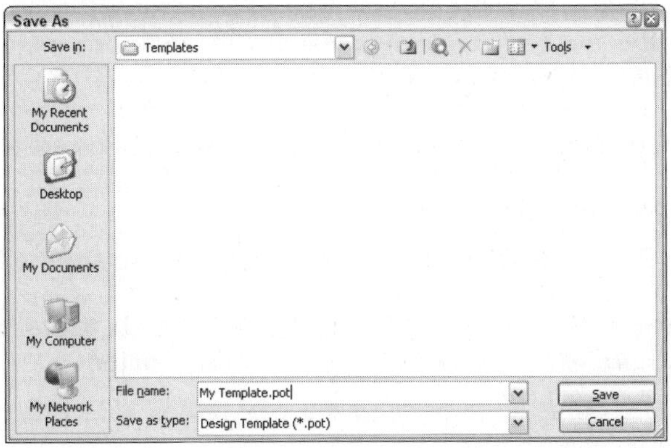

**Figure 4-13:** Save as Design Template.

Microsoft has created a distinction between masters and templates in the file format within which they're saved:

- ✔ **Regular PowerPoint presentations are usually named with the `.ppt` or `.pps` extensions** — and such presentations can include masters.

- ✔ **Templates are saved with the `.pot` extension.**

  Templates can include both masters and Color Schemes.

## Customizing templates

PowerPoint ships with many ready-made templates — you can customize these as required to create new templates. Such customization of templates is a good idea because most existing PowerPoint templates look so canned anyway — you've probably seen all PowerPoint templates at one meeting or another by now!

Beyond Microsoft's own offerings, hundreds of other vendors create templates — a simple online search will provide several links to both free and commercial sites. You can find many such resources at this book's companion site:

    www.cuttingedgeppt.com/templates

This book's accompanying CD contains over a hundred free PowerPoint templates that you can use.

You can opt for ultimate customization by commissioning your own PowerPoint template — many professional template designers can do this for you. Or you can evolve your own templates from your own masters and Color Schemes.

## Applying templates

Applying templates can be fun. I love to watch a presentation metamorphose into a new look with one click.

The steps to apply a template depend on your version of PowerPoint.

### PowerPoint 2002 and 2003

If you have PowerPoint 2002 or 2003, follow these steps to apply a template:

1. **With a presentation open, make sure you're in Slide Sorter view, as shown in Figure 4-14, by choosing View⇨Slide Sorter.**

2. **If you want to apply a template to selected slides, select them individually in Slide Sorter view.**

   Use the Ctrl or Shift keys to select more than one slide.

   If you want to apply a template to all slides, don't select any slides in Slide Sorter view.

3. **Choose Format⇨Slide Design.**

   The Slide Design task pane appears. Previews of available templates appear in the Available For Use section.

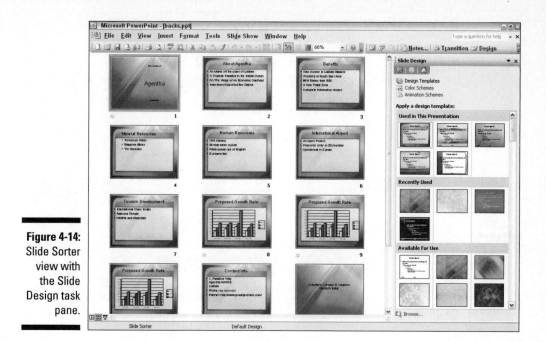

**Figure 4-14:**
Slide Sorter
view with
the Slide
Design task
pane.

4. **Click a preview to apply the template.**

   You aren't limited to using the templates that show up in the Slide Design task pane. If you want to apply another template from your hard drive, just click the Browse link below the previews and choose any PowerPoint template (.pot) on your computer.

   You aren't limited to using a PowerPoint template (.pot) file as a template, either. You can browse to any PowerPoint presentation (.ppt) file on your computer and apply that as a template to a presentation!

If you inadvertently click a preview icon that you don't like, press Ctrl+Z to undo the change.

### PowerPoint 2000

If you have PowerPoint 2000, follow these steps to apply a template:

1. **With a presentation open, choose Format⇔Apply Design Template.**

   This summons the Apply Design Template dialog box, which you can see in Figure 4-15.

2. **Choose any of the templates available and then click the Apply button.**

If you inadvertently click a preview icon that you don't like, press Ctrl+Z to undo the change.

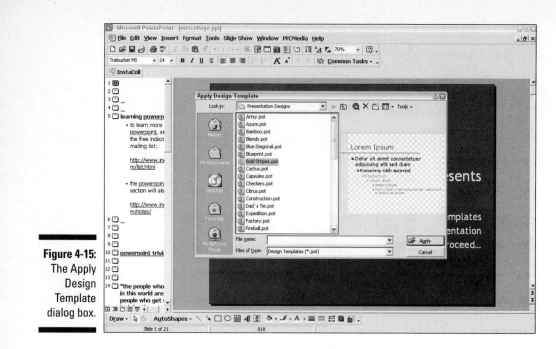

# Creating templates from existing presentations

If you like the look of an existing presentation, you can save it as a template. Yes, PowerPoint allows you to choose any `.ppt` file on your computer and convert it to a template.

It's easy to create a template from an existing presentation — you might first want to create a backup copy of the presentation involved:

1. **Delete all slides within the active presentation.**

2. **Insert two blank slides — press Ctrl+M twice and accept the defaults.**

   PowerPoint automatically inserts one slide based on each of the Title and Slide Masters. Leave these slides unaltered.

3. **Save as a PowerPoint template (`.pot`) file:**

   a. Choose File➪Save As.

   b. Select Design Template (*.pot) in the Save as Type drop-down list (refer to Figure 4-13).

   c. Click Save.

## Blank or default templates

When you start PowerPoint, you can create a blank presentation.

Such blank presentations are based on PowerPoint's default blank template that has just one Slide Master and uses Arial as the default font.

The best part of this blank presentation ability is that you can use any template to create your blank presentation. Imagine how much time you could save if PowerPoint would default to your own custom template that you use all the time.

Assuming you have formatted your default presentation exactly as you want, follow these steps to create your own default template:

1. **Choose File⇨Save As.**

2. **Choose Design Template (*.pot) as the file type.**

   PowerPoint saves the template in the default templates folder.

   Don't change the location!

3. **Name your template.**

   The name is version-specific:

   - If you're using PowerPoint 2002 or 2003, name your template **Blank.pot**.

   - If you're using PowerPoint 2000, name your template **Blank Presentation.pot**.

4. **Click the Save button.**

Sometimes you might apply a custom template to a presentation but then want to go back to a plain template presentation — something that contains black text on a white background. To do this, create a boilerplate "blank" template (under a different name than the default template) and apply this to the active presentation.

# Why bother with templates?

Joye Argo of Studio F, a company that creates PowerPoint templates, shares some of her thoughts.

"Why is it so important to select the right PowerPoint template or background? Most people dread giving presentations. Sure, a few natural speakers with incredible charisma relish the thought of an audience, but most of us don't fall into that category. Public speaking is the most common fear among adults. So we all need every confidence builder we can get. Using professional slide graphics is a confidence builder in two ways. You're more confident because your presentation looks great, and your audience has more confidence in you.

"When I get up to make a presentation, there's an unspoken agreement — the audience will give me their attention as long as I am credible. And every component of my presentation will contribute to or diminish my credibility. I know my audience will recognize professional design because we all get constant visual stimulation . . . from TV advertising and movies to print ads. That's the kind of visual stimulation our audiences are used to. And that's the standard for design we're measured against when we ask for someone's time and attention during a presentation.

"Most of us have read or at least heard about the *Dress for Success* book. Think of buying high-end graphics for your presentations as an extension of the dress-for-success concept, but in this case you're dressing your presentation for success.

"Presenters may say 'content is king,' and that's true, but think about the last time you visited your favorite fine restaurant. You went there for food, so why was so much attention paid to the decor, the waitperson's dress and manner, the arrangement of food on the plate, the lighting? It didn't change the actual taste of the food . . . but great presentation makes the experience memorable.

"I would like to ask your readers to do an experiment over the next couple of days. Really pay attention to presentation — on TV, in print ads, and at retail stores they visit. Notice the graphic design, use of color, layout, and arrangement. I believe they will be amazed at how frequently presentation affects the decisions they make in everyday life."

Joye has agreed to provide several of Studio F's award-winning templates to all readers of this book. To download these templates, visit this book's companion site at `www.cutting edgeppt.com/studiof`.

# Part II
# Achieving Visual Appeal

The 5th Wave                    By Rich Tennant

# In this part . . .

This part is all about the visual element in PowerPoint. From the basic building blocks of PowerPoint to the text content, and pictures to diagrams, this part covers all the stuff that you see on a typical PowerPoint slide.

# Chapter 5

# AutoShape Magic

. . . . . . . . . . . . . . . . . . . . . . . . . . . . . . . . . . . . . . . . . . . .

. . . . . . . . . . . . . . . . . . . . . . . . . . . . . . . . . . . . . . . . . . . .

**P**resentation graphics can emphasize your essential message and keep your audience's attention. But great presentation graphics often take time that you can better spend elsewhere in your business (especially if you aren't already an expert designer — or maybe you just need more time to study astronomy).

PowerPoint AutoShapes can give your presentations the pop you need with just a few simple steps. This chapter shows how you can quickly create and customize presentation graphics with AutoShapes.

AutoShapes use PowerPoint's basic line, color, and font tools. If a tool in this chapter is unfamiliar, it's covered elsewhere in this book. Colors, for example, are covered in Chapter 3; fonts and text are in Chapter 7.

# Why AutoShapes?

*AutoShapes* are preset, intelligent shapes like circles, arrows, stars, and call-outs that you can use to draw almost anything inside PowerPoint. Figure 5-1 shows some of these AutoShapes. Combine these shapes to create amazing visual content so fast that your colleagues will be left blinking and dazzled.

With AutoShapes, you can

- ✔ **Draw circles, rectangles, arcs, hexagons, cubes, and many other shapes.**
- ✔ **Place a thought bubble beside a picture of Aunt Eliza and make her think (for a change).**
- ✔ **Combine several shapes to create diagrams, charts, and timelines.**
- ✔ **Draw an exotic thunderbolt shape fit for Harry Potter's forehead.**
- ✔ **Draw stars with more points than you can count.**

If you want to create better presentations, you'll love AutoShapes.

You can create professional-looking drawings on your slides even if you have led an uneventful, boring, or sinister life that required no artistic expression. If you have led a moral and eventful life full of artistic vision, you'll still love AutoShapes because Microsoft beta-tested this technology with all sorts of guinea pigs (er, users).

Although AutoShapes are versatile, you can't get too far in your presentations by using them as they are. After all, how much impact can a set of green shapes on a white background make? Not to worry — in this chapter, you find out how to combine them with exotic fills. In fact, you discover the easiest route to create cutting-edge PowerPoint presentations that scream *wow!*

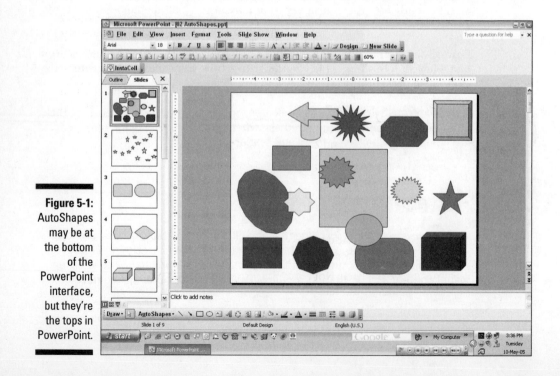

**Figure 5-1:**
AutoShapes
may be at
the bottom
of the
PowerPoint
interface,
but they're
the tops in
PowerPoint.

# Types of AutoShapes

Each type of AutoShape is accessed from the AutoShapes toolbar, as shown in Figure 5-2.

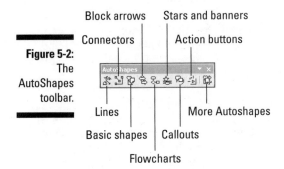

**Figure 5-2:**
The
AutoShapes
toolbar.

PowerPoint offers nine types of AutoShapes:

✓ **Lines:** Lines (with or without arrows), curves, freeform paths, and scribbles.

Chapter 6 shows you more about drawing lines and paths.

✓ **Connectors:** Connect AutoShapes with straight and curved connectors. You can have arrowheads on either, none, or both ends of the connectors.

✓ **Basic Shapes:** Create circles, rectangles, cubes, hearts, and many not-so-basic shapes.

✓ **Block Arrows:** An assortment of arrow styles will make sure that you move in the right direction.

✓ **Flowcharts:** Create a number of standard flowchart shapes, such as *process, decision,* and *data.*

✓ **Stars and Banners:** Draw stars, explosions, scrolls, and banners.

✓ **Callouts:** Insert comic book–style and line callouts.

✓ **Action Buttons:** Add push-style buttons that allow you to add navigation between slides. See Chapter 14 for more information on navigation.

✓ **More AutoShapes:** Not really an AutoShapes, this option opens the Clip Art Organizer and lets you use clip art as an AutoShape.

# Drawing AutoShapes

AutoShapes can be found in the Drawing toolbar. If you can't see the Drawing toolbar within PowerPoint, choose View⇨Toolbars⇨Drawing. By default, the Drawing toolbar lives at the bottom of the PowerPoint interface (refer to Figure 5-1), but you can move the toolbar anywhere you want.

Click the AutoShapes icon in your Drawing toolbar and then drag the handle to spawn a standalone AutoShapes toolbar (refer to Figure 5-2). You'll find nine icons on the toolbar. All but the last one open their own flyout menus that can be dragged off by their handles to create new toolbars.

Before you get enthusiastic about keeping these toolbars open all the time, remember that PowerPoint can spawn enough toolbars to make the combined population of China and India appear sparse. For proof, look at Figure 5-3, which shows all the AutoShape toolbars on display. Fortunately, Microsoft placed icons to draw lines, rectangles, and ovals right on the Drawing toolbar, so you needn't encounter all the menus and toolbars before you get to these common shapes.

**Figure 5-3:**
If you can find a place to work after opening all the AutoShape toolbars, you're either an optimist or have a very large monitor.

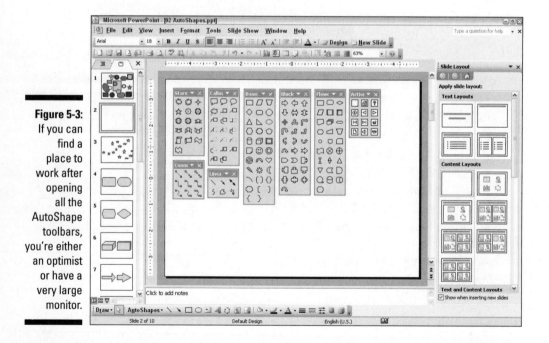

You can draw an AutoShape in two ways:

- ✔ Choose any shape and click on the slide to place a default-sized AutoShape.

- ✔ Choose any shape and then drag-and-draw on the slide to place an AutoShape of the size and proportion you require.

PowerPoint automatically applies a default fill and line to the AutoShape. Yes, those defaults can be changed. (See the sidebar, "Changing default fills and lines," later in this chapter.)

## Text within AutoShapes

To add text to an AutoShape, draw an AutoShape and start typing. Anything you type shows up within the AutoShape.

You can't just create an AutoShape and start typing for some AutoShape types such as lines, connectors, and Action Buttons.

To type or edit text within an existing AutoShape, follow these steps:

1. **Select the AutoShape.**

2. **Right-click and choose either Add Text or Edit Text.**

3. **Start typing your text.**

In many ways, AutoShapes function in the same way as regular text placeholders. That isn't surprising; any new text box you create on a slide is actually just a rectangle AutoShape with special characteristics.

You even use AutoShapes when you aren't aware. Many elements, like tables and charts, are special types of AutoShapes. In fact, if you ungroup a table or chart, you end up with a collection of AutoShapes, as I discuss in the section, "A tale of tables," later in the chapter.

## "Sticky" AutoShapes tools

Sometimes, you want to pull your hair out because PowerPoint insists on making you work more. This is particularly true if you want to draw a hundred stars on your slide. PowerPoint will insist that you reselect the Star AutoShape after drawing each star. That means you're clicking within the AutoShape menu a hundred times! Maybe it's just easier to imagine a sky without stars?

Or maybe you should tame PowerPoint and get your work done fast — I show you how in this section.

PowerPoint changes the AutoShape crosshair cursor to the default arrow cursor soon after you draw an AutoShape. If you want to draw a hundred stars, don't go back to the Basic Shapes flyout menu a hundred times. Do this instead:

1. **Select the AutoShapes menu on your Drawing toolbar and open the category you need (such as Stars & Banners).**

2. **Drag the handle of the flyout menu to create a standalone toolbar.**

3. ***Double*-click the AutoShape you need and the icon remains "sticky."**

4. **Draw your hundred or so AutoShapes.**

5. **Click the star icon once again (or any other icon) or just press the Esc key to get your hands off this "sticky" mess.**

## Supernatural AutoShape abilities

AutoShapes have special attributes and supernatural powers. Some of them are such show-offs — they even sport yellow diamonds when selected. You can't steal those diamonds, but you can certainly put them to good use. For example:

✔ Dragging the diamond above a rounded rectangle AutoShape from left to right (or top to bottom) increases the "rounded" value of the rectangle, as shown in Figure 5-4.

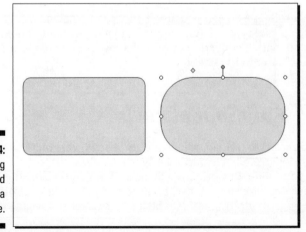

**Figure 5-4:**
Increasing the rounded value of a rectangle.

✔ Dragging the diamond down or toward the right on a parallelogram, octagon, hexagon, or trapezoid alters the shape further. Drag toward the left (or top) and you have almost a rectangle — look at Figure 5-5.

✔ Dragging the diamond down or toward the right on a cube, bevel, or can (otherwise known as a cylinder) alters the three-dimensional angle of the shape. Drag toward the left (or top) to make the shape more two-dimensional, as illustrated in Figure 5-6.

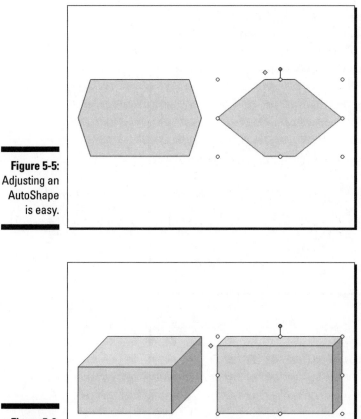

**Figure 5-5:**
Adjusting an
AutoShape
is easy.

**Figure 5-6:**
Controlling
the third
dimension.

✔ You can adjust the size of the various parts of an Arrow by dragging its yellow diamond, as shown in Figure 5-7.

✔ All stars except the 5-Point star have diamonds — pull them toward the center to create a star with a smaller center. Drag outward to create larger centers. In fact, if you drag the 32-Point star's diamond outward, you end up with an oval — almost. Figure 5-8 shows you more.

✔ With callouts, pulling the diamond around the shape moves the tail of the callout. See Figure 5-9.

Experiment with any AutoShape you use in a presentation. You never know what unique shapes those diamonds can cause!

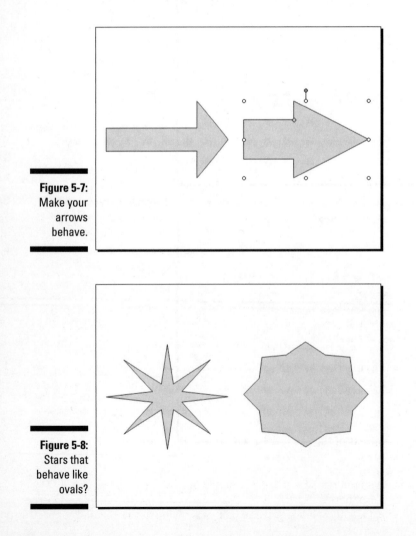

**Figure 5-7:**
Make your
arrows
behave.

**Figure 5-8:**
Stars that
behave like
ovals?

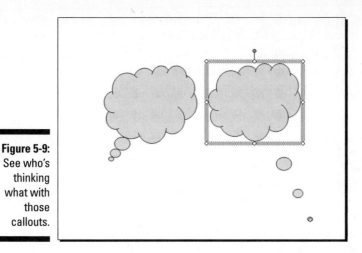

**Figure 5-9:**
See who's
thinking
what with
those
callouts.

## Changing AutoShapes

Sometimes you end up drawing the wrong AutoShape. By the time you realize
the mistake, you've already added a fill and applied some animation and
don't want to delete and start again.

Here's a solution: Select the AutoShape on the slide, choose Draw⇨Change
AutoShape in the Drawing toolbar, and choose the AutoShape you want to
change to.

# Keeping Your AutoShapes Tidy

On the CD, you'll find a full version of *AutoShape Magic,* my PowerPoint add-
in. I got so frustrated repeating certain tasks that I created this add-in to
make life simpler and happier for all PowerPoint users.

To install AutoShape Magic, read the documentation included in the same
folder as the setup file on the CD. When you have completed the installation,
AutoShape Magic shows up as a toolbar inside PowerPoint, as shown in
Figure 5-10.

Throughout the rest of this chapter, I refer often to the add-in and how to use
particular options.

Although I discuss the resize, rotate, flip, nudge, move, align, and distribute
options using AutoShapes, bear in mind that most other slide elements, including photos, charts, and even videos, can be manipulated in the same way.

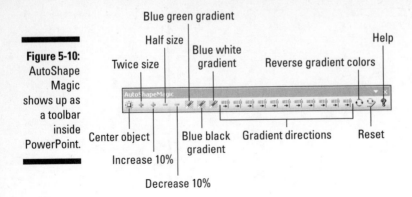

**Figure 5-10:**
AutoShape
Magic
shows up as
a toolbar
inside
PowerPoint.

Double-click any AutoShape and you'll be face-to-face with the venerable
Format AutoShape dialog box with six tabs (see Figure 5-11). You can also
summon this dialog box by selecting an AutoShape and choosing
Format⇨AutoShape. In the Size tab, you'll find options to resize and rotate
AutoShapes. Unless you need to enter exact coordinates or resize percent-
ages, there are faster and easier ways of keeping your AutoShapes in order.
For now, click Cancel to get rid of the Format AutoShape dialog box.

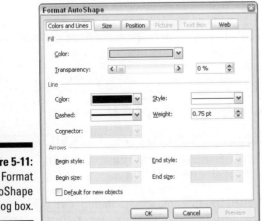

**Figure 5-11:**
The Format
AutoShape
dialog box.

# Orientation

Most AutoShapes have eight resize handles around them — four handles on
the corners and four more on the sides, as you can see in Figure 5-12. Another
green rotation handle can be found over the top-middle handle. All these handles help you change the orientation of your shapes, as I show you next.

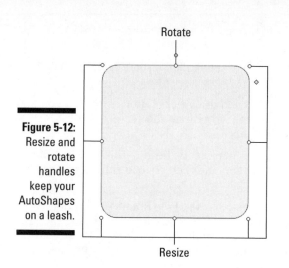

Rotate

**Figure 5-12:**
Resize and
rotate
handles
keep your
AutoShapes
on a leash.

Resize

## Resize

It's easy to make AutoShapes teeny-tiny or humongous. Here are your options:

- ✔ **Drag one of the eight handles to resize the shape.**

- ✔ **To resize while maintaining the shape's proportions,** hold the Shift key while you drag one of the four corner handles.

- ✔ **To resize from the center of the AutoShape,** hold the Ctrl key while you drag one of the four corner handles.

- ✔ **To resize from the center and still maintain proportions,** hold both the Shift and Control keys while you drag one of the four corner handles.

- ✔ **To resize only one side,** drag the corresponding side handle.

- ✔ **To resize opposite sides,** hold the Ctrl key while you drag a side handle.

- ✔ **To resize your AutoShape in 10-percent increments,** use the "+" and "–" buttons on the AutoShape Magic toolbar (the add-in found on the CD). The other set of "+" and "–" icons allows you to double or halve your AutoShape size with just one click.

- ✔ **To enter exact coordinates and resize percentages,** double-click the AutoShape to summon the Format AutoShape dialog box, click the Size tab, and enter specific coordinates or measurements in the various text boxes.

## Rotate

To rotate AutoShapes, select an AutoShape and do the following:

- ✔ Drag the green rotation handle toward the right or left to rotate around the center of the AutoShape.

- Hold the Shift key and drag the rotation handle to rotate in 15-degree increments.

- Hold the Ctrl key and drag the rotation handle to rotate around the bottom of the AutoShape.

- Hold both the Shift and Ctrl keys and drag the rotation handles if you want to rotate around the bottom (rather than the center) of the AutoShape in 15-degree increments.

- If you want to rotate in 90-degree increments, head to the Drawing toolbar and choose Draw⇨Rotate or Flip and then choose either Rotate Left 90° or Rotate Right 90°.

- The Draw⇨Rotate or Flip menu also has the Free Rotate option that essentially puts four rotation handles on the selected AutoShape rather than just one. If you hold the Ctrl key while you drag one of these rotation handles, the shape rotates around the corner opposite the one you're dragging.

- You'll find a selected AutoShape's rotation value within the Size tab of the Format AutoShape dialog box. You can enter a new value here or type in a zero rotation value to restore the original placement. Double-click the AutoShape to summon the Format AutoShape dialog box.

### Flip or mirror

Start flipping your AutoShapes like pancakes:

- **Select any of the side handles of a selected AutoShape and drag toward the AutoShape.** Keep dragging beyond the AutoShape on the other side to flip an object. Although this is quick and easy, I prefer the next option because it more precisely maintains the AutoShape's size.

- **In the Drawing toolbar, choose Draw⇨Rotate or Flip and then choose either Flip Vertical or Flip Horizontal.**

## Positioning

The position of an object on a slide in relation to itself and other objects can be manipulated by using these options.

### Group and ungroup

Many PowerPoint tasks can be performed easier and faster with grouped objects. Perhaps you want to animate a group of shapes all at once, or you want to move every shape an inch to the left. PowerPoint provides functional grouping and ungrouping abilities:

✔ *Grouping* in PowerPoint places more than one object in a collection so that you can change the characteristics of objects contained within the group at one go.

✔ *Ungrouping* in PowerPoint breaks a grouped collection back into individual objects.

Follow these steps to group your shapes (or anything else):

1. **Select all the shapes you want to group.** You can

   • Select one shape, then hold down the Shift or Ctrl keys while you select other shapes.

   • Drag a marquee around the shapes you want to be grouped.

2. **Group the shapes by choosing Draw⇨Group in the Drawing toolbar.**

   Now you can change the position, color, size, and various other attributes of all the grouped items simultaneously.

Follow these steps to ungroup your grouped shapes:

1. **Select the grouped shape you want to ungroup.**

2. **Choose Draw⇨Ungroup in the Drawing toolbar.**

## Nudge or move

PowerPoint provides more than one way to nudge or move your shapes:

✔ Select an AutoShape and press the arrow keys on the keyboard to nudge the shape.

✔ To nudge in even smaller increments, hold down the Ctrl key while you press the arrow keys.

✔ From the Drawing toolbar, choose Draw⇨Nudge and then choose either Up, Down, Left, or Right. You guessed right — the Nudge flyout menu can be dragged off to form a floating toolbar, as shown in Figure 5-13.

✔ To move the AutoShape around, just select and drag it anywhere on or off the slide.

✔ To move in a straight line, hold the Shift key and then select the AutoShape and drag it horizontally or vertically.

**Figure 5-13:**
The Nudge
toolbar.

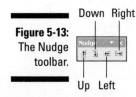

Down   Right

Up   Left

## *Align*

Before you align your AutoShapes, or any other element in a PowerPoint slide, make sure that the Align or Distribute toolbar (shown in Figure 5-14) is visible by choosing Draw⇨Align or Distribute and dragging the Align or Distribute menu's handle onto your work area. In PowerPoint, everything is on a toolbar!

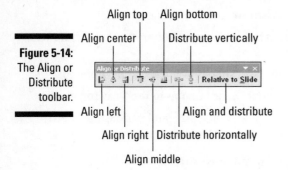

**Figure 5-14:**
The Align or
Distribute
toolbar.

Let us assume you have three AutoShapes on a slide. Select all three shapes (by clicking the first one and then Shift-clicking the other two) and click any of the six align icons on the Align or Distribute toolbar.

- ✔ **Align Left:** Aligns the left edge of all the AutoShapes.

  The leftmost AutoShape determines the left anchor. See the second column of AutoShapes in Figure 5-15.

- ✔ **Align Center:** Aligns all AutoShapes vertically along their centers.

  The anchor is determined by the median center of all the AutoShapes. See the first column of AutoShapes in Figure 5-15.

- ✔ **Align Right:** Aligns the right sides all the AutoShapes.

  The rightmost AutoShape determines the right anchor. See the third column of AutoShapes in Figure 5-15.

- ✔ **Align Top:** Aligns the tops of all AutoShapes.

  The topmost AutoShape determines the top anchor.

- ✔ **Align Middle:** Aligns all AutoShapes horizontally along their midlines.

  The anchor is determined by the median center of all the AutoShapes.

- ✔ **Align Bottom:** Aligns the bottoms of all the AutoShapes.

  The bottommost AutoShape determines the bottom anchor.

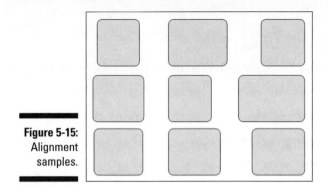

**Figure 5-15:**
Alignment
samples.

## Center an AutoShape

Follow these steps to center an AutoShape on a PowerPoint slide:

1. **Select the AutoShape.**
2. **Make sure that the Relative to Slide option is selected in the Align or Distribute toolbar.**
3. **Click the Align Center and the Align Middle icons.**

 If you have installed AutoShape Magic (the PowerPoint add-in available on this book's CD), just select the AutoShape and click the Center icon.

Follow these steps if you need to center several AutoShapes on a PowerPoint slide without altering their distances from each other:

1. **Select all the AutoShapes.**
2. **Group the AutoShapes.**

   Choose Draw➪Group in the Drawing toolbar.
3. **Make sure that the Relative to Slide option is selected in the Align or Distribute toolbar.**
4. **Click the Align Center and the Align Middle buttons.**
5. **Ungroup the selected AutoShapes (if required) by choosing Draw➪Ungroup in the Drawing toolbar.**

 If you have AutoShape Magic installed, just select the grouped AutoShapes and click the Center icon.

## Distribute

Distributing AutoShapes is a great way to make sure that they're perfectly lined up. For example, if you want a row of 12 evenly spaced stars, you use the Distribute command. Figure 5-16 illustrates how distributed AutoShapes look. Assume that you have three AutoShapes on a slide.

To distribute horizontally:

1. **Place all three shapes beside each other.**
2. **Select the shapes and choose Draw⇨Align or Distribute⇨Distribute Horizontally.**

To distribute vertically:

1. **Place all three shapes one below the other.**
2. **Select the shapes and choose Draw⇨Align or Distribute⇨Distribute Vertically.**

Undistributed row

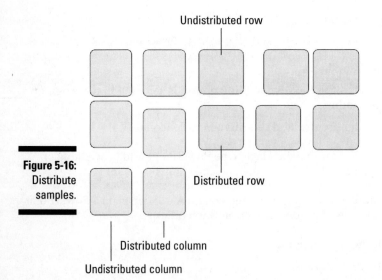

**Figure 5-16:**
Distribute
samples.

Distributed row

Distributed column

Undistributed column

### Order

Ordering brings your shapes behind or above each other. Select any shape and choose any of the four ordering options. These can be found in the Draw⇨ Order option of the Drawing toolbar:

- ✔ **Bring to Front:** Moves the object in front of *all* objects on the slide.
- ✔ **Send to Back:** Moves the object behind *all* objects on the slide.
- ✔ **Bring Forward:** Moves the object *up* one layer.
- ✔ **Send Backward:** Moves the object *down* one layer.

The Order toolbar can be dragged off to spawn a standalone toolbar, as shown in Figure 5-17.

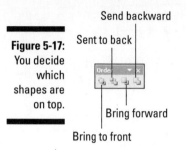

Send backward

Sent to back

**Figure 5-17:**
You decide
which
shapes are
on top.

Bring forward

Bring to front

# The Format Painter

You just formatted an AutoShape with the fill and line you want, and the text inside the AutoShape is formatted using a particular font style and color. Now you need to apply the same formatting to 25 more shapes within the presentation. What do you do?

You could format each AutoShape the same way and have no time for lunch. Or you could use the Format Painter and also have time for dessert and coffee.

Follow these steps to use the Format Painter:

1. **Select the AutoShape whose attributes you want to copy.**

2. **Copy the attributes:**

   • If you want to apply the attributes to one AutoShape, click the Format Painter icon.

   • If you want to apply the attributes to several AutoShapes, double-click the Format Painter icon so that it remains selected ("sticky").

3. **Click the AutoShape(s) where you want the attributes copied.**

4. **If you double-clicked the Format Painter to make it sticky, get rid of the stickiness.** You can

   • Click the Format Painter button again.

   • Click any other icon.

   • Press Esc to get rid of the stickiness.

Here are some guidelines for using the Format Painter:

✔ **The Format Painter can be used to copy attributes to other AutoShapes on the same slide, the same presentation, or across other presentations.**

✔ **The Format Painter works beyond AutoShapes.** You can use the Format Painter to copy characteristics of placeholders, tables, and charts.

# Working with Fills and Lines

PowerPoint's ability to present richly colored and textured elements is based on the OfficeArt fill and line technology. OfficeArt is a shared graphic component used across the Microsoft Office suite.

 Apart from AutoShapes, PowerPoint's fills and lines work the same way across other slide elements, such as WordArt, backgrounds, and charts. In fact, they even work the same way in other Microsoft Office programs because they're all based on OfficeArt technology. So you can use all the tricks you learn here in Word and Excel!

 Although fills and lines can be used for almost all PowerPoint elements in the same way, there are subtle differences. For example, backgrounds can't have a transparent fill, and pictures can only be formatted for lines.

## PowerPoint's fills

PowerPoint provides five types of fills:

- ✔ Solid Colors
- ✔ Gradients
- ✔ Patterns
- ✔ Textures
- ✔ Pictures

Color Plate 5-1 shows how versatile the fills can be.

 By default, any AutoShape you draw has a solid fill. You can change the fill either through the icons on the Drawing toolbar or through the Format AutoShape dialog box.

 I suggest you use the Drawing toolbar because

- ✔ It's quicker.
- ✔ The fill and line color icons on the Drawing toolbar remember the last settings you used for solid fills and lines.

  If you want to repeat a fill or line color again, you just click the icon.

### Default fills and Color Schemes

Whenever you create a new shape, PowerPoint uses a default fill color. This color is determined by the default fill color specified in PowerPoint's *Color Schemes* option for the active open presentation. Color Schemes are covered in Chapter 3 — however, you can follow the rest of this chapter even without reading that section now.

The advantage or disadvantage (whichever way you look at it) of using a default color from a Color Scheme is that when you change the Color Scheme, all your fill colors change, too. If you don't want your fill colors to change, don't use a color from the Color Scheme swatches in the Fill Color toolbar.

### The Fill Color toolbar

To access the Fill Color toolbar:

1. **Click the downward-pointing arrow next to the Fill Color icon in the Drawing toolbar to open a flyout menu.**

2. **Drag this menu off the Drawing toolbar to create a floating Fill Color toolbar within PowerPoint, as you can see in Figure 5-18.**

Default fill color

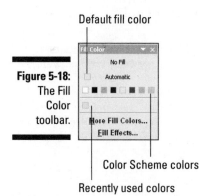

**Figure 5-18:** The Fill Color toolbar.

Color Scheme colors

Recently used colors

## Changing default fills and lines

You can override Color Schemes and change the default fill and line colors for AutoShapes in any presentation:

1. Draw any AutoShape or select an existing AutoShape.

2. Format the fills and lines as required.

3. Double-click the AutoShape to summon the Format AutoShape dialog box.

4. In the Colors and Lines tab, check the option that says "Default for new objects."

### Solid fills

Follow these steps to change or apply a solid fill:

1. **Select the AutoShape.**

2. **On the Fill Color toolbar (see Figure 5-18), choose from**

    • Eight Color Scheme swatches

    • Eight recently used color swatches

    • An absolute color value by clicking More Fill Colors

Clicking the More Fill Colors option opens the standard Windows color picker dialog box, where you can choose or mix any RGB color — that means you have almost 16 million color choices.

The PowerPoint color picker has two tabs, Standard and Custom, as shown in Figures 5-19 and 5-20.

    • The **Standard tab** (see Figure 5-19) offers 127 colors, black, white, and 14 shades of gray. You can also change the transparency value of the color, so that whatever is behind your AutoShape shows through.

    • In the **Custom tab** (see Figure 5-20), you can click a color from a spectrum and then adjust the color's *luminosity* with the slider on the right. You can also enter specific HSL or RGB values to create a specific fill color.

    For the skinny on RGB and HSL, refer to the relevant sidebars in Chapter 3. And check out the Color Plates for Chapter 3 as well.

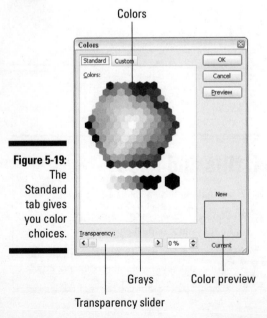

Colors

**Figure 5-19:**
The Standard tab gives you color choices.

Grays

Color preview

Transparency slider

Color picker    Luminosity

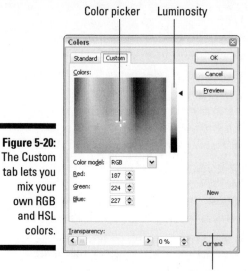

**Figure 5-20:**
The Custom
tab lets you
mix your
own RGB
and HSL
colors.

Color preview

## Gradient fills

To change or apply a gradient fill, select the AutoShape and choose Fill
Effects from the Fill Color toolbar (refer to Figure 5-18). Click the Gradient tab
in the Fill Effects dialog box and you see the dialog box shown in Figure 5-21.

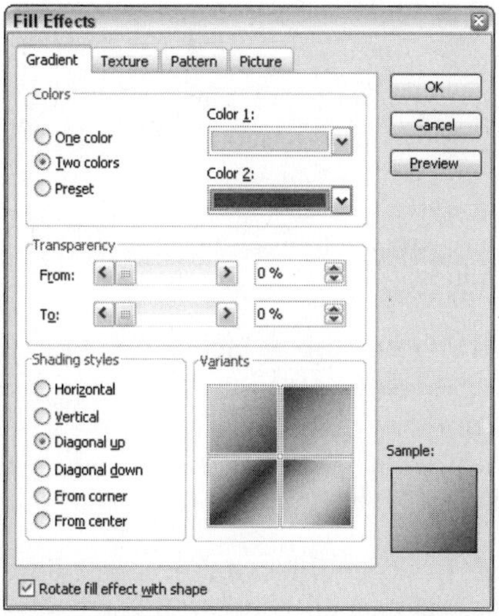

**Figure 5-21:**
The
Gradient tab
of the Fill
Effects
dialog box is
chock-full of
options.

You can create gradients from three color systems:

- ✔ **One Color gradients** allow you to use a graduated fill that merges between one color and either black (dark) or white (light).
- ✔ **Two Color gradients** allow you to merge shades between any two colors.
- ✔ **Preset gradients** are part of PowerPoint's fill engine. Some of these gradients use more than two colors. You can't alter or edit any presets.

In addition to choosing colors, you can choose the direction of the gradient. In all, you can choose from 11 gradient directions. Reverse the gradient colors and you end up with 22 gradient styles.

You can also choose a transparency level for each gradient (supported only in PowerPoint 2002 and 2003).

Creating gradients can take so much time. The CD attached to this book contains over 1,000 gradient swatches for you to copy and use. All gradient swatches are contained in a PowerPoint presentation. Follow these steps to use these swatches:

1. **Copy any swatch you like and paste it in your active presentation.**

2. **With the copied swatch selected, click once on the Format Painter icon on the standard toolbar.**

3. **Click an AutoShape to apply that gradient to the AutoShape.**

4. **Delete the copied swatch.**

### Changing the gradient direction

You can change the gradient direction in the Fill Effects dialog box. This normally involves five to six clicks. You probably don't want to experiment with all 22 styles if they need five clicks each!

AutoShape Magic comes to the rescue again! It allows you to play with 11 gradient directions with only one click.

If you want to play with the other 11 directions, just click the Reverse Colors icon!

### Design guidelines

Follow these guidelines for gradient fills:

- ✔ **Experiment with gradients between hues of the same color.** I often use a medium to dark blue gradient as a fill — this works great if I need to place some white text inside the AutoShape.

Make sure that any gradient fill you use works well with either black or white text.

✔ **If you don't need to place any text in the AutoShape, you can use gradients composed of light and dark colors.**

✔ **If you need to focus attention on a single AutoShape in a slide that contains many elements, use a gradient fill with a contrasting color.** For example, in a slide filled with blue gradient elements, I would use a red-to-black gradient to focus on a single AutoShape.

✔ **Experiment with using white as one of the gradient colors.** This works especially well if you're creating a presentation with a white background.

### Texture fills

In PowerPoint parlance, *textures* tile across to form a fill. It goes without saying that such textures need to be *seamless*. PowerPoint includes 24 textures, and you can import more by using the Other Texture button.

Seamless textures wrap all over the slide to create an uninterrupted pattern when tiled. If your texture isn't seamless, or if you don't want to tile it, you can always use picture fills (discussed later in this chapter).

Here's how you change or apply a texture fill:

1. **Select the AutoShape.**

2. **On the Fill Color toolbar (see Figure 5-18), choose Fill Effects and open the Texture tab in the Fill Effects dialog box (see Figure 5-22).**

3. **Choose from one of the existing textures or click the Other Texture button and choose a texture saved on your hard drive.**

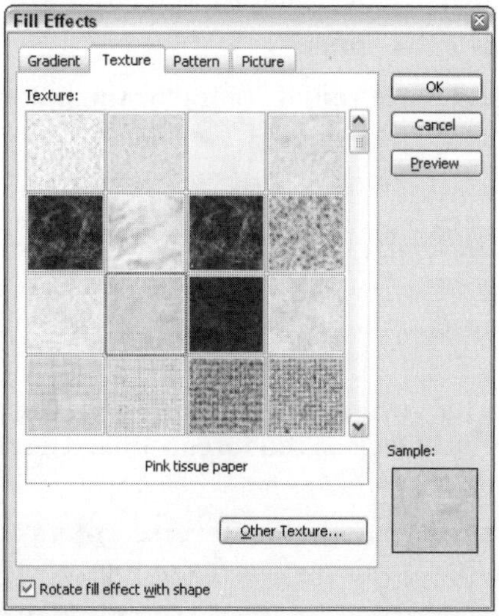

**Figure 5-22:**
The Texture tab of the Fill Effects dialog box.

The CD that accompanies this book contains more than 100 seamless textures ready for you to use as fills in your presentations. To use these textures, click the Other Texture button and navigate to the folder on the CD that contains these textures. You can also copy the entire folder to your hard drive.

Because textures are small files that tile seamlessly across an AutoShape, using textures will not balloon up your PowerPoint file size.

Follow these guidelines for texture fills:

- **Don't use textures as fills for AutoShapes that also contain text.**
- **If you want to design your own seamless textures,** use an application like Corel Painter that has specific features suitable for their creation.
- **You can find tons of seamless textures available on the Internet.** Check out www.ppted.com/001100/back for a collection of over 800 seamless textures.
- **Create design elements with small, texture-filled AutoShapes.** Often, you can enliven a drab presentation by inserting such shapes in the corners or sides of the slide area. You can also use seamless textures as fills for charts.

### Pattern fills

Patterns are two-color designs comprising lines, dots, dashes, and checks. In all, PowerPoint includes 48 patterns, such as Plaid, Weave, Shingle, and Zig Zag.

Here's how you change or apply a pattern fill:

1. **Select the AutoShape.**
2. **On the Fill Color toolbar (see Figure 5-18), choose Fill Effects and open the Pattern tab in the Fill Effects dialog box (see Figure 5-23).**
3. **Choose from one of the existing patterns.**
4. **Choose the foreground and background colors for the pattern from the drop-down lists.**
5. **Click OK.**

Follow these guidelines for pattern fills:

- **Patterns work well for presentations that need to be printed as handouts, especially for black-and-white prints.**
- **If you need to print black-and-white slides with pattern fills, use white as the background color and black as the foreground.** The reverse doesn't print too well.

- **To reverse pattern colors, you can use the Reverse Colors option on the AutoShape Magic toolbar.** You'll find a copy of the add-in on the CD with this book.

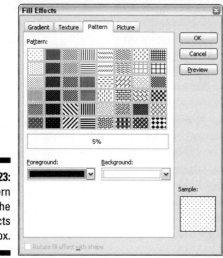

**Figure 5-23:**
The Pattern
tab of the
Fill Effects
dialog box.

## Picture fills

Pictures make great fills — you can obtain pictures from digital cameras, scans, online photo galleries, or CD-ROM clip-art collections. Many pictures are included within Clip Organizer, a media cataloging program that's part of Microsoft Office.

Here's how you change or apply a picture fill:

1. **Select the AutoShape.**

2. **On the Fill Color toolbar (see Figure 5-18), choose Fill Effects and open the Picture tab in the Fill Effects dialog box (see Figure 5-24).**

3. **Click the Select Picture button and select a picture saved on your hard drive.**

    The CD with this book contains several royalty-free pictures for you to use. You can access the pictures from the CD, or you can copy all the picture folders to your hard drive and access them from there.

4. **Select the Lock Picture Aspect Ratio check box if you don't want your picture proportions to change.**

    This option is available only in PowerPoint 2002 and 2003.

5. **Deselect the Rotate Fill Effect with Shape check box if you want to keep your picture right-side-up when you rotate the AutoShape — by default this option is selected.**

    This option is available only in PowerPoint 2002 and 2003.

6. **Click OK.**

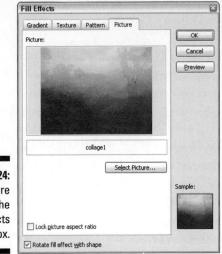

**Figure 5-24:**
The Picture
tab of the
Fill Effects
dialog box.

Follow these guidelines for picture fills:

✔ **Although you can insert pictures directly inside PowerPoint, there are inherent advantages in using a rectangular AutoShape filled with a picture.** Such pictures can rotate with the AutoShape, and changing the picture is as easy as changing the fill. You can't make a picture transparent, but an AutoShape with a picture fill can be made transparent.

✔ **Picture fills can increase the PowerPoint file size.**

Use PowerPoint's compression feature to bring your file size in order. You can find more information about compression in Chapter 8.

## PowerPoint's lines

PowerPoint provides an amazing diversity of options for creating and editing lines (outlines), as shown in Figure 5-25.

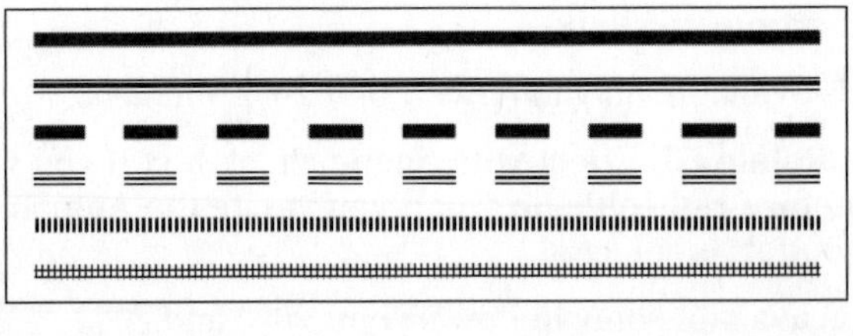

**Figure 5-25:**
Options for
line styles
are nearly
limitless.

Unlike fills, line styles don't require a closed area like a rectangle, circle, or background. They can be used in shapes that don't close.

## *Line attributes*

On PowerPoint's Draw toolbar, you'll find four icons that can be used to format lines:

- ✔ **The Line Color icon** opens a flyout menu similar to the Fill Color icon. This menu can be dragged off the Draw toolbar to spawn the Line Color floating toolbar (see Figure 5-26).

- ✔ **The Line Style icon** opens a flyout menu with different line styles. These include thin and thick lines and double-ruled lines (see Figure 5-27).

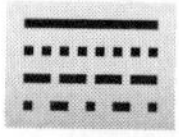

- ✔ **The Dash Style icon** opens a flyout menu with different dash styles (see Figure 5-28).

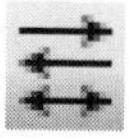

- ✔ **The Arrow Style icon** opens a flyout menu with different arrow styles for lines (see Figure 5-29).

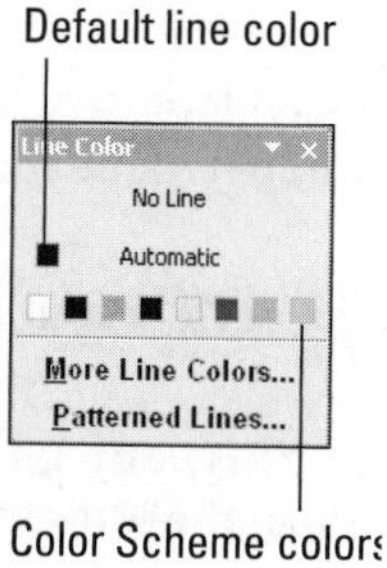

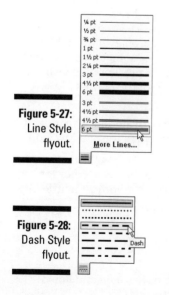

**Figure 5-26:** Line Color flyout.

**Figure 5-27:** Line Style flyout.

**Figure 5-28:** Dash Style flyout.

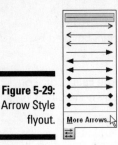

**Figure 5-29:**
Arrow Style
flyout.

## Applying a line style

Follow these steps to apply or edit a line style:

1. **Select the element (shape, drawing, line).**

2. **Choose a color for the line from the Line Color flyout (see Figure 5-26) on the Draw toolbar.**

3. **Choose a line style from the Line Style flyout (see Figure 5-27) on the Draw toolbar. Choose More Lines if you want to tweak beyond the presets available.**

4. **Choose a dash style (if required) from the Dash Style flyout (see Figure 5-28) on the Draw toolbar.**

5. **Choose an arrow style (if required) from Arrow Style flyout (see Figure 5-29) on the Draw toolbar. You can choose the More Arrows option if you want larger or smaller arrowheads.**

Follow these guidelines for lines:

✓ Just because PowerPoint includes a line by default on every AutoShape you draw is no reason to live with it. Let's face it — sometimes lines just get in the way. If that's the case with some of your presentation visuals, set the line attribute on the Colors and Lines tab of the Format AutoShape dialog box to No Line.

✓ Taking this further, you can achieve a great effect by adding a shadow to an AutoShape that has no line. To add a shadow, click the Shadow icon in the Drawing toolbar.

✓ Sometimes, you can achieve a nice effect by using the same color for both line and fill. You might want to darken the line color just a little bit.

✓ Explore patterned lines. They make great frames for images — you can discover them in the next section.

## Patterned lines

What's a patterned line? Every element in PowerPoint has a fill and line attribute — patterned lines are just another line attribute.

Figure 5-30 shows some samples of patterned lines. Color Plate 5-2 shows more patterned lines.

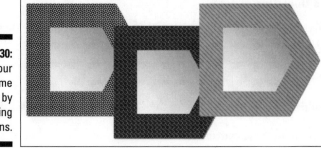

**Figure 5-30:** Give your lines some pizzazz by adding patterns.

Follow these steps to apply or edit a patterned line:

1. **Draw an AutoShape on the slide and choose Format➪AutoShape.**

   This presents you with the Format AutoShape tabbed dialog box. By default, the Colors and Lines tab is active.

2. **Click the Line Color drop-down list and choose Patterned Lines.**

   The resultant Patterned Lines dialog box that you see in Figure 5-31 gives you 48 patterns to choose from.

Patterned Lines
Pattern
Pattern:
OK
Cancel
5%
Foreground:
Background:
Sample:
Foreground color
Pattern preview
Background color

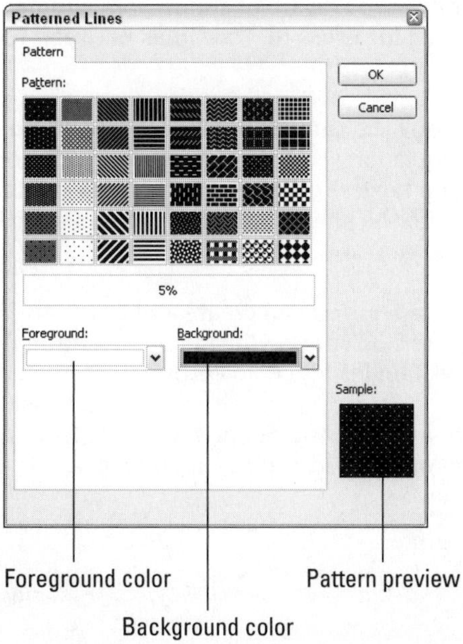

**Figure 5-31:** Creating patterned lines.

3. **Select a pattern and choose two colors that provide a nice contrast and then click OK.**

   This returns you to the Format AutoShape dialog box.

4. **Choose a thick line weight.**

   I normally choose a thickness between 15 and 40 points, depending on the size of the shape. If you choose anything thinner than that, the patterned lines really won't show the patterns!

5. **Click OK.**

You'll find samples of patterned lines on the CD that's included with this book.

Follow these guidelines for patterned lines:

✔ Patterned lines can help persons with color-vision deficiency differentiate between objects.

✔ Patterned lines look good only if you use lines with at least 15-point thickness.

✔ Patterned lines are ideally suited for creating quick frames for pictures inserted in PowerPoint.

# Smart Connectors

Many PowerPoint users simply aren't aware of connectors and how they differ from lines. It isn't unusual for users to draw lines between two shapes to show a relationship.

Lines and connectors might look the same in some instances, especially if all you need is to draw something linking two shapes. In reality, there are subtle differences between them. The biggest difference is that if you attach a connector to a shape, it moves with the shape. Attach a line to a shape and it will never move with a shape.

Using connectors and basic shapes, you can create any type of relationship chart inside PowerPoint. Figure 5-32 shows you an unconventional diagram that was created using just rectangles and connectors.

Although connectors are just another AutoShape type, they have no fill attributes. All line formatting options, including line thickness, dash styles, and arrowheads, are available.

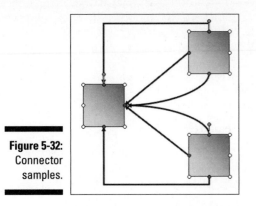

**Figure 5-32:**
Connector
samples.

# Types of connectors

PowerPoint provides three types of connectors:

✔ Straight connectors

✔ Elbow connectors

✔ Curved connectors

Each connector style has three variants:

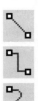

✔ No arrowheads on either side

✔ Arrowhead on one side

✔ Arrowheads on both sides

# Drawing connectors

Draw the connectors only after your shapes are in place. To draw a connector between shapes, follow these steps:

1. **Select a connector style from the Connectors flyout menu on the AutoShapes menu in the Drawing toolbar.**

   The flyout can be dragged out by its handle to spawn a new toolbar.

   The minute you move your cursor near a shape, you'll find several blue, square handles highlighted on the shape, as you can see in Figure 5-33.

2. **Click the cursor on one of the handles to determine the start point of the connector.**

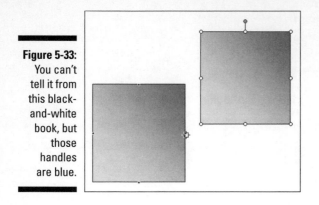

**Figure 5-33:**
You can't
tell it from
this black-
and-white
book, but
those
handles
are blue.

Move toward the shape you want to connect, and the blue squares are
highlighted on that shape.

**3. Click any of the blue handles to set the connector's closing point.**

### Changing the connector type

To change the connector type, right-click the connector and choose the new
connector type from the flyout menu, as shown in Figure 5-34.

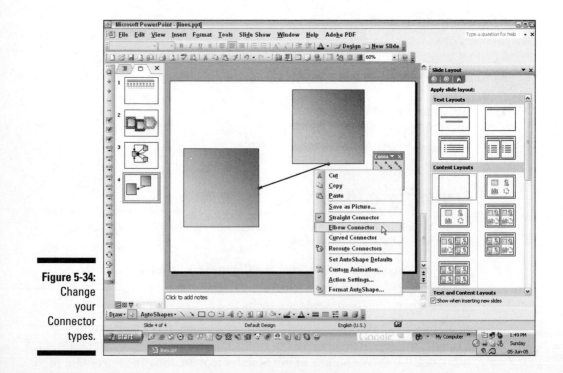

**Figure 5-34:**
Change
your
Connector
types.

### Using the yellow diamonds

Curved and elbow connectors, when selected, sport yellow diamonds that allow you to change the elbow location in elbow connectors and the curvature in curve connectors. Straight connectors need no manipulation.

After manipulating the curve and elbow connectors, you might want to change their shapes back to the original forms. Just right-click the connector and choose Reroute Connectors from the resultant context menu.

### Adding, changing, or reversing arrowheads

You might want to add or remove the arrowheads from a connector. You might also want to reverse the arrowheads in a connector.

Follow these steps to add, change, or reverse arrowheads:

1. **Select the connector that you want to edit and choose Format⇨AutoShape (or just double-click the connector).**

   This summons the Format AutoShape dialog box.

2. **In the Colors and Lines tab, the bottom third of the dialog box is concerned exclusively with arrowheads.**

   You can set the begin and end styles for the arrowheads and also make the arrowheads smaller or larger.

3. **When you're done, click OK.**

There are many ways to get to the Format AutoShape dialog box, but the easiest route is to double-click any AutoShape (including connectors).

### Moving connectors and shapes

Follow these guidelines:

- ✔ When you move a shape with an attached connector, the connector moves with the shape and automatically becomes longer or shorter to accommodate the distance between shapes.

- ✔ Connector ends attached to a shape have a red circle handle. Connector ends unattached to a shape have a green circle handle.

- ✔ To move a connector, first select the connector and then drag one of the ends to another shape or leave it unconnected.

### Expanding your chart horizons

You can combine shapes and connectors to create any sort of chart in PowerPoint. For most data-based charts, you can use PowerPoint's own charts. However, for other types of charts, the shape-and-connector approach works very well.

Some examples of this approach include

- ✔ Relationship charts
- ✔ Mind maps
- ✔ Flowcharts
- ✔ Callouts
- ✔ Concept charts

### Connectors: Design guidelines

Follow these guidelines to create better connectors:

- ✔ **Experiment with connector formatting options — especially line thickness and color.** Dark-color connectors work well over light background colors, and vice versa.

- ✔ **Use a consistent line color and thickness for the shapes and connectors on the same slide to maintain a unified design look.**

- ✔ **Animate connectors in sequence with the shapes to create a sequential chart build.**

# More AutoShape Ideas

Almost everything on a PowerPoint slide has something to do with AutoShapes. Even then, some ideas are better than others. Here are some of my favorite AutoShape ideas.

## Transparent fills

This only works with PowerPoint 2002 and 2003.

All fill styles can be made transparent to varying degrees. To change the transparency value:

1. **Double-click the AutoShape to open the Format AutoShape dialog box.**

2. **In the Colors and Lines tab, drag the Transparency slider to show any value between 0 and 100 (see Figure 5-35).**

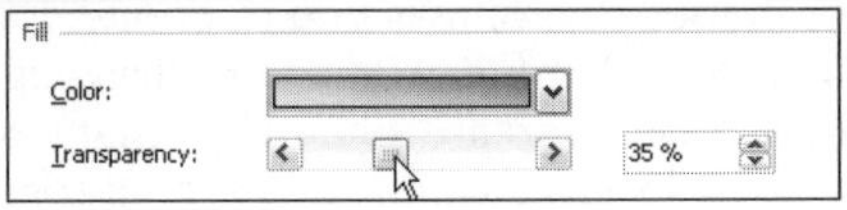

**Figure 5-35:**
Creating
AutoShape
ghosts with
the Trans-
parency
slider.

| Fill | |
|---|---|
| Color: | |
| Transparency: | 35 % |

# A tale of tables

PowerPoint's native tables can't be animated in sequence one row or column at a time. To do this, you have to convert a table to AutoShapes first. Follow these steps to convert a table into AutoShapes:

1. **Draw your table and select it or choose an existing table.**

   *Duplicate* the slide so you can get your old table back!

2. **Choose Draw⇨Ungroup on the Drawing toolbar.**

   PowerPoint warns you that you're about to discombobulate a table, but that's one warning you can ignore if you don't need to add more new columns or rows to your table.

3. **If your table isn't yet ungrouped to AutoShapes, choose Draw⇨Ungroup once again.**

   You're now free to animate the individual cells of the table as you see fit.

# Quick drawings

You can combine AutoShapes to create quick drawings even if you need to use them outside of PowerPoint. For example, you can combine

- ✔ Five or six ovals to create a flower
- ✔ Several hexagons to create a honeycomb pattern
- ✔ Two or more donuts to create a target for darts

Other quick drawings you can create with AutoShapes include clocks, road maps, and geometric abstracts. This can be a very helpful and quick alternative to conventional clip art.

# Callouts

Callouts are a category of AutoShapes that allows you to create comic book–style text and thought balloons. Combine them with drawings or photos of human or animal characters to create something that's different, yet universally appealing. Figure 5-36 shows you how this coin-tossing man is coping with three callouts!

**Figure 5-36:**
Call out for
callouts.

To use a callout:

1. **Draw or insert the character associated with the callout.**

2. **In the Drawing toolbar, choose AutoShapes⇨Callouts and select the callout style you need.**

3. **Just click anywhere on the slide.**

   Don't drag-and-draw callouts. The text in the callouts doesn't reflow on its own if you do that!

4. **Type text inside the callout shape and format the font as required.**

5. **Resize the callout to fit the entire text content.**

6. **Drag the diamond handle of the callout toward the character associated with the callout.**

# Export your AutoShapes

You might end up creating something that needs to be used outside of PowerPoint. Follow these steps to export shapes to a graphic file format in PowerPoint 2002 and 2003 — this trick doesn't work in older versions:

1. **Select all the shapes and then group them by choosing Draw⇨Group on the Drawing toolbar.**

2. **Right-click the graphic and choose Save Picture As.**

3. **In the Save As dialog box, choose the graphic format you need from the Save as Type drop-down list.**

  4 **Type a name for your graphic in the File Name text box and then click Save.**

If you're using PowerPoint 2000, you can simply select your group of shapes, copy it (Ctrl+C), and then paste it (Ctrl+V) into another Microsoft Office application.

While this regular copy-and-paste routine works well most of the time, designers often need to move their compositions to high-end drawing and page-layout applications. To export your graphic to an industry standard format, such as EPS, you need to have Adobe Acrobat (the full version, not just the Reader) and Adobe Illustrator installed on your system. This trick works in all versions of PowerPoint:

1. **Select your shapes and choose Draw⇨Group in the Drawing toolbar.**

2. **Print the slide(s) to PDF.**

   Print your slide containing the AutoShape to a PDF document by using the Acrobat printer driver.

   Make sure that each slide that contains your composition is saved as a separate PDF document. All versions of Adobe Illustrator can't import multipage PDFs.

3. **Edit outside PowerPoint.**

   Open the single-page PDF inside Adobe Illustrator. Edit as required before you save to an EPS graphic. EPS graphics can be used in page-layout programs like Adobe InDesign and Quark XPress.

## *Beyond AutoShapes*

If you love the AutoShape concept, you might want to explore Microsoft Visio and SmartDraw. Both applications use the shape metaphor to create diagrams. Both Visio and SmartDraw work very well with PowerPoint.

You'll find an evaluation version of SmartDraw on the CD attached to this book. I've often used SmartDraw to create quick charts, timelines, and tree diagrams. These charts can then be used within PowerPoint.

# Chapter 6

# Drawing in PowerPoint

• • • • • • • • • • • • • • • • • • • • • • • • • • • • • • • • • • • • • • • • • • • •

*In This Chapter*

▶ Get organized with rulers, grids, and guides

▶ It's a drawing application!

▶ Easy selection ideas

▶ Shadows in PowerPoint

▶ 3-D effects

• • • • • • • • • • • • • • • • • • • • • • • • • • • • • • • • • • • • • • • • • • • •

*P*owerPoint isn't a drawing program, but it still gives you enough flexibility to let your creative juices flow. From curves and guides to shadows and 3-D effects, PowerPoint has them all!

In this chapter, I first show you how you can use rulers, guides, and grids as the building blocks of a structured presentation. I then move to PowerPoint's drawing abilities — you learn all about lines, curves, and points. And then I show you how to select all the teeny-weeny stuff on your slides. The chapter ends with a look at PowerPoint's shadows and 3-D effects.

This chapter won't make a Disney or Picasso out of you, but if you keep playing with PowerPoint's drawing tools, inspiration is never far away.

# *Rule Your Slides with Grids and Guides*

If you want to create a structured presentation that maintains consistency of layout, look to PowerPoint's rulers, grids, and guides. With these tools, you can make PowerPoint's slide objects stay in their places all the time. For instance, you can

> ✔ **Position text boxes and other elements identically across slides and presentations.**

> ✔ **Control ruler tabs.**

✔ Manipulate the spacing between bullets and text in text placeholders and boxes.

✔ Control the snap options in PowerPoint so that slide objects snap and align to each other.

# Rulers

Rulers let you determine and measure where your objects are placed in relation to each other on one or more slides.

Rulers are found to the left and above the slide area in Normal view, as shown in Figure 6-1. If your rulers aren't visible, you need to enable them.

## Displaying rulers

Follow these steps to view or hide your rulers:

1. **Choose View⇨Normal to make sure you are in Normal view.**

2. **Show or hide your rulers by choosing View⇨Ruler.**

   As you can see in Figure 6-1, this toggle option alternates between showing and hiding the rulers.

   If you can't see the Rulers option in your View menu, hold the menu for a while to expand it; the option will become visible.

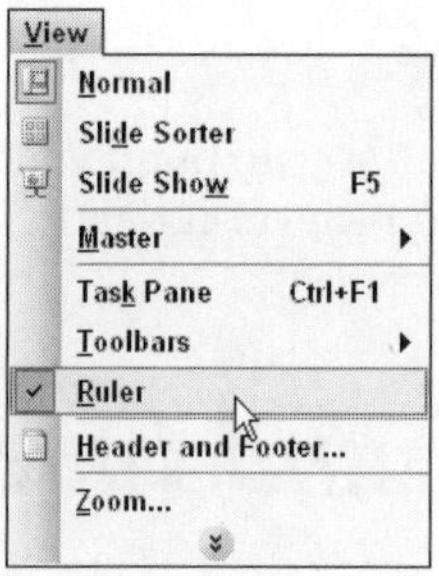

**Figure 6-1:**
PowerPoint's
rulers.

## Using rulers

Rulers can be used to

✔ Find and then change the position of guides

✔ Tweak the tab settings in text placeholders and boxes

✔ Position the spacing between the bullets and the text parts in text placeholders and boxes

Copy text into a PowerPoint placeholder from another application and you'll find that all the text formatting is goofed up. The solution is to tweak the tabs and bullets by using the ruler, as I show you next.

Follow these steps to change the tabs and bullet placements:

1. **Show your rulers if they aren't visible (see the preceding section).**

2. **Make sure you have a placeholder with bulleted text on your slide:**

   Placeholders are covered in Chapter 7.

3. **Select the text you want to alter the spacing for.**

   You can select either

   - All the bulleted text (if you want to tweak the entire placeholder)
   - A single bullet or sentence

4. **Use the two sliders (carets) on the top ruler to adjust spacing between the text and the bullets or the distance between tabs.**

   Figure 6-2 shows you the sliders that you need to pull. When you pull (or drag) any of those sliders, the selected text dynamically rearranges itself to the new spacing.

   - The left slider controls the distance between the placeholder margin and the bullet.
   - The right slider controls the distance between the bullet and the text.

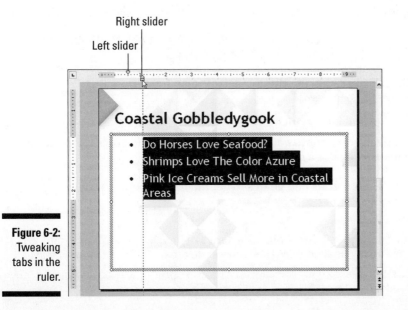

**Figure 6-2:**
Tweaking
tabs in the
ruler.

## Give 'em an inch, and they'll take a kilometer

If your ruler displays inches but you want it to display centimeters — or vice versa — don't start exploring the options in PowerPoint! This setting is outside of PowerPoint. PowerPoint shows inches or centimeters based on how your operating system is set up.

To change the default units in a Windows XP system, follow these steps:

1. Choose Start➪Settings➪Control Panel➪ Regional Settings (or Regional Options or Regional and Language options).

2. Click the Customize button to open another dialog box.

3. Tweak the settings in the Measurement Settings box under the Numbers tab.

The process is similar in other Windows versions.

To add a new tab to a text placeholder or box, select all the text, then click the exact position on the ruler where you want to set a tab.

## Getting friendly with grids and guides

Think of grids and guides as a framework that lets you

- ✔ Align, anchor, and snap your slide objects in place.
- ✔ Apply the same changes to similar elements on all slides in a presentation.

The tool you should use depends on how important object placement is to you and which version of PowerPoint you are using.

- ✔ **Grid:** If you're happy with the default snap framework that PowerPoint provides, use a *grid*.

  The grid isn't as useful as guides.

- ✔ **Guide:** If you want to control the placement of slide objects to the most minute level, use a *guide*.

You can use both grids and guides to get the best of both worlds.

### Grids

Consider the *grid* in PowerPoint as a series of imaginary horizontal and vertical lines equally spaced over the entire slide area.

The grid can help you place slide elements in the same position in all your slides. The grid isn't as helpful as the guides because you really can't alter the placement of gridlines.

The steps to view the grid and change its settings depend on your PowerPoint version.

### PowerPoint 2002 and 2003

Follow these steps in PowerPoint 2002 and 2003 to change the grid settings and to view the grid on-screen:

1. **Choose View⇨Grid and Guides to summon the Grid and Guides dialog box.**

2. **Change the snap options.**

   Check (or uncheck) the option to snap objects to the grid, as shown in Figure 6-3.

   The Snap Objects to Grid option is like a magnet that attracts slide objects to *evenly spaced points* on the slide. Move your objects on the slide, and you'll find them attaching a wee bit off from where you stopped moving them. That's the Snap to Grid feature at work.

3. **Change the grid settings.**

   You can either

   • Change the default grid spacing from several preset choices in the Spacing drop-down list box.

   • View the grid on the slide by selecting the relevant option (see Figure 6-3).

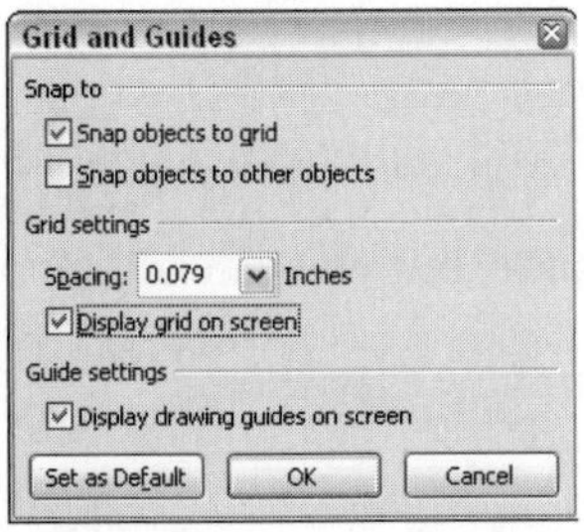

**Figure 6-3:**
**The Grid and Guides dialog box.**

Grid and Guides

Snap to
☑ Snap objects to grid
☐ Snap objects to other objects

Grid settings
Spacing: 0.079 ▾ Inches
☑ Display grid on screen

Guide settings
☑ Display drawing guides on screen

Set as Default    OK    Cancel

In PowerPoint 2002 and 2003, you can toggle the visibility of the grid by pressing Shift+F9.

Even if you can't view the grid, the Snap to Grid option might be active.

### PowerPoint 2000

To either enable or disable the grid-snapping feature in PowerPoint 2000, follow these steps:

1. **If your Drawing toolbar isn't visible, choose View⇨Toolbars⇨Drawing.**

2. **Choose Draw⇨Snap⇨To Grid from the Drawing toolbar.**

   This toggle option is used for both enabling and disabling the grid snapping.

Activating the Snap to Grid feature only snaps objects you move after it's selected. Previously placed objects don't snap to the grid unless you move them.

If you want to place an image manually without any grid-snapping, just turn off the option and place your image. Turn on the snap to grid option again when you're done.

PowerPoint 2000 uses a grid, but it's less capable than the grid in newer PowerPoint versions:

✔ **You can't change any of the predefined spacing settings.**

✔ **You can't view the grid on the slide.** Even though you can't view the grid, it's still active!

## Guides

Guides are much more than grids, but you can consider them as grids that can be moved, added, or deleted.

You can have as many as eight horizontal and eight vertical guides in a presentation. By default, PowerPoint defaults to one horizontal and one vertical guide that intersect at the center of the slide, but you can add more manually.

To make sure that the guides are visible, follow these steps:

1. **Choose View⇨Grid and Guides.**

2. **Select the Display Drawing Guides on Screen check box (refer to Figure 6-3).**

To quickly toggle the visibility of your guides, press Alt+F9. This shortcut works only in PowerPoint 2002 and 2003.

If you need to use the same guides in all your presentations, insert them in the Master slide and save the presentation as a template. The guides show up in all presentations that you create using the template. You can learn more about masters and templates in Chapter 4.

### Creating new guides

Follow these steps to create new guides:

1. **Make sure that the guides are visible on the slide.**

2. **Place the mouse cursor over a visible guide, press Ctrl, and drag in the direction required.**

   As you drag the new guide, you see the coordinates of the guide, which tell you how much you've dragged it away, as you can see in Figure 6-4. You can also view the coordinates within the ruler.

   If the rulers aren't visible, choose View⇨Ruler.

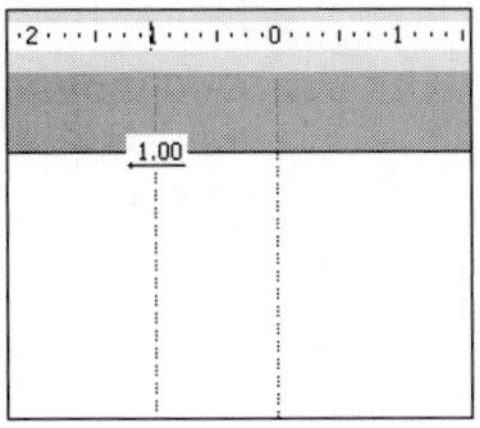

**Figure 6-4:**
Drag and
you can see
the
coordinates.

There's no Snap to Guide option that you can turn on and off. If you set your guides to be visible, they snap all objects that venture close enough!

### Moving and removing guides

To remove a guide, just select it and drag it off the slide.

Sometimes, you might select a slide element rather than a guide and drag it off by mistake, especially if the slide is crowded. In that case, press Ctrl+Z to undo the original move and then pull the guide from outside the slide area.

To move a guide, just drag it to wherever you want.

# Drawing Castles and Skyscrapers

Here are the facts about drawing in PowerPoint:

- ✔ PowerPoint doesn't have the amazing power of dedicated drawing programs, such as Adobe Illustrator, CorelDRAW, and Macromedia Freehand.

- ✔ If you need a quick doodle or a simple drawing within your presentation, PowerPoint is best.

If you don't know how to use advanced drawing programs, don't enroll for professional training now. PowerPoint's drawing tools may be all you need.

PowerPoint can help you draw castles in the clouds. However, castles are passé — so, in the following sections, you create skyscrapers in the skies.

## Line up those tools

Follow these steps to create a toolbar of PowerPoint's line-drawing tools:

1. **Get to those lines.**

   If the Drawing toolbar isn't visible, choose View⇨Toolbars⇨Drawing to access the toolbar.

   In the Drawing toolbar, choose AutoShapes⇨Lines. This reveals the Lines flyout.

2. **Drag the handle on the top of Lines flyout off the menu to create a Lines toolbar (see Figure 6-5).**

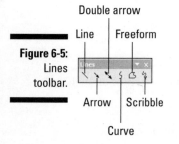

**Figure 6-5:**
Lines
toolbar.

The Lines toolbar has icons for six types of lines:

✔ These options let you create straight lines:

   • Line

   • Arrow (arrowhead at one end of the line)

   • Double Arrow (arrowheads at both ends of the line)

✔ These options let you create all sorts of lines:

   • Curve

   • Freeform

   • Scribble

# Lines and points

Most dedicated drawing programs don't give you six types of line tools. PowerPoint does just that so that you'll know exactly the type of line you'll end up with.

### Points

In their simplest form, all lines connect two points. Before you get acquainted with lines, you must know more about points.

- ✔ A point is a *node* on any of the line types. Sometimes, these points are also called *vertexes*.

  Every line type has a starting point and a closing point.

- ✔ For some lines that end up as closed shapes, the starting point is the same as the closing point. Of course, there are many more points in between.

- ✔ There are several other points in between the starting point and the ending point, especially for lines that can be rounded.

  These in-between points can either be

  - *Smooth points* (smooth curves)
  - *Corner points* (sharp angles)

Using any of the line tools is as simple as

1. Clicking the icon of the line type you want.

2. Using a combination of clicking and dragging to create the points that are connected by lines.

In the following sections, I assume that you have the Lines toolbar visible, as explained in the preceding section.

### Line

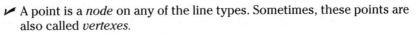

Follow these steps to draw a line in PowerPoint:

1. **Choose the line tool and click where you want to create the starting point of the line.**

   Don't let go of the mouse button.

2. **Drag the cursor to wherever you want to create the closing point of the line.**

3. **Let go of the mouse button.**

### Arrow and Double Arrow

Lines can automatically end with arrows:

🗸 An *arrow line* has an arrowhead on one end.

🗸 A *double arrow line* has arrowheads on both ends.

You draw the arrow and double arrow lines just like any other line.

The line, arrow, and double arrow options are all interchangeable. Just select any of these drawn lines on a slide and click the Arrow Style icon on the Drawing toolbar to reveal a flyout menu. The top three options let you change the type of line.

### Curve

Drawing a curve in PowerPoint is easy and intuitive. Follow these steps to create a simple shape with the Curve tool:

1. **Select the Curve tool.**

2. **Click anywhere on the slide to create a starting point.**

3. **Move the cursor down and to the right of the first point in a 45-degree angle and click again, as you can see in Figure 6-6.**

**Figure 6-6:**
Get them
curved in
PowerPoint.

4. **Move leftward in a straight line and click again, as shown in Figure 6-6.**

5. **Click over the first point to close the shape.**

If you don't want to close the shape, just double-click wherever you want to place the closing point of the curve.

As you just discovered, you are drawing with curved points rather than the corner points created by the Freeform Lines option. However, you can create a shape that contains both curved and corner points by using the Curve tool — just Ctrl-click to create a corner point rather than a curve point.

To see how points can be edited even after you finish drawing a shape, check the Edit Points video tutorial (`editpoints.exe`) on the *Cutting Edge PowerPoint Presentations For Dummies* CD. The video shows you how you can convert a curved (smooth) point into a corner point.

### Freeform Line

Despite its name, the Freeform Line tool can create both freeform lines and straight lines.

Its best capability may be a sequence of straight lines that form a shape or drawing.

Follow these steps to create freeform lines with the Freeform Line tool:

1. **Select the Freeform Line tool.**
2. **Click the mouse cursor where you want to create the starting point.**

   Don't release the mouse button yet.
3. **Drag and draw the same way you would with a pencil on paper.**
4. **End your freeform line with these options:**
   - To *stop* drawing, just double-click.
   - To *close* the shape, click the starting point once.

Follow these steps to create straight lines (and skyscrapers) with the Freeform Line tool:

1. **Select the Freeform Line tool.**
2. **Click anywhere on the slide to mark the starting point of your drawing.**
3. **Click anywhere on the slide to create another point.**

   PowerPoint draws a straight line connecting both the points.
4. **Keep adding nodes with connecting lines to create your own shape.**

   To do that, keep clicking to create new points and lines in between the points. Think of this as working in the same way as those connect-the-dots drawing books!
5. **When your drawing is done, click the first node (the starting point) to close the shape.**

   If you don't want a closed shape, just double-click the last node.

Figure 6-7 shows how I created a skyscraper by using this technique.

All closed shapes can be formatted with PowerPoint's fills and lines; shapes that aren't closed can be formatted with PowerPoint's line attributes. Chapter 5 has more information on PowerPoint's fills and lines.

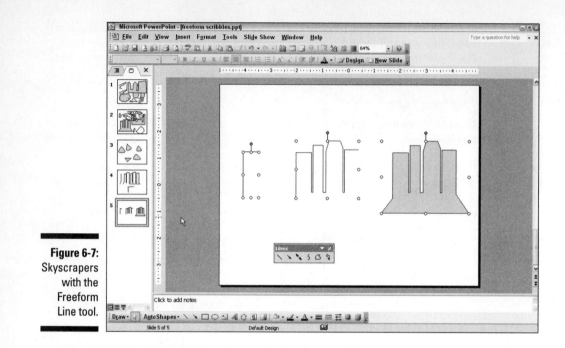

**Figure 6-7:**
Skyscrapers
with the
Freeform
Line tool.

## Scribble Line

The Scribble Line option works the same way as the Freeform Line option but with one difference: You don't need to double-click to stop drawing — just stop dragging the cursor and the drawing ends at that position — just like a pencil!

# Draw better with Tablets

However good you might be at controlling the mouse, it's not as intuitive as drawing with a pen or pencil on paper. To draw more accurately and artistically, consider using a *drawing tablet* or a *Tablet PC platform* rather than a conventional mouse.

A drawing tablet functions as a mouse replacement and lets you use a special pen over a magnetic tablet surface. Drawing tablets are often used as mouse replacements (or even coexist with mice) for desktop computers. Wacom creates the best drawing tablets — in fact, Wacom's

technology is part of the Microsoft Tablet PC platform. You can find more information at

www.cuttingedgeppt.com/wacom

A Tablet PC is a notebook computer that allows the screen to work as the tablet. This means you draw on the screen itself using a special pen — this is the closest simulation to paper and pen in the computer world. Microsoft creates a Tablet PC version of Windows that creates a seamless tablet interface. Find out more at

www.cuttingedgeppt.com/
tabletpc

## The Select Multiple Objects tool

PowerPoint has a hidden tool called the *Select Multiple Objects tool*. The only way you can access it is through PowerPoint's customization feature. Follow these steps to access the Select Multiple Objects tool:

1. **Choose View➪Toolbars➪Customize to access the Customize dialog box.**

2. **Click the Commands tab and select the Drawing category in the left pane.**

3. **Drag the Select Multiple Objects tool icon from the right pane to anywhere on your Drawing toolbar.** (I placed mine right next to the Select Objects icon.)

Follow these steps to use the Select Multiple Objects tool:

1. **Click the Select Multiple Objects tool.**

   This activates the Select Multiple Objects dialog box, which you can see in the figure here.

   This dialog box has cryptic names for every object on the slide, so you might not immediately be able to identify which name represents which object.

2. **To identify an object, select each name and then click OK to see which object gets selected.**

   You can select multiple objects this way.

3. **When you are done selecting the objects, click OK to get back to the slide with the checked objects selected.**

   This isn't an intuitive way of doing things, but sometimes this is the only solution when you can't select an object by using conventional selection tools.

Shape Console is a PowerPoint add-in that displays a miniature floating window indicating the selected shapes on the slide. You can download a free copy from this book's companion site:

`www.cuttingedgeppt.com/shape console`

# Selecting All the Teeny-Weeny Stuff

This happens so often! You draw a hundred shapes on your PowerPoint slide, make them all sing and dance — and then fumble when you want to do something as simple as selecting a shape. Fortunately, here's all the help you need.

These selection techniques are almost always taken for granted:

✓ **To select an individual object, just click it.**

✓ **To deselect all objects on a slide, just click anywhere outside the slide area where no object is placed.**

✔ To select multiple objects that aren't next to each other, Shift-click each consecutive object.

✔ To select multiple objects next to each other, follow these steps:

    *a. Make sure nothing is selected.*

    *b. Drag a marquee around the objects.*

    To drag a marquee, click your mouse button on one corner of the area and drag diagonally (an angle of around 45 degrees) until all your objects are selected. You can even start dragging from outside the slide area.

✔ To highlight each individual object on the slide, keep pressing the Tab key on your keyboard until your object is selected.

    The Tab key files through the slide objects.

# Shadow Boxing

Seeing shadows from nowhere in the middle of the night can be eerie. PowerPoint, which has no ghosts in the cupboard, makes you feel more secure with its shadows.

Did you hear the squeak of the cupboard door? Don't get paranoid — that was just a PowerPoint animation!

## Adding shadows

PowerPoint lets you add shadows to all sorts of objects, including AutoShapes, text, and pictures. Follow these steps to add a shadow to any object:

1. **Select the object.**

2. **Click the Shadow icon on the Drawing toolbar to open the Shadow flyout menu, which you can see in Figure 6-8.**

    If you can't see the Drawing toolbar, choose View➪Toolbars➪Drawing to make it visible.

3. **Choose any of the shadow preset styles in this flyout menu.**

    If you don't find the exact style you need, click the Shadow Settings option to spawn a toolbar of the same name (see the upcoming Figure 6-9). The next section shows how you can create softer shadows.

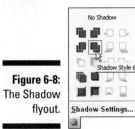

If you want to remove a shadow from an existing object, click the No Shadow option in the flyout menu (refer to Figure 6-8).

**Figure 6-8:**
The Shadow
flyout.

## Adjusting shadow

PowerPoint's default shadows are nice — and the presets allow you to add them quickly and easily. But if you want to create more convincing (or just call it eerie!) shadows, you'll love the Shadow Settings toolbar (see Figure 6-9).

To access the Shadow Settings toolbar, click the Shadow icon in the Drawing toolbar and then choose Shadow Settings from the flyout menu.

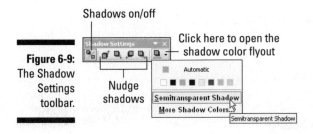

**Figure 6-9:**
The Shadow
Settings
toolbar.

The Shadow Settings toolbar holds six icons that allow you to tweak the shadows:

- ✔ The leftmost icon on this toolbar toggles between shadow and no shadow.

- ✔ The middle four icons nudge the shadow up, down, left, and right in one-pixel increments.

   This can be very helpful if you don't want to use PowerPoint's default shadow styles or if you want to tweak one of the default styles.

✔ The rightmost icon is the Shadow Color icon. Click the arrow next to the icon to access a flyout menu (see Figure 6-9) that lets you choose from

  • The default shadow color (Automatic) or any of the eight colors contained in the active Color Scheme

  • A semitransparent shadow

   Choose this option again to make the semitransparent shadow toggle.

  • More Shadow Colors (which opens PowerPoint's default color picker and lets you choose any shadow color)

The *Cutting Edge PowerPoint Presentations For Dummies* CD contains a sample presentation that uses shadow styles.

# Adding Depth and Perspective

Dimension adds depth and makes objects look closer or farther away than they actually are. Dimension also adds perspective, so appearance depends upon the angle from which an object is viewed. PowerPoint has an advanced 3-D engine working behind the scenes that is surprisingly simple and intuitive to use. It provides all the depth and perspective you might expect.

PowerPoint's 3-D engine works only with AutoShapes. This leaves out pictures, but you can get around that limitation: Just use a rectangle AutoShape with a picture fill!

Follow these steps to add a 3-D style to an AutoShape:

1. **Select the AutoShape and click the 3-D Style icon on the Drawing toolbar (see Figure 6-10) to open the 3-D flyout menu.**

   If you can't see the Drawing toolbar, choose View➪Toolbars➪Drawing.

2. **Choose from any of the preset styles in this flyout menu.**

   If you don't find the exact style you need, click the 3-D Settings option to spawn a toolbar of the same name. (See Figure 6-11.)

   If you want to remove 3-D from an existing object, click the No 3-D option in the flyout menu.

**Figure 6-10:**
The 3-D
Settings
flyout.

3-D style icon

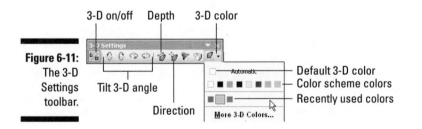

**Figure 6-11:**
The 3-D
Settings
toolbar.

3-D on/off   Depth   3-D color

Tilt 3-D angle

Direction

Default 3-D color
Color scheme colors
Recently used colors

The 3-D Settings toolbar is a mini-application in itself. (See Figure 6-11.) It has these options:

- ✔ The leftmost icon lets you enable or disable the 3-D attribute.
- ✔ The second, third, fourth, and fifth icons allow you to tilt the 3-D angle down, up, left, and right, respectively.
- ✔ The Depth and Direction icons allow you to play with the 3-D extrusion.

✔ The Lighting icon lets you change the direction of the light. You can also choose Bright, Normal, or Dim lighting.

✔ The Surface icon lets you choose from different surface styles, such as Wire Frame, Matte, Plastic, and Metal.

✔ The rightmost icon is the 3-D Color icon. Click the arrow next to the icon to reveal a flyout menu that lets you choose from

  • The default 3-D color (Automatic) or any of the eight colors contained in the active Color Scheme

  • Recently used colors

  • More 3-D Colors, which opens PowerPoint's default color picker, allowing you to choose any color

A sample presentation containing various 3-D styles can be found on the *Cutting Edge PowerPoint For Dummies* CD.

# Chapter 7

# Dressing Up the Text Stuff

- - - - - - - - - - - - - - - - - - - - - - - - - - - - - - - - - - - -

*In This Chapter*

▶ Placeholders, text boxes, and outlines

▶ Behold Microsoft Word

▶ Text box tweaks

▶ Fun with fonts

▶ Research with references

▶ Wisdom with WordArt

- - - - - - - - - - - - - - - - - - - - - - - - - - - - - - - - - - - -

*I*f content is king, then nothing relates to content like text in a presentation. This chapter is all about the text part of PowerPoint.

In this chapter, I explain what all those text terms like *placeholder, text box,* and *outline* really mean — and how you can use them best. I also show you how you can create presentations from content already available as a Microsoft Word document.

You discover more about all those text niceties such as line spacing, margins, and case, and get your bullets and numbered lists polished.

And then there are fonts. You find out how to use them as symbols and how you can make them look beautiful with WordArt.

## Using Text in PowerPoint

A presentation bereft of text is like a body without a soul. Yes, you can have photo album presentations without text, but even those need text captions. If this prompts you to fill all your slides with 400 words of text in 10-point Arial, you need to realize that too much of anything (including text) isn't a good thing. These presentation guidelines for text usage will help:

✔ **Prepare your text before you begin creating a presentation.**

This chapter shows you how to create a presentation from a Word document.

✔ **Every presentation needs a storyboard — use storyboarding principles.** This subject is beyond the scope of this book, so I've put up the content on the companion Web site:

> www.cuttingedgeppt.com/story

The *Cutting Edge PowerPoint For Dummies* CD includes a single-page storyboarding template. Print copies of the template and use it to evolve your storyboard.

✔ **Don't use PowerPoint slide text smaller than 24 points.**

You can use smaller text for things you really don't want the audience to read, such as copyright notices or silly captions!

✔ **Don't use more than four bullet points on a slide.**

If your bulleted items are *short,* five bullets may be okay on a slide.

If you have longer lists, either

- *Combine* bulleted items.
- *Divide* the content over two or more slides.

✔ **Consider not using bullets altogether!** Although most presenters swear by slides filled with bulleted items, not using bullets might give you more flexibility in designing and delivering your presentation.

# All Those Text Terms

This section shows all the text nomenclature that PowerPoint uses. After you and PowerPoint start using the same language, you'll be on the same wavelength!

## Placeholders and text boxes

All placeholders are text boxes, but not all text boxes are placeholders:

✔ **Any container of text is called a *text box.***

✔ **PowerPoint includes several layouts.** Most of these layouts include text boxes. Because these text boxes are part of a slide layout, they're known as *placeholders.*

To view the layouts, choose Format➪Slide Layout. Depending on the version of PowerPoint you are using, you might either see a dialog box or a task pane with thumbnail representations of all slide layouts.

✔ **Other text boxes that you insert within a slide aren't placeholders;** they're mere text boxes.

To insert a text box in a slide, choose Insert➪Text Box. Depending on the version of PowerPoint you are using, you might get an option to insert either a horizontal or vertical text box. Your cursor transforms into an insertion point. You can either

- Place the cursor anywhere on the slide to create a text box that resizes to fit any text you type.

- Drag and draw with the cursor on the slide to set the size and location of the text box.

✔ **All text boxes and placeholders are part of the AutoShapes family.** You can use all the formatting options associated with AutoShapes (such as fill, transparency, and lines) to spiff up your text boxes.

Chapter 5 includes more information about how you can format your AutoShapes with fills — and also how you can manipulate them for size, position, and orientation.

## *Outlines*

The outline of a presentation is merely all the titles and bulleted text that you see on your slides.

All the text that you include within the title and text placeholders is part of the presentation's outline.

Any text outside the placeholders doesn't become a part of the outline. Include as much text content in the outline (and placeholders) as you can because most third-party tools for PowerPoint use only the text contained within the outline and ignore everything else! Even if you want to send your text to Microsoft Word, it will ignore everything outside the outlines.

How you view a presentation's outline depends on your version of PowerPoint:

✔ *In PowerPoint 2002 and 2003,* click the Outline tab in the left pane of the PowerPoint window.

If you want a better view of the outline in PowerPoint 2002 and 2003, drag the vertical line between the slide and outline panes to resize it as required.

✔ *In PowerPoint 2000,* click the second view button (Outline View) in the lower-left corner of the PowerPoint window.

# *Putting Microsoft Word to Good Use*

Creating and editing an outline in Word is easier than in PowerPoint. You can create a new PowerPoint presentation in an instant from a properly formatted Word outline. Only two conditions need to be met:

- ✔ **Both Word and PowerPoint must be installed on the same machine.** Word and PowerPoint collaborate best when they have the same version number.

- ✔ **Your Word outline needs to be formatted using Heading styles.** These styles correspond directly to PowerPoint's Title and Bullets attributes.

For the following brief tutorial, you need a Word document with some text in it. You can use the sample document called `small.doc` on the *Cutting Edge PowerPoint For Dummies* CD.

Follow these steps to create a Word document that successfully translates to a PowerPoint presentation:

1. **Remove all the gobbledygook.**

   PowerPoint often requires much less text than a Word document:

   - Remove repetitive text.

   - Prune your sentences.

   - Break long sentences into smaller sentences.

   Repeat this process any number of times to end up with a slick and effective outline.

2. **Include a return (press Enter) after each title or sentence.**

   Place only one return after each sentence. More than one return makes *blank* PowerPoint slides after the conversion!

3. **Apply Word's paragraph styles.**

   Select the text you need to apply the style to and then choose a style from the Style drop-down box in the Formatting toolbar (see Figure 7-1).

   I've included an edited Word file, `edited.doc`, with the styles applied on the *Cutting Edge PowerPoint For Dummies* CD.

   Use only the following styles; PowerPoint ignores anything else. These Word styles translate to PowerPoint equivalents:

   - Heading 1 becomes Title.

   - Heading 2 becomes Bullet Level 1.

   - Heading 3 becomes Bullet Level 2 (a sub-bullet).

   - Heading 4 becomes Bullet Level 3 (a sub-bullet of a sub-bullet).

- Heading 5 becomes Bullet Level 4.

- Heading 6 becomes Bullet Level 5.

**4. Save your outline document — preferably under a new name.**

**5. Choose File➪Send To➪Microsoft PowerPoint.**

This opens the Word document in PowerPoint, formatted as a proper presentation with titles and bulleted items. Wasn't that cool?

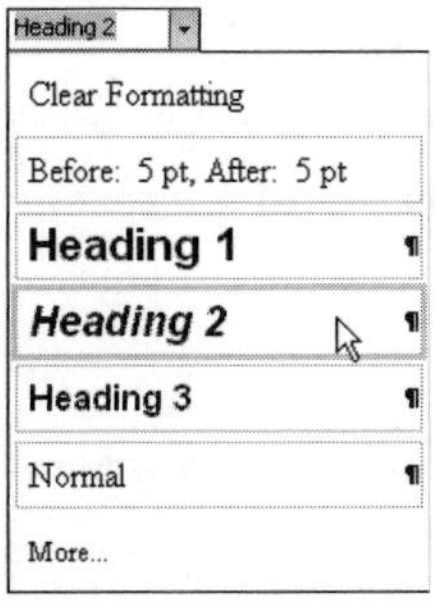

**Figure 7-1:** Applying styles in Word.

Presentations created with Word outlines are pretty basic: a default font style in black over a white background. Rarely do you want your presentation in such a bare state.

The easiest way to provide a sophisticated look to such a presentation is to apply a template. Chapter 4 has more information on applying PowerPoint templates.

You can choose from one-hundred PowerPoint templates on the *Cutting Edge PowerPoint For Dummies* CD!

# Formatting Text Boxes

Text in a presentation might be within a placeholder, an AutoShape, or a text box.

All text boxes (or the text that they contain) have these formatting attributes:

- ✔ Line spacing
- ✔ Case
- ✔ Margins
- ✔ Bullets and numbering

The following sections show how you can use these text attributes.

# Line spacing

*Line spacing* denotes the spacing between sentences and paragraphs in a text box. Efficient use of line spacing is one of the most neglected options in presentations. Fortunately, it is one of the easiest things to manage in PowerPoint.

Follow these steps to tweak line spacing:

1. **Select the text to change.**

   You can select either

   - The entire text box (to change spacing for all the text in the box)
   - Just the text you want to format

2. **Choose Format⇨Line Spacing.**

   The Line Spacing dialog box (as shown in Figure 7-2) appears.

   If the dialog box covers your text box, move the dialog box to another position so that you can preview any changes you make.

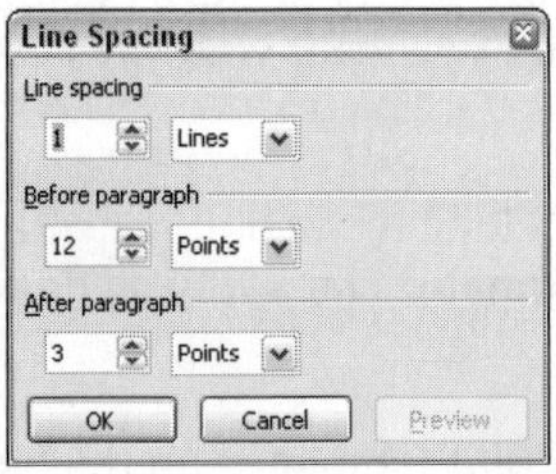

**Figure 7-2:**
Change line
spacing to
make text
more
readable.

| Line Spacing | ✕ |
|---|---|
| Line spacing | |
| 1 | Lines |
| Before paragraph | |
| 12 | Points |
| After paragraph | |
| 3 | Points |
| OK | Cancel | Preview |

3. **Change the line spacing options:**

   - The Line Spacing option changes the spacing between lines of the same sentence or paragraph.
   - The Before Paragraph option changes the spacing in the area above the paragraph.
   - The After Paragraph option changes the spacing in the area below the paragraph.

4. **Click the Preview button to see how the changes affect your text box.**

5. **If you like the changes, click OK.**

   Otherwise, tweak the options some more and then click OK. To exit without any changes, click Cancel.

Reducing the line spacing value is a great idea when you need to squeeze a single, extra line on an existing text box. However, don't do this too much because reducing the line spacing might affect readability.

## Changing case

How often have you inherited a presentation that was created by someone who seemed to love typing in ALL CAPS? If this frustrates you as much as it frustrates me, you'll love PowerPoint's Change Case option, which puts the case in your court!

Follow these steps to set your cases in order:

1. **Select the text to change.**

   You can select either

   - An entire text box (to change capitalization for all text in the box)

   - Only the text you want to format

2. **Choose Format➪Change Case.**

   The Change Case dialog box appears. (See Figure 7-3.)

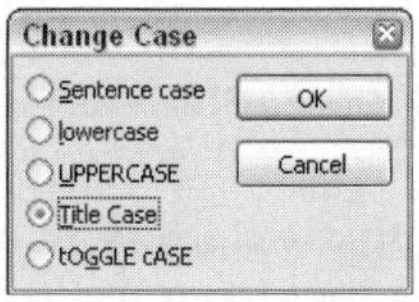

**Figure 7-3:**
What case
can I
provide?

3. **Choose any of the five *case* (capitalization) options:**

   - **Sentence case:** Capitalizes the first letter of the first word in a sentence and uses lowercase for everything else

   - **Lowercase:** Changes the entire selection to lowercase letters

   - **Uppercase:** Changes everything selected to uppercase

     This is my worst case nightmare come true! Never use it unless there is a sound reason to do so.

   - **Title case:** Capitalizes the first letter of each word in a selection.

     Yes, it capitalizes the *by*s and the *a*s. Change them back manually to lowercase after using this option.

- **Toggle case:** Reverses every letter's original case.

  For instance, PowerPoint would become pOWERpOINT.

4. **Click OK to accept your choice or click Cancel to exit without changes.**

## Margins

Margins are the bare areas on the perimeter of the text boxes that provide some breathing space to the text.

If your text suffers from a lack of oxygen, follow these steps to let it breathe more easily:

1. **Select the text box and choose the relevant Format option.**

   Depending on whether you choose a placeholder, text box, or AutoShape, the Format menu in PowerPoint (or the right-click menu) provides you with one of these three options:

   - Format Placeholder
   - Format Text Box
   - Format AutoShape

2. **In the resulting dialog box, click the Text Box tab (as shown in Figure 7-4).**

3. **Change the left, right, top, and bottom margin values as required for your selected text.**

4. **If you want to alter the direction in which the text flows in a text box, change the *text anchor point* in this dialog box from the Text Anchor Point drop-down menu.**

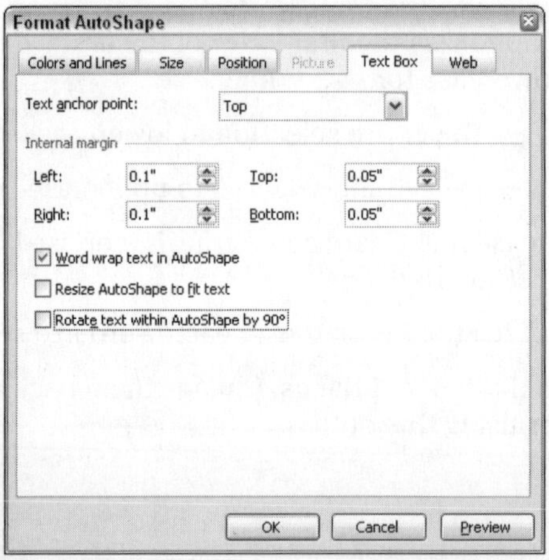

**Format AutoShape**

| Colors and Lines | Size | Position | Picture | Text Box | Web |

Text anchor point:    Top

Internal margin

Left:    0.1"        Top:    0.05"

Right:   0.1"        Bottom: 0.05"

☑ Word wrap text in AutoShape
☐ Resize AutoShape to fit text
☐ Rotate text within AutoShape by 90°

OK    Cancel    Preview

**Figure 7-4:**
Margin
magic.

5. **Click the Preview icon to see the changes reflected.**

6. **Click OK to accept the changes.**

   Click Cancel to exit without any changes.

The same dialog box offers more formatting options for niceties like word wrap and text rotation. Play with these options and review the changes immediately by clicking the Preview button.

## Bullets and numbering

Do you take all those bullets and numbering for granted just because PowerPoint takes care of them seamlessly? Truly, you don't know what you are missing. Try experimenting with some of the style options to find great new ways to make your presentation look unique.

### Bullets

Follow these steps to change the bullet style:

1. **Select the text to be changed.**

   You can select either

   - Bulleted items that you want to format
   - A sentence without bullets that you want to be bulleted

2. **Choose Format⇨Bullets and Numbering.**

   The Bullets and Numbering dialog box opens, as shown in Figure 7-5.

3. **Select your bullet character.**

   To choose a preset bullet style, just select one and click OK.

   To choose a picture bullet, follow these steps:

   a. *Click the Picture button.*

      A dialog box opens with many picture bullets.

   b. *Select a picture bullet, then click OK to apply it.*

   To use another symbol as the bullet character, follow these steps:

   a. *Click the Character (PowerPoint 2000) or Customize (PowerPoint 2002 and 2003) button.*

      The Bullet (PowerPoint 2000) or Symbol (PowerPoint 2002 and 203) dialog box opens.

   b. *Use the dialog box to select any character from any installed font as the bullet.*

Preset bullet styles

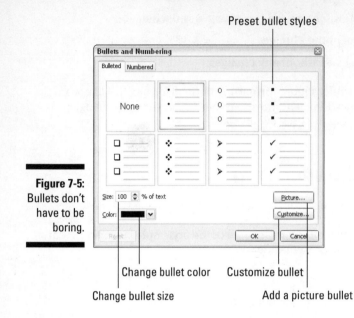

**Figure 7-5:**
Bullets don't
have to be
boring.

Change bullet color    Customize bullet

Change bullet size    Add a picture bullet

**REMEMBER**

Use a common font like Wingdings for your bullets. This ensures that all recipients of your presentation can view the bullets as you intended. If you use an uncommon font, recipients of the presentation who don't have the font installed on their computers might not see the bullet. They might end up seeing an annoying box!

4. **If required, use the Bullets and Numbering dialog box (refer to Figure 7-5) to change the bullet color or size:**

    • The bullet size option lets you increase or decrease the bullet size in proportion to your text size.

**TIP**

By default, the bullet size is 100 percent of the text size because it makes so much design sense. Don't change it to 40% or 400% unless you have a compelling need for variation in size!

    • The bullet color option lets you change the bullet color from the default text color.

**REMEMBER**

If you change the color, you can change it back to the *default* with the Automatic color option here. Make sure that the bullet color contrasts well with your slide background.

5. **Click OK to accept or click Cancel to exit without any changes.**

## Numbering

Changing the format of numbered bullets gives you an excuse to choose from a small mob of numbering styles. Follow these steps to change the number style:

1. **Select the text you want to format with a numbered list:**

   • Numbered items that you want to format

   • Sentences that you want numbered

   • A bulleted list that you want to convert to a numbered list

2. **Choose Format⇨Bullets and Numbering.**

   This opens the Bullets and Numbering dialog box shown earlier in Figure 7-5.

3. **Click the Numbered tab, as shown in Figure 7-6.**

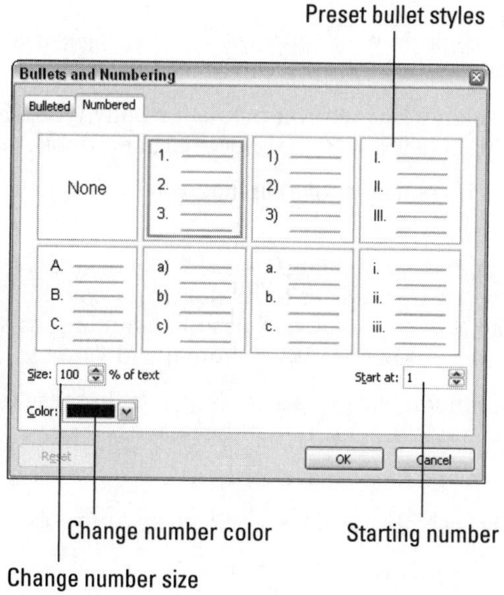

Preset bullet styles

**Figure 7-6:**
Are your
bullets
numbered?

Change number color        Starting number

Change number size

4. **Choose your options.**

   Choose from any of the preset styles. You can choose a different color and size for the number, as explained in the preceding "Bullets" section.

5. **Choose a starting number.**

   This allows you to start your numbered list from 6,754 rather than the default 1 so that the next number in the list is 6,755, not 2.

6. **Click OK to accept or click Cancel to exit without any changes.**

# Playing with Fonts

Did you ever end up using a font that looks like the letters are running away! Or maybe the font you used looks just like a movie title? It might look good on a home poster, but use it in a presentation and the audience might run away. Using the right fonts for your presentation is very important.

## Font types

Fonts can be classified into five types:

- **Serif** fonts are typefaces that have *serifs* (little hook edges that make them easier to read). Figure 7-7 shows you a few serif fonts.

  Serif fonts are used mainly by the print media for body type. Examples of such fonts include Times New Roman, Georgia, and Book Antiqua.

- **Sans serif** fonts, which are also shown in Figure 7-7, are typefaces without serifs.

  Sans serif fonts are suited for headings and electronic media (such as PowerPoint) because they are easier to read on your computer screen. In addition, they also project well. Examples of common sans serif fonts include Arial, Helvetica, Trebuchet MS, Tahoma, and Verdana.

- **Monospace** fonts are much like typewriter imprints. In these fonts, all characters are the same width, including the spaces.

  Courier is an example of a monospace font.

- **Script** fonts typically resemble brush scripts, calligraphy, or handwriting.

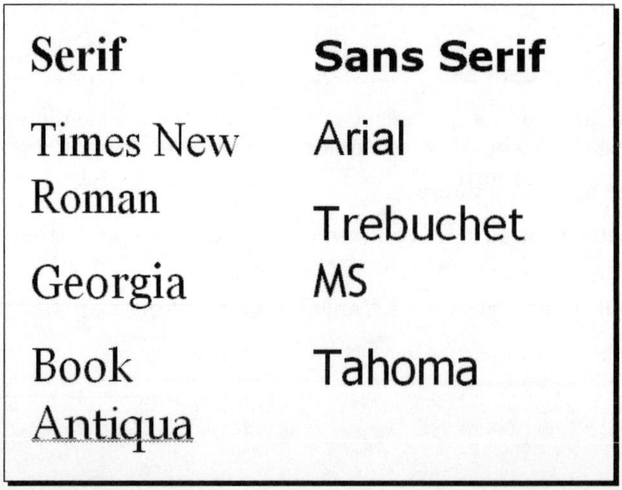

**Figure 7-7:**
Serif and
sans serif
fonts.

| Serif | Sans Serif |
|---|---|
| Times New Roman | Arial |
| Georgia | Trebuchet MS |
| Book Antiqua | Tahoma |

These normally aren't suitable for PowerPoint presentations.

✔ **Dingbats** are character fonts that don't include the alphabet. Each keystroke produces a basic line drawing or illustration.

A quick search of the Internet reveals thousands of free dingbat sets that you can download. In PowerPoint, dingbats are used for bullets. Examples of such fonts include Wingdings and Webdings.

## Font formats

All fonts in Windows are actually files that can be found by double-clicking the Font icon inside the Control Panel.

Table 7-1 lists the common font formats for Windows PCs.

| Table 7-1 | Common Windows Font Formats |
|---|---|
| *Format* | *Windows Versions* |
| TrueType | XP, 2000, NT, 98, 95 |
| Type 1 PostScript | XP, 2000, NT, 98, 95 (older versions require Adobe Type Manager) |
| OpenType | XP |

## Font guidelines

Follow these font guidelines to ensure that your presentations look sophisticated and cutting-edge:

✔ **Avoid using more than two font types in a presentation.** I normally use just one font type and provide the variation component by using different colors, sizes, and formatting attributes like bold and italic.

✔ **Using two sans serif styles in a PowerPoint presentation is perfectly acceptable.** For instance, your title and body text can each be composed in a different sans serif style.

✔ **If you can't read the text in your presentation from about two meters (about six feet) from your computer, use a larger font size.**

Avoid using a font size smaller than 24 points for any text.

Fonts with the same "point size" may be different actual sizes. For example, 24-point Times New Roman is smaller than 24-point Arial.

✔ **Use fonts that are installed on most systems by default, such as**

- Arial
- Comic Sans
- Courier New
- Georgia
- Symbol
- Tahoma
- Times New Roman
- Trebuchet MS
- Verdana
- Wingdings

✔ **If you use an uncommon font, consider embedding it in the presentation.**

Only TrueType fonts can be embedded. Find the whole scoop about embedding fonts in the next section.

## Embedding TrueType fonts

PowerPoint lets you embed a copy of a TrueType font in a presentation. But this isn't a solution to all your font problems. Sometimes, embedding a font creates more problems than solutions. Trust me — you don't want to know more about these problems until you run into them! If that made you more curious, you can find out more at

```
www.cuttingedgeppt.com/fontembedproblems
```

How you embed TrueType fonts within a presentation depends on your version of PowerPoint.

### PowerPoint 2002 and 2003

Follow these steps to embed a TrueType font within a presentation in PowerPoint 2003 or 2002:

1. **Choose File⇨Save As.**

   You're presented with the Save As dialog box.

2. **In the Save As dialog box, choose Tools⇨Save Options, as shown in Figure 7-8.**

   This opens the Save Options dialog box, as shown in Figure 7-9.

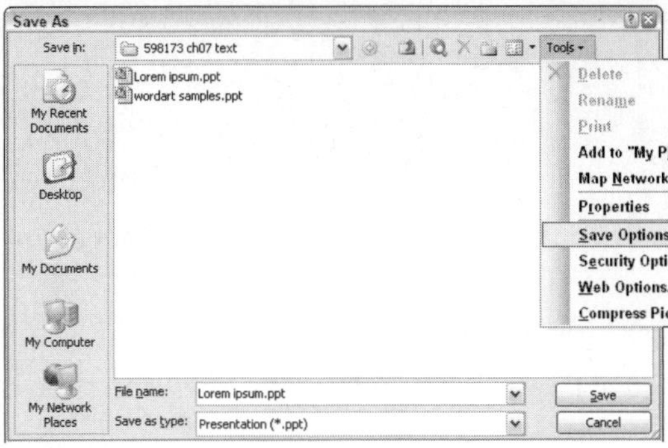

**Figure 7-8:**
The Save As
dialog box is
where you
embed
fonts.

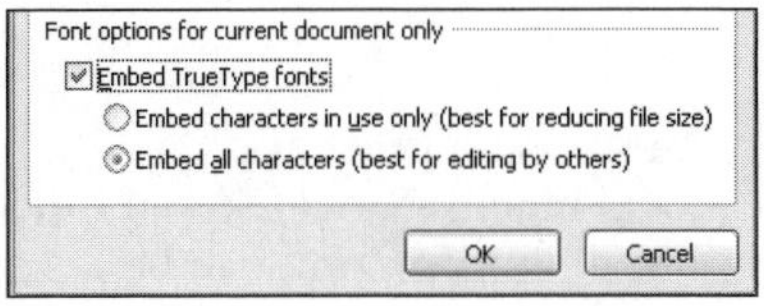

**Figure 7-9:**
Font
embedding
options.

3. **Select the Embed TrueType Fonts option.**

   The Save Options dialog box has two other noteworthy options:

   • **Embed Characters in Use Only** embeds just the font characters
     you have used in the presentation. This means that if you haven't
     used the capital letter Z anywhere in the presentation, that charac-
     ter isn't embedded.

   • **Embed All Characters** embeds the entire font into the PowerPoint
     presentation.

4. **When you are done, click OK to get back to the Save As dialog box.**

5. **Give the file a new name and then click Save.**

### PowerPoint 2000

Follow these steps to embed a TrueType font within a presentation in
PowerPoint 2000:

1. **Choose File➪Save As.**

   The Save As dialog box appears. (Refer to Figure 7-8.)

2. **In the Save As dialog box, choose Tools➪Embed TrueType Fonts.**

3. **Give the file a new name and click Save.**

## Font embedding guidelines

Follow these guidelines to make sure that you don't run into any font embedding problems:

✔ If a particular TrueType font doesn't support embedding, PowerPoint warns you.

   OpenType or Type 1 fonts can't be embedded at all.

✔ If your recipients use PowerPoint on the Mac, they can't see embedded fonts.

✔ To find out if a particular font supports embedding, download the free Font Properties Extension from the Microsoft Typography site:

   www.cuttingedgeppt.com/fontextension

✔ PowerPoint 2003 won't allow you to edit a presentation with embedded fonts that aren't installed on a local machine, even if you replace the font (discussed in the next section). More information can be found at this book's companion site:

   www.cuttingedgeppt.com/fontembedproblems

## Replacing fonts

You might receive a presentation that uses fonts that look better on a garage-sale poster, or you might inherit a presentation with a zillion font styles. Luckily, it's a snap to set the fonts in order — follow these steps to replace your fonts:

1. **Choose Format⇨Replace Fonts.**

   This opens the Replace Font dialog box, as shown in Figure 7-10.

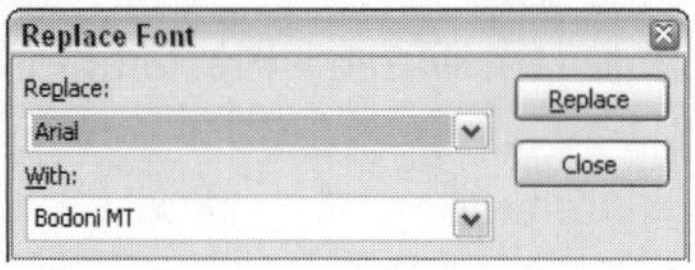

**Figure 7-10:** Replace fonts.

| Replace Font |
|---|
| Replace: Arial |
| Replace |
| With: Bodoni MT |
| Close |

2. **In the Replace drop-down list box, select the name of the font you want to change.**

3. **In the With drop-down list box, select the name of the font that you want to use.**

4. **Click the Replace button.**

5. **Repeat the process to replace more fonts.**

6. **When you're done, click Close.**

# Inserting symbols

If you're mentioning a product or company name in a presentation, you might need to put in the trademark (™) or registered (®) symbol. At other times, you might require other symbols like copyright (©) or just an infinity (∝, if you're describing the meeting length) symbol. Follow these steps to insert a symbol as part of the text:

1. **Click your cursor within a text box to create an insertion point.**

2. **Choose Insert⇨Symbol to summon the Symbol dialog box, as shown in Figure 7-11.**

3. **Choose the font that contains the symbol.**

   Common symbols for trademarks and copyrights are available in most fonts; you can find more exotic symbols in dingbat fonts, which I explain earlier in this chapter in the "Font types" section.

4. **For each symbol you want to insert**

   *a. Choose the symbol.*

   *b. Click Insert.*

5. **When you finish inserting symbols, click Close.**

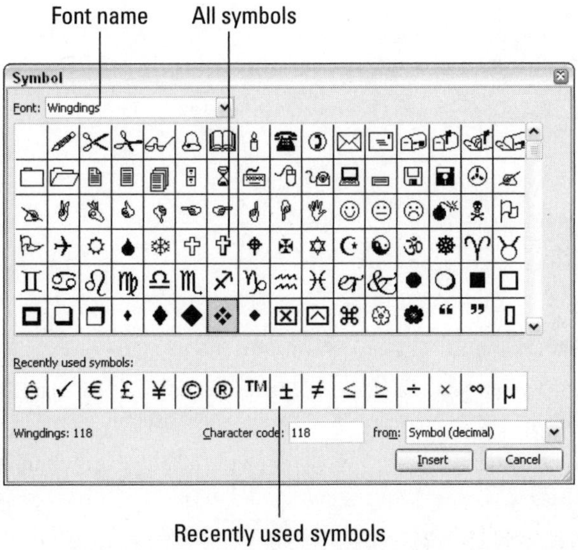

Font name        All symbols

**Figure 7-11:**
Insert
symbols.

Recently used symbols

# Doing Your Research inside PowerPoint: The World Is Your Oyster!

If you need to make your presentations more authentic, using quotes from sources as diverse as literary luminaries and stock market gurus, then look no further than the Research pane. Imagine looking for a definition, seeking alternate words in a thesaurus, searching the Web, and translating from one language to another — all from within PowerPoint!

The Research task pane is a new feature introduced in PowerPoint 2003. It isn't available in older versions.

## Accessing the Research task pane

Follow these steps to access the Research task pane in PowerPoint 2003:

1. **Choose View➪Task Pane.**

2. **Within the task pane, click the downward-pointing arrow to reveal a flyout menu.**

3. **Choose Research from the flyout menu to see the Research task pane, as shown in Figure 7-12.**

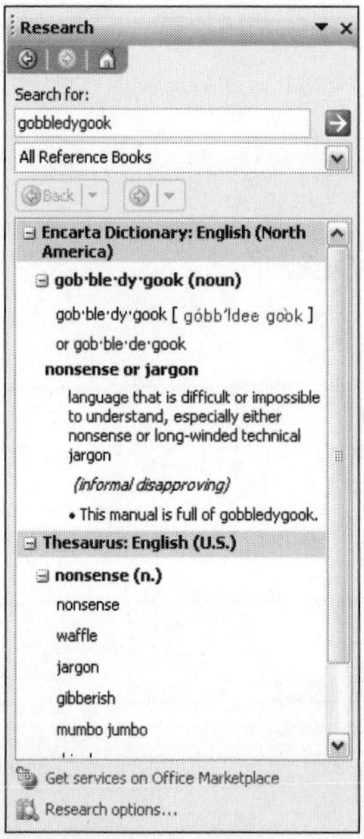

**Figure 7-12:**
Do research
inside
PowerPoint.

# References

Here is a partial list of some reference sources available within the Research pane:

- **Dictionary:** PowerPoint can access dictionaries in several languages.
- **Thesaurus:** Thesauruses are also available in multiple languages.
- **Encyclopedia:** Microsoft's award-winning Encarta Encyclopedia is available as part of the Research pane.
- **Translation:** You can translate among 12 languages, and more could be added. However, because the translation is done entirely by computers, you might end up with some hilarious results. Have fun!
- **Stock Quotes:** Yes, you can get stock quotes, change percentages, and charts for the last five years!

The Research pane is *extensible* — Microsoft and third-party developers can create extensions that allow you to search more reference sources. Most of the reference sources in the Research pane require an Internet connection to access the content.

To quickly find the definition of any word on your slide in PowerPoint 2003, right-click the word and choose Look Up from the flyout menu to search for your word in the dictionary in the Research pane.

# WordArt Wonders

WordArt is a mini-program whose *raison d'être* is to create artistic effects with ordinary words. Such words could be anything — an advertising blurb, a headline, or even an entire design all its own.

## Creating WordArt

Follow these steps to create WordArt within PowerPoint:

1. **Choose Insert⇨Picture⇨WordArt.**

   You come face-to-face with the WordArt Gallery dialog box, as shown in Figure 7-13.

2. **Choose a preset style.**

   If you can't find something you like, choose something close to your requirements. You can tweak it later.

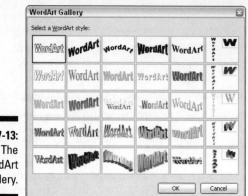

**Figure 7-13:**
The
WordArt
Gallery.

3. **Type your text.**

   You're prompted to type your text in the Edit WordArt Text dialog box.

   You can change the font style and size here.

4. **Click OK and the WordArt graphic is placed on your slide. Move or resize the WordArt graphic as required.**

## Editing WordArt

Changing WordArt text is easy — just double-click the WordArt object to summon the Edit WordArt Text dialog box. Then just change the text.

Editing other WordArt attributes is straightforward. Follow these steps to change the fills and other frivolities:

1. **When you select WordArt on the slide, you should see the WordArt toolbar. If you can't see the WordArt toolbar, choose View➪Toolbars➪WordArt.**

   The WordArt toolbar, as shown in Figure 7-14, houses several icons.

2. **Work with all the icons on the toolbar to edit the WordArt as required.**

   • The leftmost icon allows you to insert a new WordArt object.

   • The Edit Text button lets you edit the WordArt text and change font attributes like font type, style, and size.

   • The WordArt Gallery button opens the WordArt Gallery that you can see in Figure 7-13.

- The button with a paint bucket and brush opens the Format WordArt dialog box that allows you to change fill and line attributes, including the color.

- The WordArt Shape icon opens a flyout menu with several WordArt shape envelopes.

- The four rightmost icons (see Figure 7-14) let you change the letter heights, make the text vertical, align the WordArt text, and adjust the character spacing, respectively.

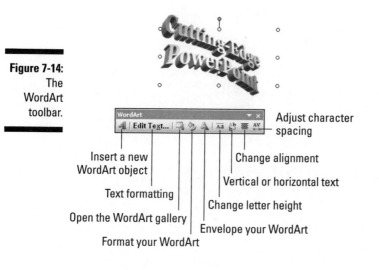

**Figure 7-14:**
The
WordArt
toolbar.

Adjust character spacing

Insert a new WordArt object

Change alignment

Vertical or horizontal text

Text formatting

Change letter height

Open the WordArt gallery

Envelope your WordArt

Format your WordArt

**3. Deselect the WordArt by clicking anywhere outside it to get back to the slide.**

To add a 3-D effect to WordArt, click the 3-D Style icon on the Drawing toolbar. More information on 3-D effects can be found in Chapter 6.

The *Cutting Edge PowerPoint For Dummies* CD contains a sample presentation that uses WordArt.

# Chapter 8

# Adding Images to Your Presentations

. . . . . . . . . . . . . . . . . . . . . . . . . . . . . . . . . . . . . . . .

## In This Chapter

▶ Parade your photos

▶ Get in the visuals

▶ Clip art galore

▶ Resolution and compression

▶ Recoloring clip art and bitmap images

▶ PowerPoint and Photoshop

. . . . . . . . . . . . . . . . . . . . . . . . . . . . . . . . . . . . . . . .

*I*n this chapter, I show you how to get those gazillion digital-camera images into your presentation in an instant and share that presentation with grandma or your colleagues at the office. The best part of images is that the content is entirely visual — that's something that spans languages and words. This is perfect for a multilingual audience.

You also find out about resolution, compression, and adding visual effects to images inside PowerPoint, as well as how to do the edits outside of PowerPoint in advanced image editors like Adobe Photoshop.

The words *image, photo,* and *picture* are used interchangeably throughout this chapter.

## Parade Your Photos

PowerPoint lets you insert pictures in numerous ways, but the easiest option is to use the Photo Album feature. Photo Album allows you to batch import tons of photos inside a presentation.

The Photo Album feature is part of PowerPoint 2002 and 2003. If you use PowerPoint 2000, you can download the free Photo Album add-in from the Microsoft site:

www.cuttingedgeppt.com/photoalbum2000

# Batch Import Pictures with Photo Album

To get started with batch importing pictures into your Photo Album presentation, you need some pictures.

I put some of my favorite pictures on the *Cutting Edge PowerPoint For Dummies* CD. Several stock vendors have also provided sample images. You can use these pictures to create your Photo Album presentation.

Although they are called Photo Albums, you can use the Photo Album feature to insert any type of graphic for your presentation, whether or not they're photos.

How you create a new Photo Album depends on your PowerPoint version.

### PowerPoint 2002 and 2003

Follow these steps to get started with Photo Album in PowerPoint 2002 and 2003:

1. **Choose File⇨New to start with a blank presentation.**

2. **Choose Insert⇨Picture⇨New Photo Album.**

### PowerPoint 2000

PowerPoint 2000 doesn't automatically include the Photo Album feature. If you need this option, install the free Photo Album add-in.

Follow these steps to get started with Photo Album in PowerPoint 2000:

1. **Choose File⇨New to start with a blank presentation.**

   PowerPoint shows the New Presentation dialog box.

2. **Choose the Photo Album option in the General tab and click OK.**

## Photo Album paraphernalia

When you create an empty photo album, PowerPoint shows you the Photo Album dialog box, which you can see in Figure 8-1. This works the same way in all PowerPoint versions.

Add pictures from scanner or camera

Add pictures from hard drive

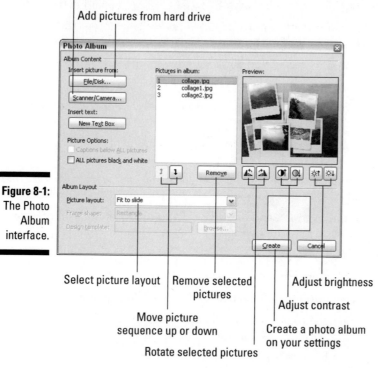

**Figure 8-1:**
The Photo
Album
interface.

Select picture layout | Remove selected pictures

Adjust brightness

Adjust contrast

Move picture
sequence up or down

Create a photo album
on your settings

Rotate selected pictures

As you can see in Figure 8-1, the Photo Album dialog box is crammed with mystifying options you might not always need. I've organized the following options into options used *frequently* and *seldom*.

### Frequently used options

These are the options that you'll want to use all the time:

1. **Click the File/Disk button to begin inserting the pictures you want to add to the album.**

   This opens the Insert New Pictures dialog box.

2. **Navigate to the folder that contains all your pictures, select them, and click Insert.**

   - If you want to insert pictures from another folder, click the File/Disk button again and repeat Step 2.

   - If you don't want to look into other niceties, either accept the default options and click the Create button or follow the extra steps to make your Photo Album more personal.

3. **Click the Move Up and Move Down buttons to reorder the sequence in which your pictures are shown.**

The picture you want to move around must be selected — the Up and Down buttons are below the picture listing (refer to Figure 8-1).

You can skip this step if you don't want to create your own sequence.

Each picture is previewed when selected. You can

- *Remove pictures* you don't need or want by selecting the picture and clicking the Remove button.

- *Rotate a selected picture* in 90-degree increments by using the relevant icons.

- If you have PowerPoint 2002 or 2003, you can *alter the contrast and brightness* values of a picture.

The rotation, contrast, and brightness icons are located directly below the picture preview window (refer to Figure 8-1).

4. **Choose a picture layout.**

Within the Picture Layout drop-down list box, you can select

- Layout options for one, two, and four pictures per slide

  If you need to have a title on each slide, you can choose the layout options for one, two, or four pictures with a single slide title.

- The Fit to Slide layout to insert full-screen images

5. **Choose a frame style.**

The Frame Style drop-down list box lets you provide specific corner styles to each picture. Choices include rectangle, rounded rectangle, beveled, oval, corner tabs, and square tabs.

6. **Choose a design template.**

Click the Browse button, which opens the Choose Design Template dialog box with your default template folder.

You can also navigate to any other folder and choose any other template.

7. **Click the Create button and watch PowerPoint weave its magic.**

You're done!

The *Cutting Edge PowerPoint For Dummies* CD contains some PowerPoint templates created especially for Photo Albums.

### Seldom used options

Here are some options that aren't used most of the time. All these options are to be found in the same dialog box shown in Figure 8-1:

✔ The Captions Below ALL Pictures option lets you add a separate caption under each picture.

✔ The ALL Pictures Black and White option (PowerPoint 2002 and 2003 only) converts all your pictures to grayscale color mode.

✔ The Scanner/Camera option lets you bring your images directly into Photo Album through a scan or from an attached digital camera.

In my opinion, this is a great time-waster because I'd rather scan all my images first and then import them into Photo Album using the File/Disk option.

✔ You can include a separate text box on each slide by using the New Text Box option. Such text boxes can include some tidbits of interesting info or memorabilia.

Most options can be added in PowerPoint 2002 and 2003 after your Photo Album is created — just choose Format➪Photo Album when your Photo Album presentation is open in PowerPoint. (This doesn't work in PowerPoint 2000.)

## Batch import images

In the preceding section, I show you how to batch import tons of pictures into PowerPoint slides in a jiffy by using the Photo Album options.

Although Photo Album provides a great way to batch import (or insert) folders full of pictures inside a PowerPoint presentation, it isn't as full-featured as third-party add-ins, which have more tricks up their sleeves.

### More ideas for Photo Album

Here are a few tips for using Photo Album to its fullest:

✔ Don't just use Photo Album to create family or vacation keepsakes. The same options let you create quick product catalogs and after-conference shows.

✔ Refine the output by adding a continuous musical score to your entire presentation. This is covered in Chapter 10.

✔ If you start with high-resolution images, your Photo Album presentation saves to a huge size — which is impractical if you want to e-mail it to others. To sidestep this problem, use the picture compression options explained later in this chapter.

✔ **Image Importer Wizard** lets you create and save your own custom templates and layouts. A free trial version that works like the full version for two weeks is available.

    www.cuttingedgeppt.com/iiw

✔ **pptXTREME Import/Export** inserts tons of pictures in an instant. It also includes niceties like updating pictures and exporting images.

    www.cuttingedgeppt.com/ppximex

# Inserting Pictures

Inserting single pictures in PowerPoint is easy, especially when you follow these steps:

1. **Navigate to the slide where you want the picture inserted.**

2. **Choose Insert➪Picture➪From File.**

3. **Navigate to wherever your pictures are saved, select one of the pictures, and click Insert.**

PowerPoint lets you insert pictures in several formats, including JPEG, GIF, BMP, WMF, EMF, and PNG.

## Between pictures and drawings

Graphics are classified into two types:

✔ **Bitmap graphics** (or just *bitmaps*) are collections of bits (pixels) that form an image. Because bitmaps are composed of pixels, they can't be scaled to more than their original size without visual deterioration (see Figure 8-2).

All photographs (pictures) are bitmaps. Typical bitmap file formats include JPEG, GIF, BMP, TIFF, PNG, and PCX.

✔ **Vector graphics** contain no pixels — they are created entirely through mathematical coordinates. These mathematical coordinates can be easily scaled to any size without any deterioration in quality (see Figure 8-2).

All line drawings and illustrations are vector graphics. Typical vector graphic file formats include WMF, EMF, EPS, AI, and CDR.

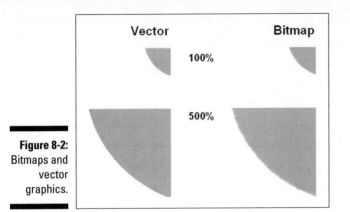

**Figure 8-2:**
Bitmaps and
vector
graphics.

# Using PowerPoint's clip art collection

PowerPoint includes an amazing collection of clip art in both bitmap and vector formats. Even more content is available online, and PowerPoint does a great job of accessing the online collections. Needless to say, you have to be connected to the Internet to access them.

Your PowerPoint version dictates the way you insert a picture from the clip art collection.

### PowerPoint 2002 and 2003

Follow these steps to access the Clip Organizer in PowerPoint 2002 or 2003:

1. **Choose Insert⇨Picture⇨Clip Art.**

   This activates the Clip Art task pane, which you can see in Figure 8-3.

   If this is the first time that you are using this option, you might be prompted to catalog all the media files on your computer. For now, just click the Later button to get rid of this dialog box.

2. **In the Search For box, set up the following search options and then click Go:**

   • Enter some keywords that describe the type of picture you're looking for. For example, I typed **prism**.

   • In the Search In drop-down list box, choose whether you want to search on your system or online — or both (see Figure 8-3).

   • In the Results Should Be drop-down list box, choose whether you want to search for clip art or photographs.

   PowerPoint also allows you to search for movies and sounds through the Clip Art task pane.

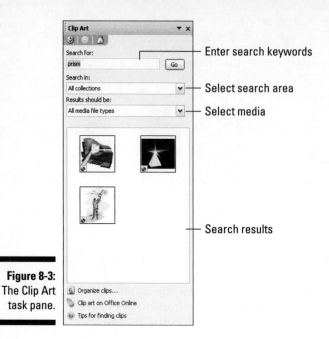

Enter search keywords

Select search area

Select media

Search results

**Figure 8-3:**
The Clip Art
task pane.

All your search results show up as thumbnail-size previews.

3. **To insert the actual clip art, drag a preview thumbnail onto a slide.**

### *PowerPoint 2000*

Follow these steps to access the Clip Gallery in PowerPoint 2000:

1. **Choose Insert⇨Picture⇨Clip Art.**

   This activates the Insert ClipArt dialog box, as shown in Figure 8-4.

2. **In the Search for Clips text box, enter some keywords that describe the type of picture you're looking for.**

   For example, I typed **skyscraper**. Your search results show up as thumbnail-size previews.

3. **To insert a clip, right-click the thumbnail preview and choose Insert from the flyout menu.**

To browse and search for more clip art, click the Clips Online button in the Clip Art task pane or the Insert ClipArt dialog box to access additional content through the Office Online Web site. You need to be connected to the Internet to use this option.

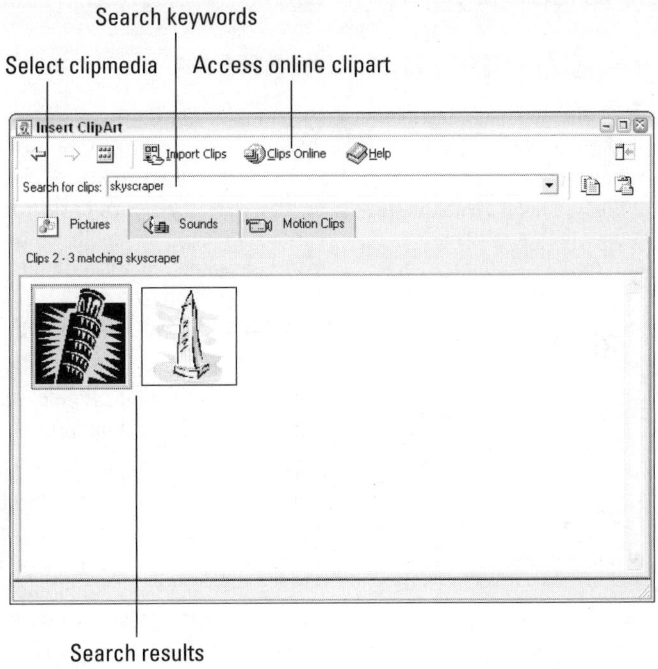

Search keywords

Select clipmedia  |  Access online clipart

Search results

**Figure 8-4:**
The Insert
ClipArt
dialog box.

By default, the Clip Gallery opens in Categories view, which allows you to browse all the clip art in a particular category — this is a great way to get a feel for the type of content available in PowerPoint's clip art collection.

# All about Resolution and Compression

PowerPoint is often the glue that binds visual content from various sources, such as

- An image created or edited in an image-editing program like Adobe Photoshop or Corel Painter
- A picture or document scanned in a scanner
- A photograph from a digital camera
- A picture from a clip art collection
- A picture saved from the Internet

In every case, you should make sure that the content you're using is copyright-free.

# Design considerations

Inserting a visual on a PowerPoint slide is extremely easy — and with the amount of clip art that Microsoft provides, everyone seems to be taking advantage of the free lunch! But don't insert visuals just because they are available, without any consideration of aesthetics or design.

Follow these guidelines to ensure that your visuals look professional:

✔ Don't use visuals at all if you don't have a graphic that adds relevance to the slide content.

✔ Try to use coordinated visuals.

All visuals in a presentation should use the same design style.

✔ Experiment with PowerPoint's picture effects. While a picture is selected, PowerPoint's Picture toolbar is activated, as shown in the figure here. You can find various icons on this toolbar that allow you to increase and reduce brightness and contrast. In addition, you can change the picture to grayscale or a watermark.

If you cannot see the Picture toolbar, just right-click any picture and choose the Show Picture Toolbar option.

✔ Sometimes, you might want to show a process, a detail, or an event through a picture. Including captions for such pictures is a good idea (especially if the presentation will be distributed to audiences who are going to view the presentation without a live presenter).

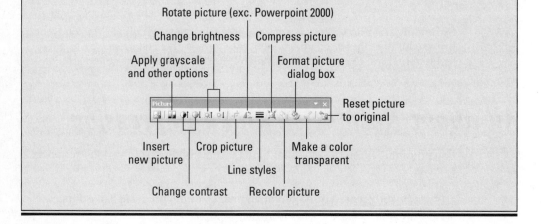

Rotate picture (exc. Powerpoint 2000)

Change brightness    Compress picture

Apply grayscale and other options    Format picture dialog box

Reset picture to original

Insert new picture    Crop picture    Make a color transparent

Line styles

Change contrast    Recolor picture

Because all this visual content can originate from so many disparate sources, you need to know about *resolution* and *compression*.

✔ Knowledge of **resolution** ensures that you bring only optimized visual content into PowerPoint.

✔ Knowledge of **compression** helps you optimize your existing visual content that's already part of a PowerPoint presentation.

## All the dpi stuff

*dpi* stands for *dots per inch*. In the print world, dpi reigns supreme for obvious reasons. A higher density of dots per inch translates into sharper, higher-quality prints.

*ppi* stands for *pixels per inch*. Although there's so much disagreement in this world about the relation between dpi and ppi, you can assume that a pixel is almost a dot. It won't hurt, but don't argue about this with your prepress people!

Most of the print world uses 300 dpi. Your screen begs to differ, though, as you shall soon discover.

A lot of confusion exists between the different versions of Windows and PowerPoint, and I want to shield you from all the stuff you don't need to know.

Assume that the resolution of your monitor is 72 dpi. Even if you bring a 300-dpi image into PowerPoint, the program won't use all those extra pixels.

Here's the math: 72 dpi is about a fourth of 300 dpi, which means that 300-dpi images are about four times larger than the screen resolution images that PowerPoint needs. More importantly, such high-resolution images mean that your presentation file sizes are getting more bloated than the most obese of our species.

PowerPoint delivers only 72 dpi screen resolution images, even if you use higher-resolution images — so where's the question of your projector showing anything better? And 72 dpi images project so well!

So, if you import a 300 dpi image into PowerPoint, it is going to show and project no better than a 72 dpi image. In the PowerPoint world, only the picture dimensions in pixels matter — all that dpi stuff is going down the drain as far as PowerPoint is concerned.

## Resolution in Photoshop

Here I show you how to set image resolution in Photoshop. Most other image editors work the same way.

Follow these steps to create a new image in Photoshop with a set resolution:

1. **Create a new image.**
2. **Choose File⇨New to view the New dialog box, as shown in Figure 8-5.**

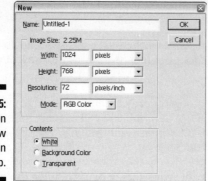

**Figure 8-5:**
Resolution
for a new
image in
Photoshop.

3. **Choose 72 pixels/inch for the Resolution.**

4. **Choose the required width and height of your image in pixels.**

   Because I'm creating a background for PowerPoint, I choose 1024 x 768 pixels — that's the same as most screen sizes.

I don't discuss how you can change the resolution of existing pictures in Photoshop here because that's automatically taken care of when you use Photoshop's Save for Web option discussed next. And if you already inserted some high-resolution images in your presentation, take a look at how to put some pressure on their bulk in the "Put the squeeze on file size" section, later in this chapter.

Other than the procedures that relate to image editing for PowerPoint presentations, I don't discuss Photoshop in too much detail in this book. You might want to look at another book about Photoshop for more detailed instructions — I recommend *Photoshop CS All-in-One Desk Reference For Dummies,* by Barbara Obermeier (Wiley).

## Exporting formats from Photoshop

Exporting images from Photoshop to a PowerPoint-compatible format is very easy. Consider these three file formats:

- **JPEG** works best for photographs and any other design composition that includes lots of shaded areas. JPEG files can be quite small.

- **GIF** works best for images that include large areas of solid colors. GIF is limited to 256 colors and supports limited transparency. In a GIF file, transparency is limited to either full or no transparency, which is why the PNG format is so much more attractive.

✔ **PNG** works best as a GIF alternative — it supports millions of colors as well as *variable transparency,* which means that it supports different levels of transparency in the same image.

Open your graphic in Photoshop and follow these steps to export to one of the three formats.

1. **Choose File⇨Save For Web.**

   This shows you the Save For Web dialog box, as shown in Figure 8-6.

2. **Choose the file format and/or export setting.**

   Photoshop shows you a live export preview, allowing you to experiment with settings and file formats. In the bottom-left corner of the dialog box, Photoshop even shows you the file size of the exported graphic.

3. **Click OK to accept the options and export the graphic.**

## Put the squeeze on file size

PowerPoint 2002 and 2003 include a compression feature that optimizes all the images in a presentation.

Select JPG, GIF, or PNG

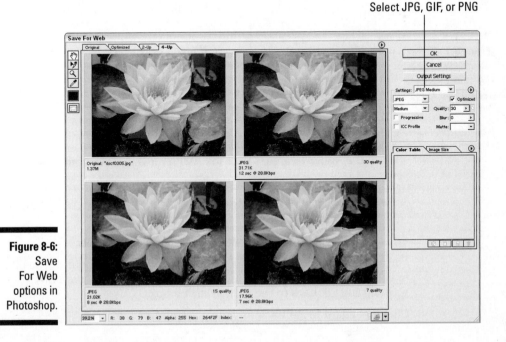

**Figure 8-6:**
Save
For Web
options in
Photoshop.

Follow these steps to put the squeeze on:

1. **Choose File⇨Save to create an updated version of your presentation.**

2. **Choose File⇨Properties to summon the Properties dialog box.**

   The General tab provides information about the file.

3. **Make a note of the file size and then click OK to close the Properties dialog box.**

4. **Right-click any picture and choose Format⇨Picture.**

   Alternatively, if you right-click an AutoShape with a picture fill, choose Format⇨AutoShape.

   This brings up either the Format Picture or Format AutoShape dialog box.

5. **Click the Picture tab in this dialog box and then click the Compress button.**

   The Compress Pictures dialog box, shown in Figure 8-7, appears.

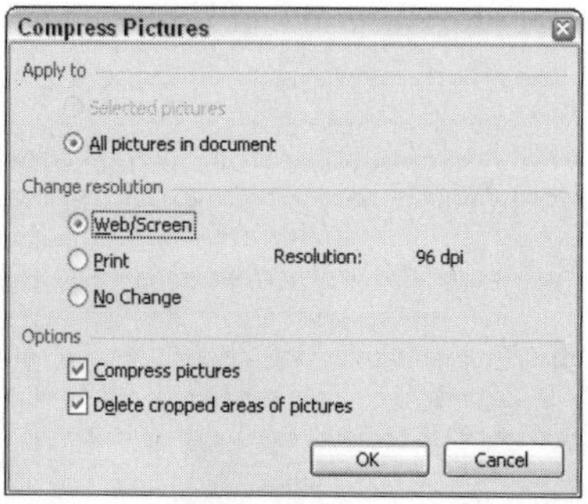

**Figure 8-7:**
Compress
pictures.

6. **Choose your compression options.**

   • In the Apply To area, select the All Pictures in Document option.

   • Change the Resolution to Web/Screen.

   • Leave the Compress Pictures and Delete Cropped Areas of Pictures options checked.

7. **Click OK; then click Apply in the successive dialog boxes.**

   You might be prompted by a dialog box that warns you about the quality of your images being reduced. Click the Apply button to ignore this warning and get back to the Format dialog box.

8. **Click OK again to get back to your presentation.**

9. **Choose File⇨Save As to save your presentation to a new file.**

   It's important to save to a new file so you can revert back to the old file if you aren't happy with the results.

10. **Make a trip again to the Properties dialog box (File⇨Properties) and check the new file size against the earlier file size.**

    If only reducing waist sizes was this easy!

# Visually Yours

PowerPoint offers several options that allow you to create coordinated visuals right inside the program.

In the following sections, you discover how to recolor clip art inside PowerPoint — in addition, an unexposed feature lets you recolor some bitmaps.

## Recoloring clip art

This is among the oldest yet most effective PowerPoint tricks. Follow these steps to recolor vector clip art inside the program:

1. **Create a blank slide.**

   You can either

   - Create a new presentation and insert a blank slide.
   - Insert a blank slide into an existing presentation.

2. **Choose Insert⇨Picture⇨Clip Art.**

3. **Select any vector clip art.**

   Search available clip art by using keywords. To find more details on how to restrict your search to vector clip art, refer to the "Using PowerPoint's clip art collection" section, earlier in this chapter.

   You can skip the preceding three steps and open the recolorone.ppt presentation from the *Cutting Edge PowerPoint For Dummies* CD.

   With the clip art selected, you should see the Picture toolbar, shown in Figure 8-8.

4. **If you can't see the Picture toolbar, choose View⇨Toolbars⇨Picture.**

Figure 8-8:
The Picture
toolbar.

Recolor picture

**5. With the clip art selected, click the Recolor Picture icon on the Picture toolbar.**

This summons the Recolor Picture dialog box, as shown in Figure 8-9. The left side of the dialog box lists all the original colors in the clip art. Each color can be individually changed to another color.

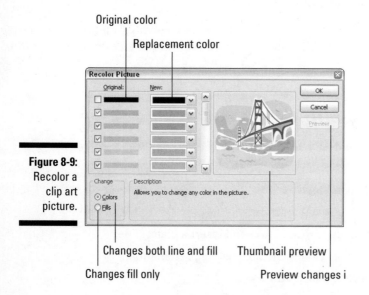

Original color

Replacement color

Figure 8-9:
Recolor a
clip art
picture.

Changes both line and fill

Changes fill only

Thumbnail preview

Preview changes i

**6. Follow these steps to change colors individually:**

*a. Place a check mark next to the color you want to change.*

*b. Click the downward-pointing arrow next to the New color swatch to open PowerPoint's default color options flyout.*

*c. Click the More Colors option to summon the Color Picker dialog box.*

*d. Choose the new color you need.*

*e. Click OK to get back to the Recolor Picture dialog box.*

Click the Preview button to see the changes reflected (see Figure 8-9).

You can change all the colors to end up with a picture that uses a completely different color palette!

You can find a sample presentation with recolored clip art on the *Cutting Edge PowerPoint For Dummies* CD.

## Recoloring bitmaps

You can easily recolor vector clip art, but PowerPoint's most well-hidden secret is its ability to recolor bitmaps. This ability was only exposed in a limited, yet-undocumented way.

Recoloring a bitmap is subject to these conditions:

✔ The recoloring is limited to bitmap images that are part of the background in a Slide Master.

✔ You can recolor only from within a few Slide Master designs that ship as part of PowerPoint 2002 and 2003.

Follow these steps to recolor bitmap images within the Slide Master:

1. **Choose File⇨New.**

   This activates the New Presentation task pane.

2. **Choose the From Design Template option in the task pane.**

   This activates the Slide Design task pane.

3. **Choose one of the special designs.**

   Scroll down the design previews. If you hover your cursor over the thumbnail previews, you see a ToolTip that identifies the name of the design.

   You can choose from any of these three designs:

   - Clouds
   - Ocean
   - Textured

   Make sure you choose one of the preceding listed designs because Microsoft exposes the image recoloring algorithm only in these templates.

4. **Choose View⇨Master⇨Slide Master.**

5. **In the Slide Master view, choose Format⇨Background to view the Background dialog box.**

6. **Click the fill drop-down list box and select the Fill Effects option.**

7. **In the resultant Fill Effects dialog box, click the Picture tab.**

8. **In the Picture tab, follow these steps to add a new picture background:**

   a. *Click the Select Picture button.*

   b. *Choose any other picture.*

   c. *Click Insert.*

   d. *Click OK in the next dialog box.*

9. **Click Apply to All in the next dialog box.**

10. **Choose View⇨Normal to get back to the default editing view in PowerPoint.**

    Your inserted picture has already been recolored.

    How does PowerPoint decide which color to use for the recoloring? That option comes from the Color Schemes, which you access in Step 12.

11. **Choose Format⇨Slide Design to open the Slide Design task pane.**

12. **Select the Color Schemes option in the Slide Design task pane.**

13. **Click various color schemes to view different two-color (any color with white) style background images on the slide.**

If you want to use a color that's not present in the Color Scheme thumbnails you see, you need to create a new Color Scheme and change its background color — Color Schemes are covered in Chapter 3.

This book's CD contains a sample presentation with recolored bitmap images.

# PhotoActive FX

PowerPlug's PhotoActive FX is a PowerPoint add-in from CrystalGraphics that lets you create several photo effects right inside PowerPoint. It also includes a video-rendering engine that creates customized video clips that integrate seamlessly within your presentation.

You can download a trial copy of PhotoActive FX from

```
www.cuttingedgeppt.com/photoactivefx
```

You need to have PhotoActive FX installed only on the machine on which you add the effects. On other machines, you can view all the still and video effects without having a copy of PhotoActive FX installed.

# PowerPoint and Photoshop

Photoshop can be used to create cool graphics for you to insert in a PowerPoint presentation. That might be an understatement because the gamut of possibilities between the two programs may justify a whole book!

The companion site has tutorials, links, and samples for you:

    www.cuttingedgeppt.com/photoshop

This section provides guidelines and design ideas to create graphics in Photoshop.

Most of the editing concepts discussed work with any image editor.

- ✔ Don't insert that bloated, eight-*megapixel* (just think of megapixels as lots and lots of pixels!) photo you shot with a digital camera into PowerPoint! Get rid of the bloat:

    1. Open the photo in Photoshop and resize it to a more realistic size.

    2. Use Photoshop's fantastic Save For Web feature, explained earlier in this chapter, to get rid of the bloat.

- ✔ Focus on what is important. If only a part of your image is required, feel free to use the crop tool in Photoshop to cut out the remaining areas.

- ✔ Play with Photoshop *layers* — think of them as sheets of transparent acetate placed over each other. When your composition is done, you can *flatten* the layers and export to a graphic file format that PowerPoint can import.

- ✔ Photoshop is a great tool for creating transparent graphics that include *alpha channels*. Such compositions, when saved in TIF or PNG formats, can be inserted on a PowerPoint slide with their transparency intact.

    More information on alpha channels can be found at

        www.cuttingedgeppt.com/alpha

- ✔ Create cool PowerPoint slide backgrounds in Photoshop. Among the easiest ways to convert a busy photograph to a useable background is to use Photoshop's Blur filter and make everything appear soft and unfocussed. Find more information at

        www.cuttingedgeppt.com/blur

# Chapter 9

# Pulling in Diagrams, Charts, Equations, and Maps

*I*nfo-graphics — the word says it all.

*Info-graphics* are more than mere graphics — these intelligent visuals help users comprehend difficult principles like figures, statistics, or even directions easily. Examples include

✔ A map that gives directions to your new office

✔ An organizational chart that explains hierarchies and power levels

✔ A chart that shows your popularity ratings shooting over the roof, or your competitor's ratings plunging

✔ A Venn diagram that shows overlapping areas of influence — or just an excuse to show how colors mix well to form new colors

If you don't know what a Venn diagram is, don't despair. This chapter covers so much more than just Venn diagrams — you also explore vistas outside PowerPoint's offerings in programs as diverse as SmartDraw, Visio, and MapPoint.

# Delectable Diagrams

Diagrams are drawings that are entirely based on logic — they help convey relationships, hierarchies, and flows through a combination of simple shapes and text. Organization charts and cycle relationship drawings are all examples of diagrams.

PowerPoint 2002 and 2003 include the Diagram Gallery, shown in Figure 9-1. The Diagram Gallery provides a quick way to work with common diagram styles.

**Figure 9-1:**
The
Diagram
Gallery.

If you use PowerPoint 2000, you can still create all diagram styles by using two types of AutoShapes: basic shapes and connectors. AutoShapes are covered in more detail in Chapter 5.

If you use PowerPoint 2002 or 2003 and want to create a diagram style that isn't included within the Diagram Gallery (such as a timeline), use AutoShapes.

## Diagram types

If asked to point out one virtue of the Diagram Gallery, I would mention its ease of use.

Follow these steps to insert a sample diagram from the Diagram Gallery:

1. **Choose Insert⇨Diagram.**

   This opens the Diagram Gallery dialog box (refer to Figure 9-1).

**Color Plate 3-1: Contrast aids readability of text over a background, whether you use lighter or darker text.**

**Color Plate 3-2: Pure colors are in center column. The tints on the left have more white and the shades on the right have more black.**

**Color Plate 3-3:** A slight change in tints and shades can significantly increase contrast and readability.

**Color Plate 3-4: Textures can be magical. These textures are infinitely more interesting than plain colors.**

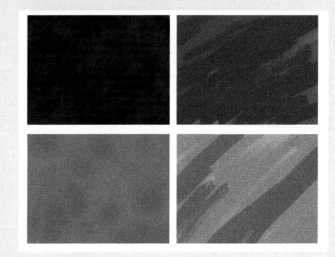

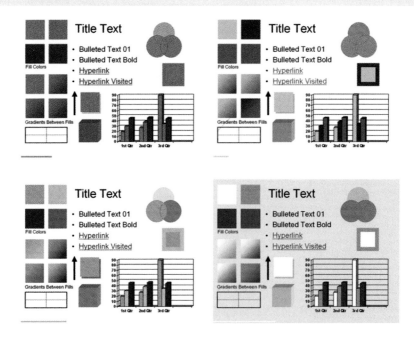

**Color Plate 3-5: Change your Color Scheme, and everything changes in a blink.**

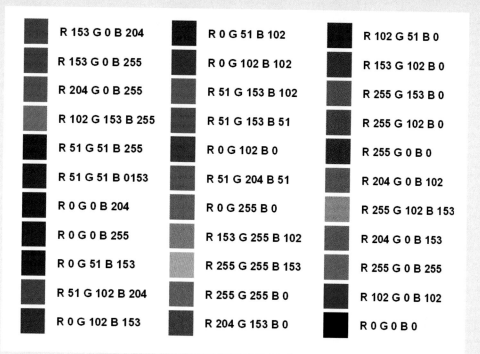

**Color Plate 3-6: RGB Color Reference Chart.**

| | | |
|---|---|---|
| R 153 G 0 B 204 | R 0 G 51 B 102 | R 102 G 51 B 0 |
| R 153 G 0 B 255 | R 0 G 102 B 102 | R 153 G 102 B 0 |
| R 204 G 0 B 255 | R 51 G 153 B 102 | R 255 G 153 B 0 |
| R 102 G 153 B 255 | R 51 G 153 B 51 | R 255 G 102 B 0 |
| R 51 G 51 B 255 | R 0 G 102 B 0 | R 255 G 0 B 0 |
| R 51 G 51 B 0153 | R 51 G 204 B 51 | R 204 G 0 B 102 |
| R 0 G 0 B 204 | R 0 G 255 B 0 | R 255 G 102 B 153 |
| R 0 G 0 B 255 | R 153 G 255 B 102 | R 204 G 0 B 153 |
| R 0 G 51 B 153 | R 255 G 255 B 153 | R 255 G 0 B 255 |
| R 51 G 102 B 204 | R 255 G 255 B 0 | R 102 G 0 B 102 |
| R 0 G 102 B 153 | R 204 G 153 B 0 | R 0 G 0 B 0 |

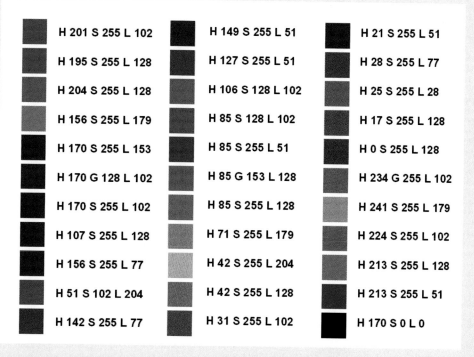

**Color Plate 3-7: HSL Color Reference Chart.**

| | | |
|---|---|---|
| H 201 S 255 L 102 | H 149 S 255 L 51 | H 21 S 255 L 51 |
| H 195 S 255 L 128 | H 127 S 255 L 51 | H 28 S 255 L 77 |
| H 204 S 255 L 128 | H 106 S 128 L 102 | H 25 S 255 L 28 |
| H 156 S 255 L 179 | H 85 S 128 L 102 | H 17 S 255 L 128 |
| H 170 S 255 L 153 | H 85 S 255 L 51 | H 0 S 255 L 128 |
| H 170 G 128 L 102 | H 85 G 153 L 128 | H 234 G 255 L 102 |
| H 170 S 255 L 102 | H 85 S 255 L 128 | H 241 S 255 L 179 |
| H 107 S 255 L 128 | H 71 S 255 L 179 | H 224 S 255 L 102 |
| H 156 S 255 L 77 | H 42 S 255 L 204 | H 213 S 255 L 128 |
| H 51 S 102 L 204 | H 42 S 255 L 128 | H 213 S 255 L 51 |
| H 142 S 255 L 77 | H 31 S 255 L 102 | H 170 S 0 L 0 |

Move this cursor up or down
to change luminosity

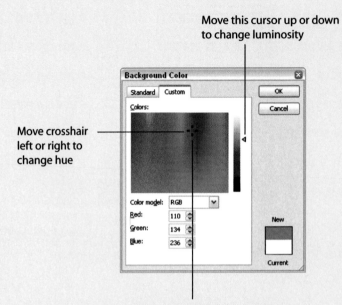

Move crosshair
left or right to
change hue

Move crosshair up or down to
change saturation

**Color Plate 3–8: The Custom tab
in the Color Chooser.**

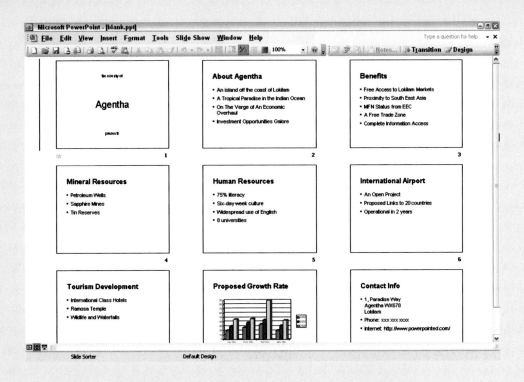

**Color Plate 4-1: Before, a basic presentation.**

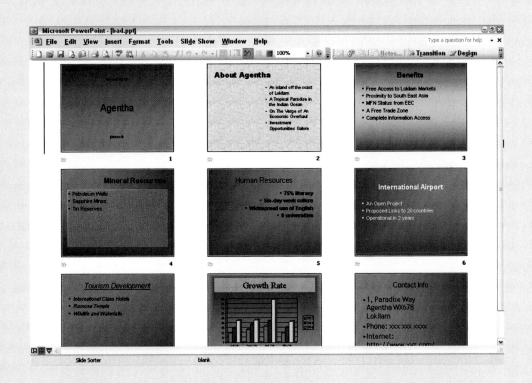

**Color Plate 4-2: Formatting without Masters is a recipe for disaster.**

Color Plate 5-1: PowerPoint's fill options control color and texture.

Color Plate 5-2: Patterned lines make great frames and borders.

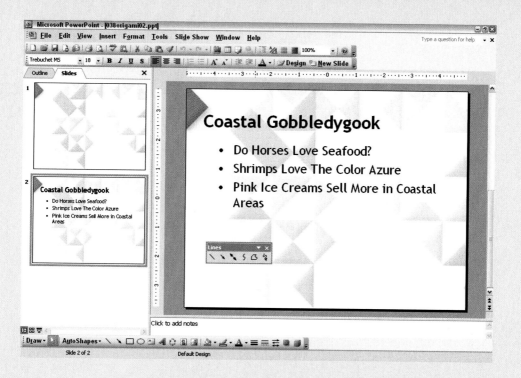

**Color Plate 6-1: The Lines toolbar.**

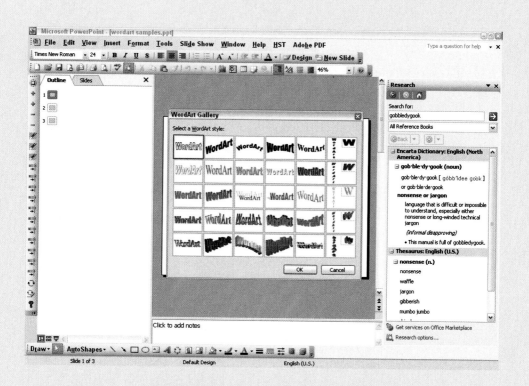

**Color Plate 7-1: The WordArt gallery.**

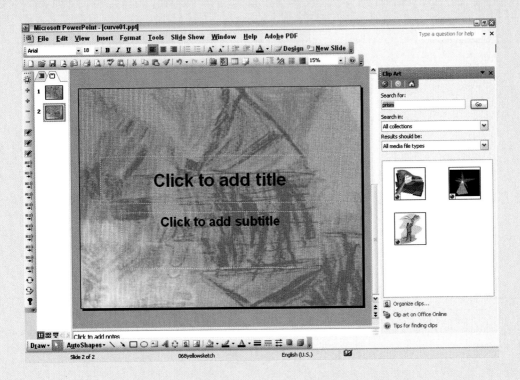

**Color Plate 8-1: The Clip Art task pane.**

**Color Plate 8-2: Save for Web options.**

**Color Plate 8-3: Save options in Photoshop.**

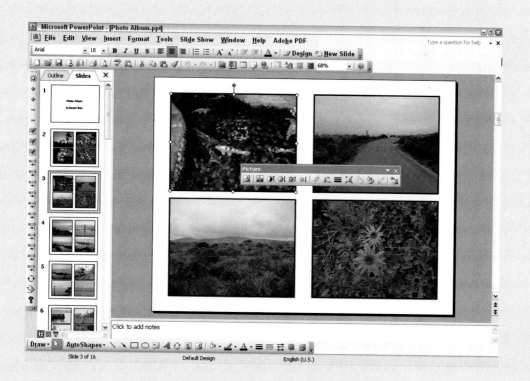

**Color Plate 8-4: The Picture toolbar.**

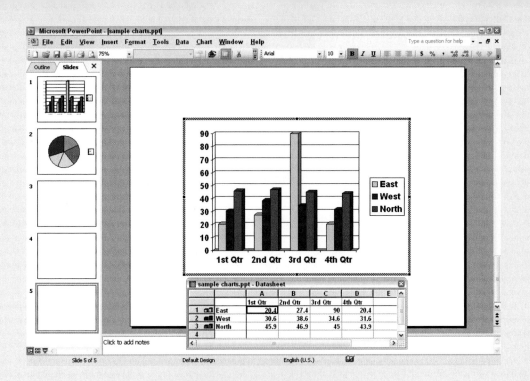
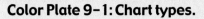

**Color Plate 9-1: Chart types.**

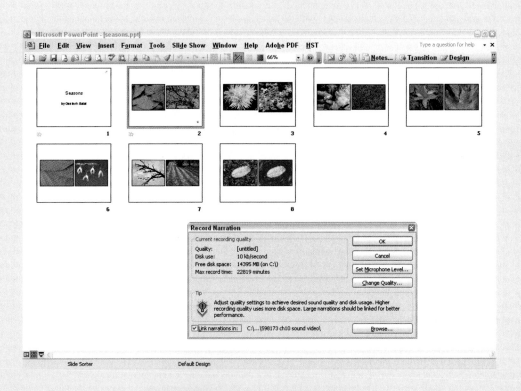

**Color Plate 10-1: Inserting video.**

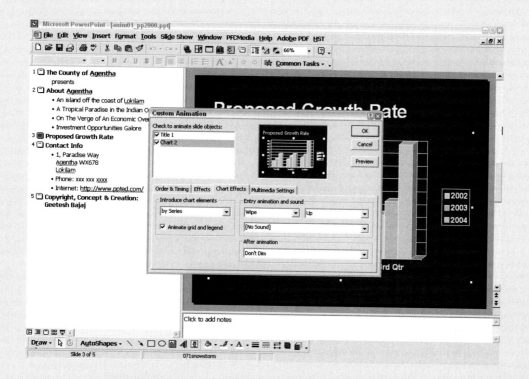

**Color Plate 11-1: Chart animation in PowerPoint.**

**Color Plate 11-2: Using the Timeline.**

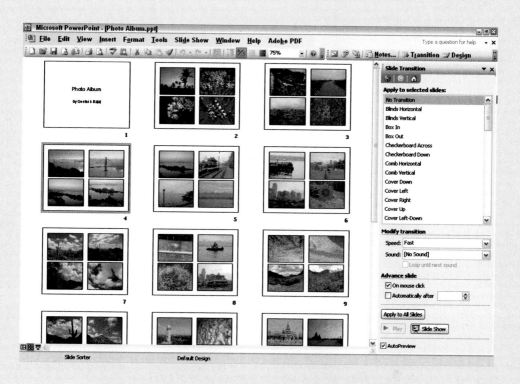

**Color Plate 11–3: The Slide Transition task pane.**

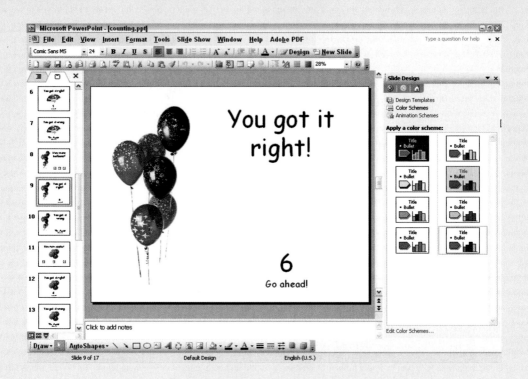

**Color Plate 12-1: Correct answer slide for a quiz.**

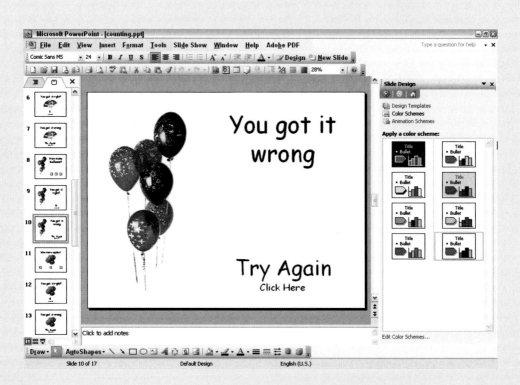

**Color Plate 12-2: Incorrect answer slide for a quiz.**

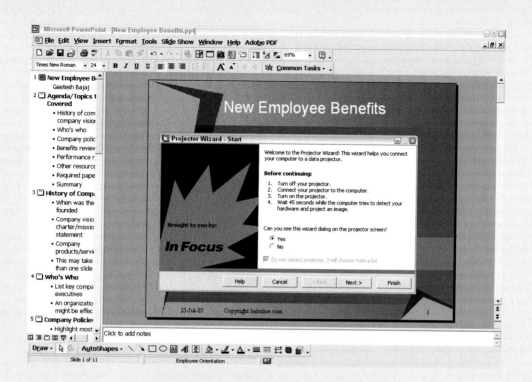

**Color Plate 14-1: The Projector Wizard.**

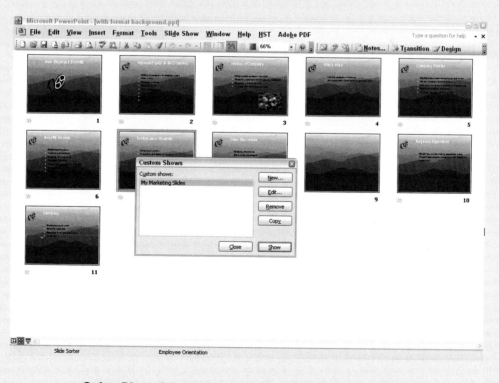

**Color Plate 14-2: Custom shows for all occasions.**

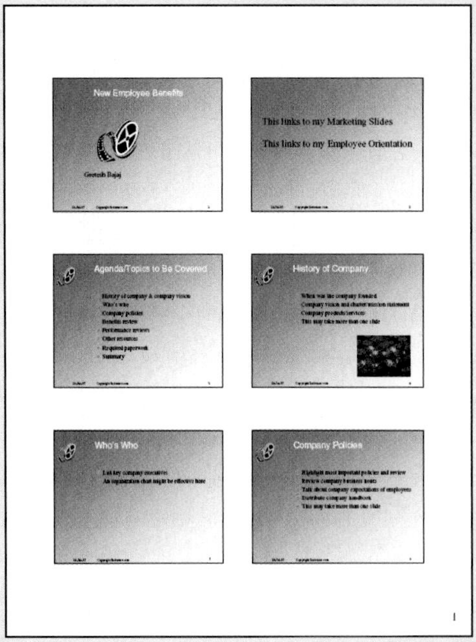

Color Plate 14-3: PowerPoint creates handouts for photocopying.

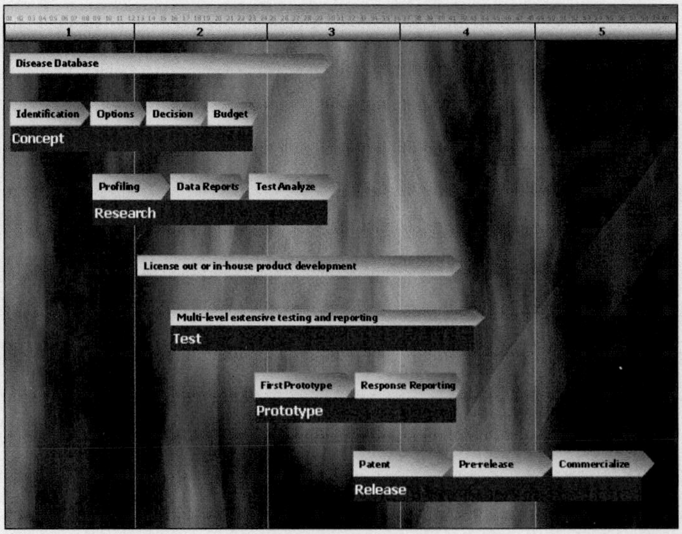

Color Plate 16-1: A timeline created in AutoShapes.

2. **Choose any of the six diagram types available.**

    After a sample diagram is placed, you can add or remove elements and change the formatting as required.

    I discuss each diagram type next.

## *Organization charts*

Organization charts, lovingly called *org charts,* are a great way to portray parent-child relationships of all sorts. Examples of org charts include company hierarchies, family trees, and product lines.

When you click the Organization Chart option in the Diagram Gallery, PowerPoint places a sample org chart ready for you to edit and enhance, as shown in Figure 9-2.

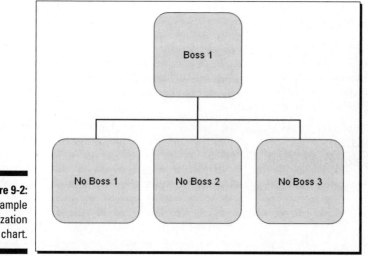

**Figure 9-2:**
A sample organization chart.

Here's the ultimate org chart tip that let's you customize the org charts to your heart's delight: Just create them without using any applets by using mere AutoShapes. Use the basic shapes to create the boxes and then link them with connectors. This is easy and works with all versions of PowerPoint!

Because the Diagram Gallery feature is limited to PowerPoint 2002 and 2003, I show you how PowerPoint 2000 manages org charts later in this chapter.

# Organization chart caveats

The Organization Chart applet has its share of miseries that provide unhelpful responses. Use the following guidelines to help you resolve the problems:

✔ If you get an insufficient memory message while you're inserting an organization chart, you might just have too many fonts installed on your system.

✔ If you're running PowerPoint 2002 or 2003 and are trying to edit an organization chart created in an earlier version, like PowerPoint 2000, be aware that that's enough to give

PowerPoint a bout of hiccups! Thankfully, all you need to do is download the free Org Chart 2 utility from Microsoft's site. Find the link here:

www.cuttingedgeppt.com/
        orgchart2

✔ Steve Rindsberg's site has tons of information on resolving Org Chart errors. Find the link here:

www.cuttingedgeppt.com/org-
        errors

Here are some working techniques for org charts:

✔ Click any shape and start typing text as required.

✔ An Organization Chart toolbar should be visible as soon as you select an org chart. Figure 9-3 shows the Organization Chart toolbar with all its layout and formatting options.

✔ You can add more shapes at three levels: Subordinate, Coworker, and Assistant.

To add a shape, follow these steps:

1. Select an existing shape and right-click it.

2. In the resultant menu, choose from either Subordinate, Coworker, or Assistant.

The same options are available from the Insert Shape menu on the Organization Chart toolbar.

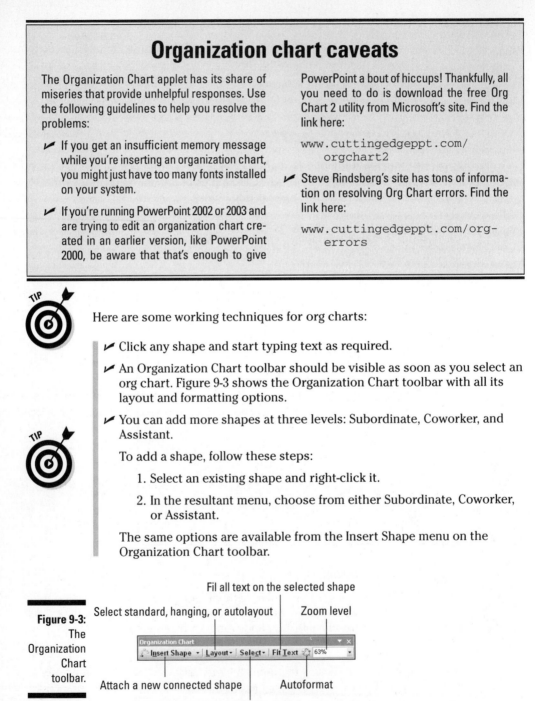

Figure 9-3:
The
Organization
Chart
toolbar.

Fil all text on the selected shape

Select standard, hanging, or autolayout

Zoom level

Attach a new connected shape

Autoformat

Select level, branch, all assistants, or all connecting

- By default, all new org charts have the AutoLayout option turned on — this prevents you from resizing individual shapes or connectors.

  To turn AutoLayout off, choose the Layout➪AutoLayout option on the Organization Chart toolbar.

- Click the Layout option on the Organization Chart toolbar and you find several placement options like Standard, Both Hanging, Left Hanging, and Right Hanging. Experiment with all of them to find what's suitable for your diagram.

- The Select option on the Organization Chart toolbar lets you select similar objects like levels, branches, or connectors — thereafter you can format and reshape all objects together.

  Most formatting options don't work unless AutoLayout is turned off.

- The Fit Text option changes the text size to match the area available in the container shape.

- The Autoformat icon activates the Style Gallery.

  You find more information on the Style Gallery later in this chapter.

## *Other diagrams*

There's a reason why I include all the five remaining diagram styles other than the Organization Chart together. That's because these five styles are interchangeable. Yes, you can change a cycle diagram to a Venn diagram with one click, and all the relationships remain unaltered.

Follow these steps to change one diagram type to another:

1. **Select a diagram so that the Diagram toolbar, shown in Figure 9-4, is visible.**

2. **In the Diagram toolbar, choose Change To and click the relevant option in the resulting menu.**

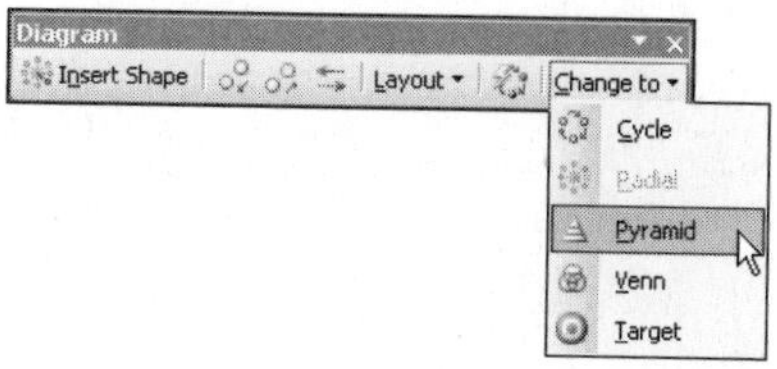

**Figure 9-4:**
Changing
the diagram
type.

### *Cycle diagrams*

Cycle diagrams are best suited for depicting continuous processes that work in conjunction with each other — these include financial transactions, trade, inventory control, and production or delivery cycles. Figure 9-5 shows a sample cycle diagram.

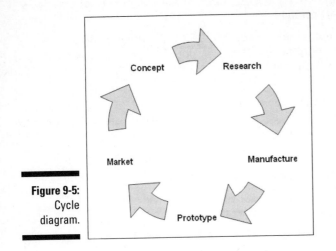

**Figure 9-5:**
Cycle
diagram.

The sample cycle diagram from the Diagram Gallery includes just three shapes. More shapes can be added by choosing the Insert Shape option in the Diagram toolbar.

### Radial diagrams

Radial diagrams contain a central hub and several spokes. These diagrams are best suited to illustrate a relationship between scattered elements and a central core element.

Examples of radial diagrams include an airline route diagram or a representation of responsibility from a core authority in a large organization like a financial or educational institution. Figure 9-6 shows a sample radial diagram.

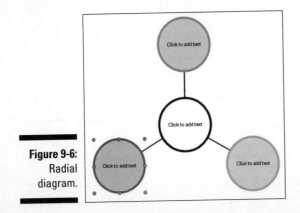

**Figure 9-6:**
Radial
diagram.

TIP

To create more hubs, just insert multiple radial diagrams. This works only if your hub and spoke requirements are fairly uncomplicated.

### Pyramid diagrams

Pyramid diagrams are typically used to illustrate layered relationships and foundation-based concepts like the classic food pyramid. Figure 9-7 shows a sample pyramid diagram.

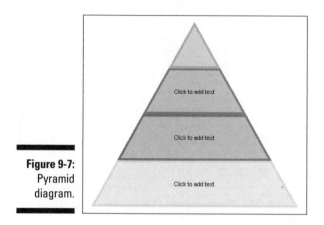

**Figure 9-7:**
Pyramid
diagram.

Pyramid diagrams are best suited for scientific info-graphics representing biospheres and environments but are also used extensively for training and regulation graphics.

### Venn diagrams

Think of Venn diagrams as a way to illustrate overlapping influences. The classical use of a Venn diagram has been to illustrate the mixing of primary colors (red, blue, and yellow) to form secondary colors (purple, green, and orange). Figure 9-8 shows a sample Venn diagram.

Use Venn diagrams wherever you need to explain synergies, reactions, or relationships.

### Target diagrams

If you have played with darts before, you already know the concept behind target diagrams! Think of dart targets without the darts themselves and you get target diagrams.

Figure 9-9 shows a sample Target diagram. Use these diagrams to illustrate goal-achievement concepts.

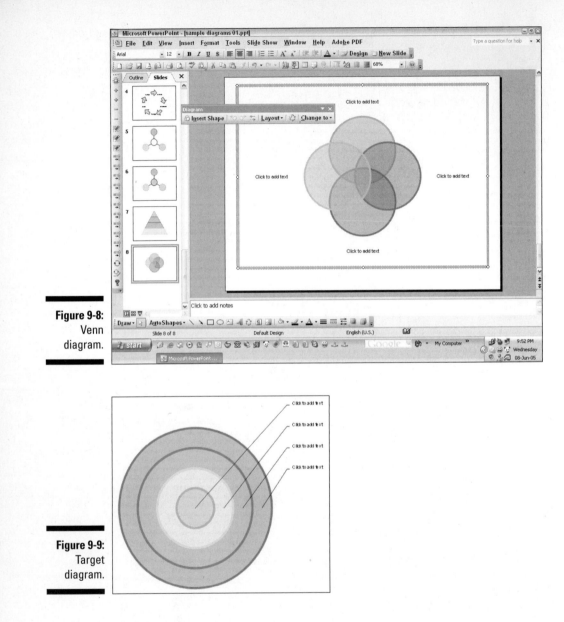

**Figure 9-8:**
Venn
diagram.

**Figure 9-9:**
Target
diagram.

### Style Gallery

The Style Gallery provides a quick way to provide your diagram with an aesthetic design style. Follow these steps to access the Style Gallery:

**1. Select any diagram so that the Diagram toolbar is visible.**

For organization charts, this would be the Organization Chart toolbar.

**2. Click the AutoFormat icon to summon the Style Gallery dialog box, shown in Figure 9-10.**

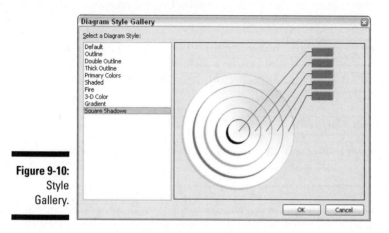

**Figure 9-10:**
Style
Gallery.

**3. Select any of the diagram styles to view a preview of the diagram with the style applied.**

**4. After you find a style you like, just click OK.**

If you don't want to apply a style, click Cancel.

### Overriding AutoFormat

Sometimes you just want to use your own colors as fills — and PowerPoint won't allow you to do that! It's entirely possible to make PowerPoint behave — just follow these steps to override the AutoFormat option:

**1. Select a diagram and then click an individual shape.**

**2. Right-click the shape.**

You might see a check mark next to the Use AutoFormat option, as shown in Figure 9-11.

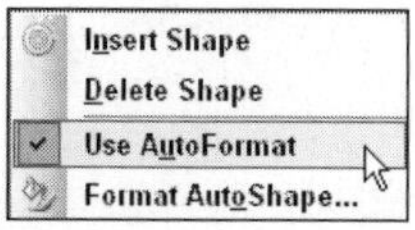

**Figure 9-11:**
Overriding
AutoFormat.

**3. Deselect the option and the shape is now a mere AutoShape.**

Format it to your heart's delight!

## Organization charts in PowerPoint 2000

PowerPoint 2000 users can use the Organization Chart applet to create org charts inside PowerPoint.

While inserting an org chart for the first time, PowerPoint might prompt you to insert the original PowerPoint or Office installation CD because the Organization Chart applet may not have been installed by default. So keep your installation media handy.

Follow these steps to create an org chart:

1. **Choose Insert➪Picture➪Organization Chart to insert an organization chart.**

   Behold the Microsoft Organization Chart applet.

   The Organization Chart applet, shown in Figure 9-12, already creates a basic organization chart for you. All you need to do is click and type the names and titles.

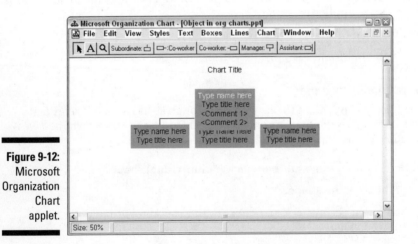

**Figure 9-12:** Microsoft Organization Chart applet.

2. **To add a subordinate, coworker, assistant, or manager,**

   a. Click the relevant icon on the toolbar.

   b. Click any of the existing boxes to establish a new relationship.

3. **When you're finished, choose File➪Exit and Return to go back to PowerPoint.**

# Charting Vistas

The easiest way to get your audience squint-eyed is to put in reams of figures in tables that use 6-point text. Nowadays, audiences are less forgiving and polite — they'll soon fire up their PDAs to check their e-mail or the latest stock quotes. Ouch!

Show the same figures by using charts and graphs to get your point across and you'll find that the audience is more receptive. Charts make it easy to visualize trends and patterns — and thus prevent people from getting squint-eyed or distracted.

Unlike diagrams that are based on logical relationships, charts are entirely based on figures. Diagrams are covered earlier in this chapter.

## Microsoft Graph

Here's a secret — PowerPoint by itself has no charting abilities! All the charts that you create in PowerPoint are actually sourced from a small application called Microsoft Graph. If you never realized this before, that's because the integration between PowerPoint and Graph is so transparent.

With Microsoft Graph, you can:

✔ Create and edit charts inside PowerPoint.

✔ Use PowerPoint's Color Schemes for chart fills. Color Schemes are covered in Chapter 3.

The terms *chart* and *graph* are used interchangeably in PowerPoint terminology. More chart terminology can be found in the following section.

## Chart elements

Before you get deeper into charts, you must be aware of some of the technical gobbledygook:

✔ **Chart Editing Mode:** You get into a special chart editing mode whenever you

• Double-click an existing chart on a slide.

• Insert a chart for the first time.

Essentially, getting into chart editing mode is the same as getting into Microsoft Graph, the small program that helps PowerPoint with charts. If you see two additional menus — Chart and Data — you know that you're using Microsoft Graph. Click anywhere outside the chart to get back to PowerPoint.

✔ **Axes:** Most charts have two axes:

  • The bottom axis (also called the *x-axis)*

  • The left axis (also called the *y-axis)*

✔ **Plot Area:** The area within the axes is called the Plot Area.

The legend and titles are normally placed outside the Plot Area.

✔ **Titles:** These include the

  • Chart titles (placed by default above the chart)

  • Axes titles (placed by default beside the axes)

✔ **Datasheet:** Every chart is influenced by underlying figures. These figures can be found and edited within the datasheet. Typically, the datasheet is visible whenever you edit a chart in PowerPoint.

You can import this data from an Excel spreadsheet — just take a peek at the "Import your spreadsheet data" section, later in this chapter.

✔ **Series:** Every row of data that's shown as a component of the chart is a series.

✔ **Values:** Values are the individual figures that constitute part of each series.

✔ **Legend:** The legend is a box placed outside the plot area that identifies the series and provides captions for them. Legends are automatically created by Microsoft Graph — you can opt to leave them out altogether if required.

## Inserting a chart

Follow these instructions to add a chart within PowerPoint:

1. **Choose Insert⇨Chart.**

   This places a dummy column chart and datasheet on the slide, as you can see in Figure 9-13. The sample chart is almost as haggard as a newborn chick, but formatting the design and data of the chart can result in much better looking specimens.

2. **Edit the chart.**

   You're now in Chart Editing mode. Edit the datasheet as required — the charts update dynamically. You can also format the fills for the individual series, format the font sizes of the values and titles, and opt to include the legend.

3. **After you finish editing your chart, just click anywhere outside the chart area to go back to PowerPoint.**

Another way to insert a chart on a slide is to use a slide layout that includes a chart placeholder. To view all the slide layouts, choose Format↪Slide Layout. Thereafter, just click the Insert Chart icon within the placeholder.

## Change the chart types

PowerPoint has many chart types to play with. Most of the time, the chart type you use is directly related to the type of data you need to portray. Nevertheless, you should experiment with various chart options before you decide what suits you best.

Data and chart menus               Chart

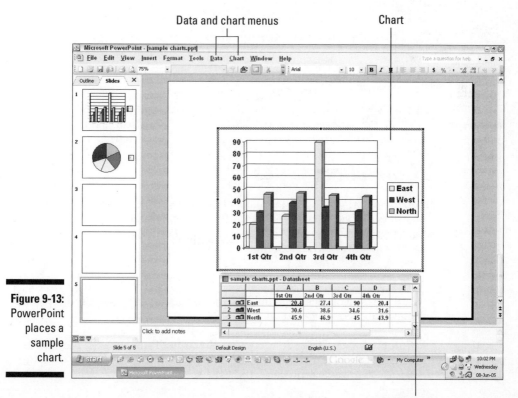

**Figure 9-13:** PowerPoint places a sample chart.

Datasheet

Follow these steps to change or preview the chart types.

1. **Double-click an existing chart to put you in Chart Editing mode, as illustrated previously in Figure 9-13.**

2. **Choose Chart➪Chart Type to summon the Chart Type dialog box, shown in Figure 9-14.**

3. **Preview all the chart types by choosing their names on the left pane.**

   The previews automatically update to show you the options possible in that type.

   To see a more detailed sample, click the Press and Hold to View Sample button.

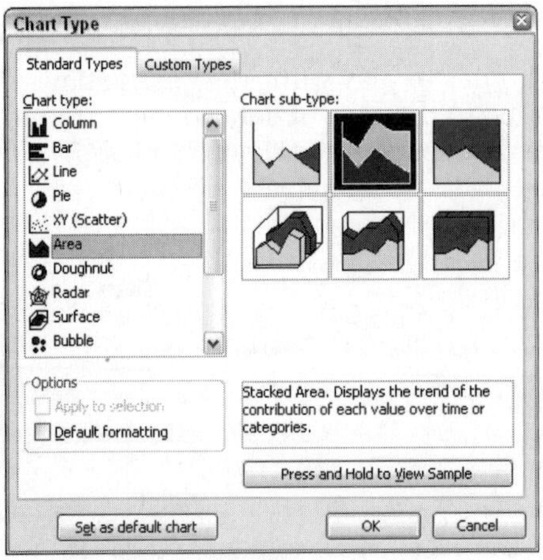

**Figure 9-14:** Behold all the chart types.

## All the chart types

Although PowerPoint provides many chart types, some charts are used more than others — I've placed them in the Simple Charts category. The other chart types are mainly used by statisticians and other geeky types — I've placed them in the Advanced Charts category.

### Simple charts

Here are the chart types you could use in your everyday work life. These are the easy and uncomplicated ones:

✓ **Column** charts are used more than any other type because they make it so easy to discern change patterns. The columns rise (or dip) from the x-axis. The y-axis represents the values.

- ✔ **Bar** charts work on the same concept as the column charts, but with the axes reversed. You have the values on the x-axis and the series on the y-axis.

- ✔ **Line** graphs use lines to connect graph points *(vertexes)*. They work best when you want to show trends over time. The 3-D version of this type uses ribbons rather than lines.

- ✔ **Pie** charts work best with percentage values — most of the time, they're used when you have just one series of values. You can also create multiple pie charts on the same slide to show relationships between two percentage-wise series. Examples include two pie charts for income and expenditure.

- ✔ **Scatter** charts are used when both the axes have numbers as the underlying data. For this reason, they're also called *XY charts*.

- ✔ **Area** charts are like stacked line graphs with the gaps filled in with individual colors or patterns. Area charts can be used when you don't have too many values — normally four to five values work best.

- ✔ **Doughnut** charts are like pie charts, but unlike pie charts, the same doughnut chart can be used to represent more than one series by using concentric doughnuts. Predictably, doughnut charts work best if you have fewer series — no more than five.

- ✔ **Cylinder, Cone,** and **Pyramid** charts are just variations of the basic column and bar charts — they use 3-D effects to make the bars and columns look like cylinders, cones, and pyramids.

### Advanced charts

These are the type of charts you encounter only once or twice a year unless you have an affinity for math and statistics.

- ✔ **Radar** charts work best when you need to compare the total values of data series. If you use a radar chart, you're on your way to becoming a chart geek — most users stay away from this complicated chart type!

- ✔ **Surface** charts work best to represent the synergistic effects of two values working together. The chart connects values in the data series to create a ribbonlike line graph.

- ✔ **Bubble** charts may look like the bubbles you blew out of soap water, but that's where the similarity ends. They compare sets of three values — it's almost like a Scatter (XY) chart on steroids:

  - Two of the series are represented on the x- and y-axes.

  - The third series is represented by the size of the bubble.

- ✔ **Stock** charts are meant to portray stock price levels, including the high, low, and closing prices.

# Data, thy name is dynamic

Although the purpose of any chart is to portray data in an easy-to-comprehend visual, data still remains more important than the chart. Follow these guidelines to make the most of the underlying data:

✔ While in Chart Editing mode, enter all your data in the datasheet.

> If you can't see the datasheet, choose View➪Datasheet.

✔ The datasheet looks like a worksheet in a spreadsheet application, such as Microsoft Excel or Lotus 1-2-3, and works in almost the same way.

> When you first insert a new chart, PowerPoint already fills in some sample data for you — change the data as required, and the chart updates dynamically.

✔ The top row and the leftmost columns in the datasheet typically contain the names or values of the corresponding x- and y-axis indicators.

## Import your spreadsheet data

If I already had all the data I needed to use for a chart available in a spreadsheet, I would rather not type it again! Call me lazy or time-productive. Follow these steps to import your spreadsheet data into the datasheet:

1. **Double-click your chart to get into Chart Editing mode. If the datasheet isn't visible, choose View➪Datasheet.**

2. **Choose Edit➪Import File.**

   You can import data from several data and spreadsheet formats, including Excel spreadsheets, text files, and Lotus 1-2-3 spreadsheets. Be aware that you can import data only from older Lotus 1-2-3 formats.

   If you select the Excel spreadsheet option, you see the Import Data Options dialog box that lets you choose which worksheet contains the data you want to import (see Figure 9-15).

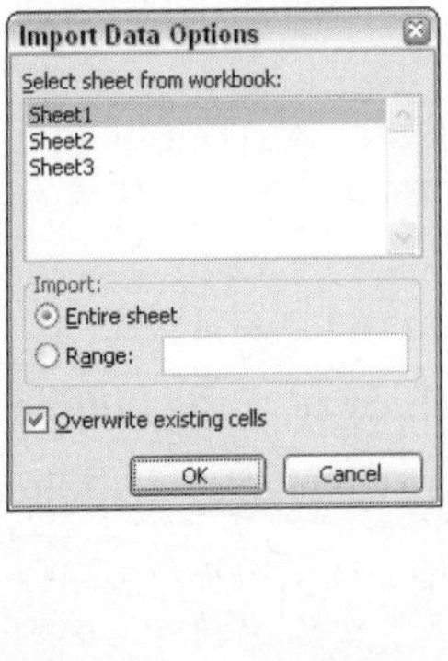

**Figure 9-15:**
Choose the
exact data
source.

## Extend your chart horizons with Excel

If you already work with Excel, you probably have charts already created on your spreadsheets. Understandably, you don't want to import the same data inside PowerPoint and duplicate the chart creation. All you want to do is reuse the whole chart — lock, stock, and barrel! That makes more sense because Excel, like PowerPoint, uses the Microsoft Graph component to create charts.

You can import your Excel charts inside PowerPoint in one of two ways, the Paste way or the Paste Special way. I discuss the benefits and problems with both the ways after I show you how to get the charts from Excel to PowerPoint.

### The Paste way

Follow these steps to paste your Excel charts inside PowerPoint:

1. **Select the chart inside Excel and choose Edit⇨Copy.**

2. **Activate PowerPoint.**

3. **Choose Edit⇨Paste to place the chart on the active slide.**

### The Paste Special way

Follow these steps to paste your Excel charts inside PowerPoint with more control:

1. **Select the chart inside Excel and choose Edit⇨Copy.**

2. **Activate PowerPoint.**

3. **Choose Edit⇨Paste Special to summon the Paste Special dialog box, shown in Figure 9-16.**

4. **Choose either of the Picture options (Windows Metafile or Enhanced Metafile) to place an image of the chart.**

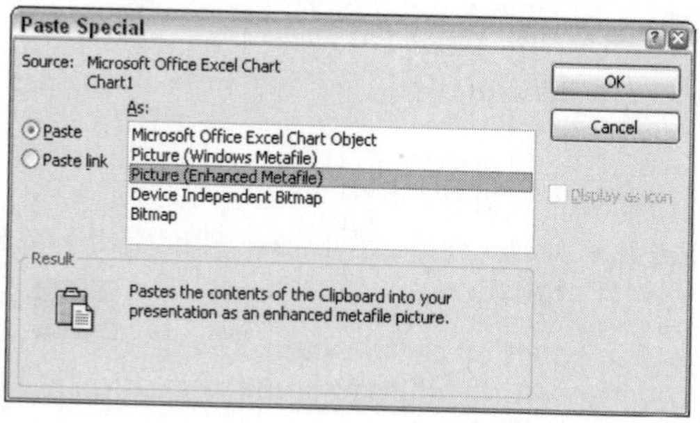

**Figure 9-16:** Paste Special options.

Although both the methods bring in the charts, the Paste way actually brings the entire Excel spreadsheet into PowerPoint 2000. This can make your PowerPoint file size huge, although it has its virtues: You can work on the data even if you lose the original Excel file.

The Paste Special way imports the chart as a graphic, keeping your PowerPoint file sizes under control.

# Slide Over to Equations

All versions of PowerPoint include *Equation Editor,* a small application that lets you insert equations in PowerPoint slides. This can be very helpful if you create lots of slides involving math, chemistry, or statistics.

Follow these steps to insert an equation inside PowerPoint:

1. **Navigate to the slide where you want to insert an equation and choose Insert⇨Object.**

   You see the Insert Object dialog box, shown in Figure 9-17.

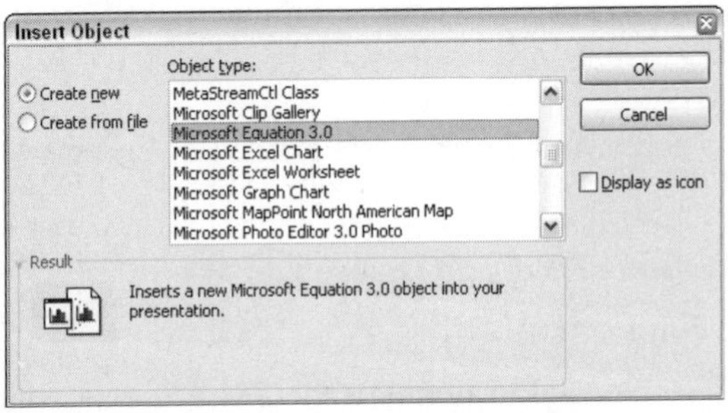

**Figure 9-17:**
Insert objects such as equations.

2. **Scroll down the choices within the Object Type box and select Microsoft Equation 3.0 (or another version) and then click OK to launch the Equation Editor.**

3. **Create your equations inside Equation Editor.**

   More details about creating equations are available on this book's companion site:

   www.cuttingedgeppt.com/eqeditor

4. **When the equation has been created, choose File⇨Exit and Return to get back to the PowerPoint slide.**

   PowerPoint inserts the equation on the slide. To edit the equation, double-click the equation on the slide to launch Equation Editor.

Equation Editor has been included with almost every version of PowerPoint. If you use equations often, you might want to insert an Equation Editor icon on one of your PowerPoint toolbars. Here's how:

1. **Choose View⇨Toolbars⇨Customize.**

2. **Click the Commands tab.**

3. **Choose the Insert option in the Categories area.**

4. **In the Commands area, select Equation Editor and then drag its icon to any location on any visible toolbar.**

If you use Equation Editor often, you might want to take a look at its big brother, MathType, which can do a lot more:

`www.cuttingedgeppt.com/mathtype`

# Go Cartographic with MapPoint

Microsoft MapPoint is a mapping application that lets you route your journeys and do much more. Microsoft makes it easy to get MapPoint maps straight into PowerPoint by including a shortcut inside PowerPoint.

Assuming that you have PowerPoint and MapPoint installed on the same system, follow these steps to insert a map on a slide:

1. **Create a new slide or use an existing one to insert the map.**

2. **Choose Insert⇨MapPoint Map.**

    PowerPoint places a basic map on the slide — which probably isn't what you want.

3. **Double-click the map and watch the magic as the map metamorphoses into an active MapPoint instance!**

    Figure 9-18 shows how all the menus and toolbars convert to the MapPoint interface.

4. **Zoom, pan, or search the map by using the toolbar controls as required until the display on the slide looks exactly how you want it.**

5. **Click anywhere outside the map to return to PowerPoint.**

If you want to find out more about MapPoint, check out *Microsoft MapPoint For Dummies,* by B. J. Holtgrewe and Jill T. Freeze (Wiley).

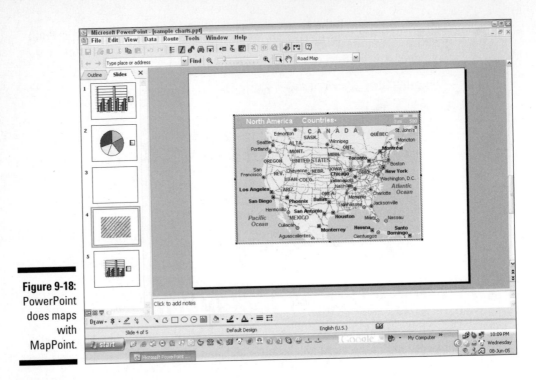

**Figure 9-18:**
PowerPoint does maps with MapPoint.

# Beyond PowerPoint

Although PowerPoint provides umpteen ways of inserting info-graphics on a slide, I still like to think of PowerPoint as a glue to hold disparate elements together. That's easy to visualize because PowerPoint can accept visual content from so many other applications. This section shows you how to incorporate content from Microsoft Visio and other applications.

## Working with Visio

Microsoft Visio is a diagramming application that's useful for everything from small home plans to complex networking prototypes.

You need to use Visio in either of these cases:

✔ PowerPoint's diagramming tools aren't sufficient for your needs.

✔ You want to reuse someone's Visio diagrams in a PowerPoint presentation.

Visio works in much the same way as PowerPoint because Microsoft has created very similar interfaces for the Office suite of applications.

PowerPoint doesn't support native drawing format. Either you need to link to an existing or newly-created Visio drawing as an object or export from Visio to a graphic format and thereafter import it into PowerPoint. Between the two methods, choose the latter if you want to transport your presentation to a system without Visio installed.

### The link option

Follow these steps to link a Visio drawing to a PowerPoint slide:

1. **In PowerPoint, choose Insert⇨Object.**

2. **In the resultant dialog box, select the Create New radio button.**

3. **Select Microsoft Visio Drawing from the Object Type list and then click OK.**

   Visio opens the Choose Drawing Type dialog box.

4. **Make your selection from the diagram categories and click OK.**

   Visio prompts you with a dialog box that asks whether you want the Visio shapes to use the PowerPoint color scheme of the host presentation.

   Accepting this option provides you with a coordinated look, so you might want to click Yes in this dialog box.

5. **Create your diagram inside Visio.**

6. **Click anywhere outside the Visio area to get back to your PowerPoint slide.**

### The insert option

This method is more straightforward. Although you can't edit the original drawing this way, the resultant presentation is more compact and portable:

1. **Open or create a Visio diagram from within the Visio application.**

2. **Choose File⇨Save As.**

   The resultant Save As dialog box lets you save the diagram in 28 different graphic formats, both vector and raster.

3. **Choose WMF or EMF from the Save as Type drop-down list.**

   WMF and EMF are the best formats to transport graphic content between Microsoft applications.

4. **In PowerPoint, choose Insert⇨Picture⇨From File, navigate to and choose the WMF/EMF file, and click Insert.**

# Info-graphics programs

Although PowerPoint has an impressive repertoire of drawing and diagramming capabilities, you should explore some third-party add-ins and companion programs that allow more possibilities:

- ✔ **SmartDraw** is a drawing application that's especially geared toward Microsoft Office users. It includes over 50,000 symbols and templates that you can use within a drag-and-draw interface that requires no artistic skill.

- ✔ **PowerPlugs: Charts** lets you create 3-D style rendered charts inside PowerPoint almost in the same way as Microsoft Graph. However, it adds niceties like anti-aliased text and high-resolution export.

- ✔ **Graphicae** adds a plethora of intelligent diagram styles and business analytical tools used by the leading MBA schools and consulting firms.

- ✔ **WowChart, Xcelsius,** and **rChart** all allow you to create Flash-based animated vector charts. These charts can then be inserted within PowerPoint slides with one click.

You can find out more about these tools at:

`www.cuttingedgeppt.com/infographics`

# Part III
# Adding Motion, Sounds, and Effects

The 5th Wave                    By Rich Tennant

# In this part . . .

This part makes PowerPoint come alive. It's about the audio-video stuff and the movement. Can you hear the humming and the foot-steps?

# Chapter 10

# Listening and Watching: The Sound and Video Stuff

. . . . . . . . . . . . . . . . . . . . . . . . . . . . . . . . . . . . . . . . . . . . . . . . . . . .

*In This Chapter*

▶ Multimedia formats

▶ Sounding off

▶ Spanning your slides with music

▶ Voice-overs in PowerPoint

▶ Putting videos in slides

▶ Media playlists in PowerPoint

▶ Codecs, codecs, codecs

▶ Making movies from your PowerPoint presentation

. . . . . . . . . . . . . . . . . . . . . . . . . . . . . . . . . . . . . . . . . . . . . . . . . . . .

*I*nserting sound and video clips into PowerPoint slides is usually easy. PowerPoint allows ample control over how they play in Slide Show mode.

Sound and video come from disparate sources — from camcorders and music CDs to stock footage libraries and in-house rendered content, not to mention downloads from the Internet. An amazing number of sound and video formats actually are entwined with an even more amazing number of *codecs*. And if you don't know what this format and codec thing means, read on and get PowerPoint to sing and dance!

Codecs are covered toward the end of this chapter. If you just need some quick codec cures, skip to the "Getting Friendly with Codecs" section.

In this chapter, in addition to the basics of adding multimedia to your PowerPoint presentations, you find out more about the nuances of multimedia — like adding fades to your sounds and using PowerPoint's amazing narration features. Finally, if you want to show DVD video clips inside PowerPoint or maybe export an entire presentation to a movie, you're reading the right chapter!

# All Those Multimedia Formats

Unless you've been living under a rock for the last decade, you have most likely been flabbergasted by the names of all those multimedia formats, such as MP3 and Windows Media. In this section, I tell you about all those wonderful multimedia formats that PowerPoint loves or hates.

## The sound brigade

PowerPoint can accept and play almost all the standard audio formats:

- ✔ **WAV:** This is the most common sound file format on Microsoft Windows. PowerPoint works well with this format.

- ✔ **MP3:** MP3s can be inserted and played inside PowerPoint but are a no-no for slide transition sounds.

- ✔ **WMA, ASF:** The same concepts that apply to MP3s apply to WMA.

  Stay away from WMA and ASF if your presentation needs to be shown on a Mac.

- ✔ **MID or MIDI:** These are actual music notations that your computer's sound card interprets and plays in real time. To enjoy this type of sound, you should have a high-fidelity sound card that retails for over a hundred dollars. Anything less than that can still do a good job, unless you start comparing the sound outputs!

- ✔ **AIFF, AU:** These are the other sound formats that PowerPoint accepts; however, it's best you leave them alone — and they'll probably leave you alone too!

## Wise up to video formats

PowerPoint can cope with a plethora of video formats:

- ✔ **AVI:** AVI has been around the longest, and PowerPoint is usually happy with this format unless it has been rendered using a nonstandard codec. (You discover more about codecs later in this chapter.)

- ✔ **MOV:** These are Apple QuickTime files that can be played easily on Windows-based machines using the free QuickTime Player application. Alas, PowerPoint isn't so benevolent — it can play only really old QuickTime content rendered using obsolete codecs from a decade ago.

  Newer QuickTime videos use more efficient codecs by default, and PowerPoint can't cope with any videos rendered in this improved format.

✔ **MPG, MPEG:** Conventional MPEG movies, also called MPEG 1 movies, play well in PowerPoint. They're the best option if you need to create a presentation that needs to be played on both the Windows and Mac versions of PowerPoint.

MPEG 2 movies are DVD-quality and aren't too PowerPoint friendly — they're extremely reliant on both hardware and software and usually don't play in PowerPoint, even if they do play well in Windows Media Player.

✔ **WMV, ASF:** WMV (Windows Media Video) works great inside PowerPoint, but stay away from it if you need your presentations to be Mac friendly. ASF is the older name for Windows Media files.

For all practical purposes, WMV and ASF are identical. When Microsoft introduced the Windows Media format, both audio and video files used the .asf extension. Later, Microsoft started using the .wmv and .wma extensions for video and audio, respectively.

✔ **Flash:** Flash isn't actually a video format. It's a vector format that supports animation. PowerPoint (and Windows itself) doesn't consider Flash a native video format. However, Flash movies can be played within PowerPoint. You can find more information about inserting Flash within PowerPoint in Chapter 13.

✔ **VCD:** VCD, or *Video CD,* files usually have the .dat extension. For all practical purposes, they're MPEG 1 videos, and several tools, including freeware applications, can convert VCD DAT movies to MPEG files without any problem. An online search for "VCD to MPEG converter" should result in several hits.

✔ **DVD:** Some third-party tools let you play DVD movies right inside PowerPoint — I cover them toward the end of this chapter.

# Inserting Sounds

Before you even insert a sound on a slide, you need to make two decisions:

✔ **Do you want the sound to play automatically as soon as the slide is shown?**

Most of the time you want to do this.

✔ **Do you want the sound to play across multiple slides?**

This is the way to go if you want to insert a background music track. Check out the upcoming section, "Sound across slides," for the lowdown.

After you answer these questions, follow these steps to insert the sounds:

1. **Navigate to the slide where you want the sound to be inserted.**

2. **Choose Insert⇨Movies and Sounds⇨Sound from File.**

   This summons the Insert Sound dialog box, shown in Figure 10-1.

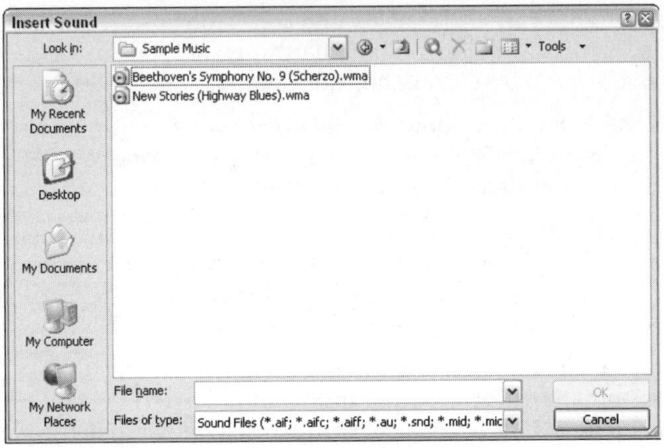

**Figure 10-1:**
Get some sound into PowerPoint.

3. **Choose a sound in any of the formats that PowerPoint accepts and click OK.**

   PowerPoint asks you whether you want the sound to play automatically in the slide show, as shown in Figure 10-2.

4. **If you want the sound to play automatically, accept the option.**

**Figure 10-2:**
Do you want PowerPoint to play the sound automatically?

PowerPoint places a sound icon in the middle of the slide. To make it invisible, just drag it off the slide area; it will still play just fine within the presentation.

## Sound across slides

Mainstream corporate presentations don't normally include a musical score that spans the entire slide presentation. However, a musical background score can be a pleasing accompaniment to a lunch-hour or tea-break presentation, especially at a convention. For example, a product photo-album presentation can benefit from an upbeat music score. Also, when the music stops, the audience knows it's time to get back to their seats.

Turning off the music in any presentation can be as easy as setting the volume bar to mute, so there's no harm in including music in any presentation, as long as the presentation doesn't include narration!

Assemble your sound files in the same folder as the presentation, even before you insert the music into a saved presentation. This ensures that PowerPoint doesn't lose its links if you move the presentation to another system — you can just copy the entire folder to another machine.

The following instructions show you how to insert a musical score that spans slides in PowerPoint. The techniques depend upon your version of PowerPoint.

### PowerPoint 2002 and 2003

Follow these steps to insert a sound that plays across slides in PowerPoint 2002 or 2003:

1. **Open a new or existing presentation in PowerPoint and navigate to the first slide.**

2. **Choose Insert⇨Movies and Sound⇨Sound from File.**

   The Insert Sound dialog box opens (refer to Figure 10-1).

3. **Navigate to and select the sound file that you want to use and then click OK.**

   PowerPoint asks you if you want the sound to play automatically. Accept this option.

   This places a sound icon on your slide.

4. **Right-click the sound icon and choose Custom Animation from the resultant context menu.**

   The Custom Animation task pane toward the right side of the PowerPoint interface activates. Your sound file is listed within the pane.

5. **In the Custom Animation task pane, choose Effect Options from the drop-down list next to your sound file.**

   The Play Sound dialog box opens (see Figure 10-3). It contains three tabs — Effect, Timing, and Sound Settings.

6. **Click the Effect tab of the Play Sound dialog box.**

7. **Type 999 in the Stop Playing After box.**

   999 is the highest slide number that PowerPoint accepts, so entering this number is the same as telling PowerPoint to play the sound throughout your presentation.

8. **Click the Timing tab.**

9. **Choose After Previous in the Start drop-down list.**

10. **Set the Delay option to 0 (zero) seconds.**

**Play Sound**

Effect | Timing | Sound Settings

Start playing
- ⦿ From beginning
- ○ From last position
- ○ From time:     seconds

Stop playing
- ○ On click
- ○ After current slide
- ⦿ After: 999 slides

Enhancements
Sound:           [No Sound]
After animation: Don't Dim
Animate text:
            % delay between letters

        OK        Cancel

**Figure 10-3:** The Play Sound dialog box.

Thereafter, you can drag the sound icon anywhere off the slide if you don't want the icon to be visible while you play the presentation.

11. **Save your presentation!**

### PowerPoint 2000

Follow these steps to insert a sound that plays across slides in PowerPoint 2000:

1. **Navigate to the first slide of the presentation.**

2. **Choose Insert⇨Movies and Sounds⇨Sound from File to summon the Insert Sound dialog box.**

3. **Navigate to and select the sound file you want to use and then click OK.**

   PowerPoint might ask you whether you want your sound to play automatically — accept this option by clicking Yes.

   A sound icon appears on your slide.

4. **Right-click the sound icon and choose Custom Animation from the resultant pop-up menu.**

   This summons the Custom Animation dialog box, shown in Figure 10-4.

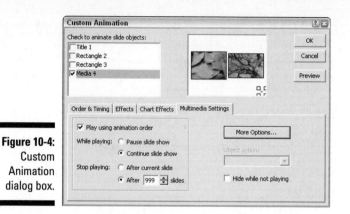

5. **Within the Custom Animation dialog box, click the Multimedia Settings tab.**

6. **Select the Continue Slide Show radio button.**

7. **Type a high number in the Stop Playing After box.**

   999 is the highest number you can type.

8. **Click OK.**

   You can drag the sound icon anywhere off the slide if you don't want the icon to be visible while you play the presentation.

The accompanying CD contains several music loops from Indigo Rose's "Liquid Cabaret" collection. Any of the loops can play continuously across slides.

The sound-across-slides feature isn't well-suited for all types of presentations:

✔ Avoid including a background musical score in a corporate presentation that has a presenter discussing issues before an audience.

✔ Unless you're a professional presentation designer or an audio-video person who is certain about the entire concept, never use a background score in a presentation that includes narration.

Watch for these opportunities to use music in presentations:

✔ You can use the sound feature in presentations that don't have a live presenter — although you should choose a soft, understated background score.

✔ For trade shows and exhibition kiosks, try to use upbeat and optimistic music instead of monotonous, weary tunes.

✔ You can use music to great advantage within presentations that are distributed on CD.

## Transition sounds

*Transition sounds* play with slide transitions. If the sound is longer than the transition, it continues to play beyond the actual transition. In fact, transition sounds can loop and play continuously across *several* slides.

If you want to find out more about transitions, they're covered in Chapter 11.

How you play transition sounds across slides depends on your version of PowerPoint.

### PowerPoint 2002 and 2003

Follow these steps to add transition sounds that play over one or more slides in PowerPoint 2002 or 2003:

1. **Navigate to the slide where you want the sound to begin.**

2. **Choose Slide Show⇨Slide Transition.**

   This activates the Slide Transition task pane, shown in Figure 10-5.

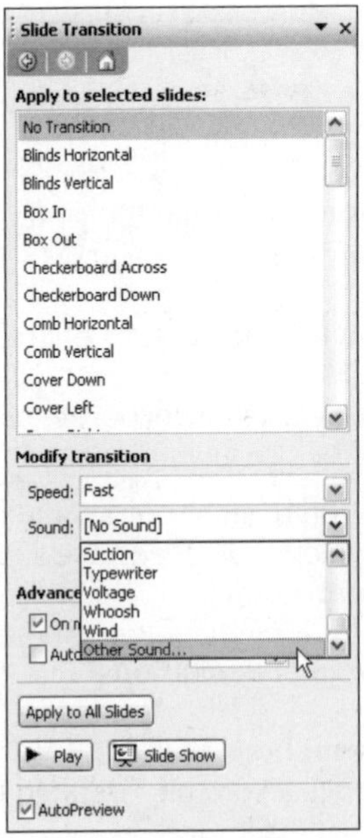

**Figure 10-5:**
Inserting
sounds in
transitions.

3. **In the Modify Transition area of the pane, choose Other Sound from the Sound drop-down menu.**

4. **Choose any WAV file.**

   This technique doesn't work with MP3, WMA, or MIDI files.

5. **Make sure you select the Loop Until Next Sound option.**

6. **Navigate to the slide where you want the sound to stop playing.**

7. **Click the Sound drop-down menu in the Transitions task pane and choose [Stop Previous Sound].**

### *PowerPoint 2000*

Follow these steps to insert transition sounds that loop in PowerPoint 2000:

1. **Navigate to the slide where you want the sound loop to begin.**

2. **Choose Slide Show⇨Slide Transition.**

   This summons the Slide Transition dialog box, shown in Figure 10-6.

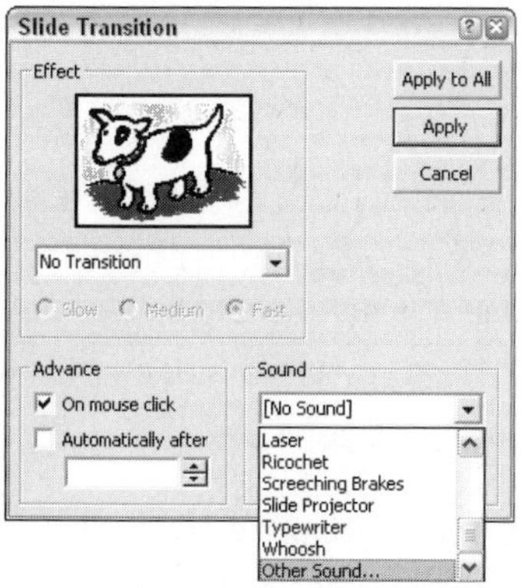

**Figure 10-6:**
The Slide
Transition
dialog box
does
sounds, too.

3. **In the Sound drop-down box, choose the Other Sound option.**

4. **Select any WAV file.**

   This technique doesn't work with MP3, WMA, or MIDI files.

5. **Make sure you select the Loop Until Next Sound option.**

6. **Click Apply to exit the dialog box.**

7. **Navigate to the slide where you want the sound to stop playing.**

8. **Choose Slide Show⇨Slide Transition to summon the Slide Transition dialog box that you saw in Figure 10-6.**

9. **In the Sound drop-down list, choose [Stop Previous Sound].**

10. **Click Apply to exit the dialog box.**

The biggest advantage to using transition sounds in a looping background score (instead of inserting sounds into the slides) is that all transition sounds are embedded as part of the presentation.

Transition sounds over 50MB are *neither embedded nor linked* — and PowerPoint doesn't even warn you, so make sure that your transition sounds aren't over that limit!

## Fading sounds in an audio editor

Many times, you don't want a sound to start playing at full volume — a sound that fades into a presentation is usually much more interesting. In the same way, you might want to end your presentation with a sound that fades out.

PowerPoint by itself has no sound-fading mechanism — you must use an external sound editor to do the fades. Plenty of good sound editors are available. My favorites are

- ✔ Sony Sound Forge
- ✔ Adobe Audition
- ✔ Audacity (freeware)

For this tutorial, I use Audacity because it is simple and free — download a free copy of the product from

```
www.cuttingedgeppt.com/audacity
```

Follow these steps to fade in and fade out your sounds in Audacity:

1. **Choose File⇨Open and navigate to wherever you have saved a sound file.**

   If you don't have a sample sound file, use one of the samples on this book's CD.

   The sound opens in a waveform view similar to what's shown in Figure 10-7.

   Stereo sounds display two waveforms; mono sounds display a single waveform.

2. **Select a part of the waveform.**

   Drag over the waveform area to select as required:

   • *For a fade-in effect,* select a small part of the beginning of the waveform.

   Fade-in sounds are ideally inserted in the first slide of the presentation.

- *For a fade-out effect,* select a small part of the end of the waveform.

  Fade-out sounds are ideally inserted in the last slide of the presentation.

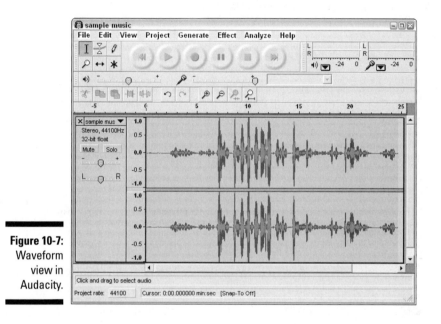

**Figure 10-7:**
Waveform
view in
Audacity.

3. **Apply the fade effect:**

   - *For a fade-in effect,* choose Effect⇨Fade In.
   - *For a fade-out effect,* choose Effect⇨Fade Out.

4. **Listen to the faded sound by clicking the big Play icon on the toolbar.**

   If you aren't satisfied with the fade effect, choose Edit⇨Undo and select a smaller or larger area of the waveform.

5. **After the fade effect is to your liking, choose File⇨Export as WAV or one of the other export options to save the sound to a new file.**

A similar tutorial for Sony Sound Forge can be found on this book's Web site:

    www.cuttingedgeppt.com/sforgefades

A trial version of Sony Sound Forge can be found on the CD attached to this book.

If you want a ready-made solution that does everything for you, including inserting sounds to play across slides with fade-ins and fade-outs, take a look at CrystalGraphics PowerPlugs: Music add-in for PowerPoint:

```
www.cuttingedgeppt.com/ppmusic
```

## Add a CD soundtrack

A CD soundtrack is great accompaniment to a picture collage or photo-album style presentation for anything from a reunion to a keepsake. And if you restrict yourself to instrumental music tracks, there's no reason why you can't use a CD soundtrack in corporate presentations.

Here's how you get PowerPoint to play CD tracks:

1. **Put your favorite CD in your CD-ROM drive.**

2. **Open a new or existing presentation in PowerPoint and navigate to the first slide.**

3. **Choose Insert⇨Movies and Sound⇨Play CD Audio Track.**

   This summons the Insert CD Audio dialog box, shown in Figure 10-8.

**Figure 10-8:**
Insert
CD audio
tracks in
PowerPoint.

4. **Choose both a start track and an end track on the CD.**

   You can start in the middle of a track by providing specific timings. In addition, you can opt to loop the sound continuously.

5. **Click OK when you're done.**

   PowerPoint asks you whether you want the sound to play automatically. Accept this option by clicking Yes or choose No if you want the tracks to play on click while presenting.

A CD icon appears on the slide. If you chose the option to play the tracks automatically in the preceding section, you can drag the icon off the slide area if you don't want it to be visible while you're playing the presentation.

After you have inserted the CD track, you can adjust it to play across slides. The steps differ depending on your version of PowerPoint.

### PowerPoint 2002 and 2003

Follow these steps to make a CD track play across slides in PowerPoint 2002 or 2003:

1. **Right-click the CD icon on the slide and choose Custom Animation from the resultant context menu.**

   The Custom Animation task pane is activated. The name of your sound file is listed in that pane.

2. **Choose Effect Options from the drop-down menu next to the name of your sound file, as shown in Figure 10-9.**

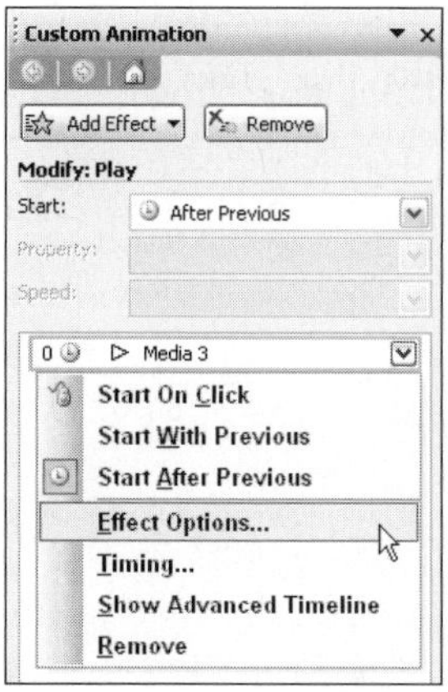

**Figure 10-9:**
Play your
CD
soundtracks
across
slides.

In the Play CD Audio dialog box that opens next, you find three tabs — Effect, Timing, and Sound Settings — as shown in Figure 10-10.

3. **Within the Effect tab, select the From Beginning radio button and type 999 in the Stop Playing Clip box.**

   999 is the highest slide number that PowerPoint accepts.

4. **Within the Timing tab, choose After Previous as the Start option, with a delay of 0 (zero) seconds.**

5. **Click OK.**

**Figure 10-10:**
Effect and
Timing.

## PowerPoint 2000

Follow these steps to play your CD tracks across slides in PowerPoint 2000:

1. **Right-click the CD icon on the slide and choose Custom Animation from the resultant context menu.**

   This activates the Custom Animation dialog box, shown in Figure 10-11.

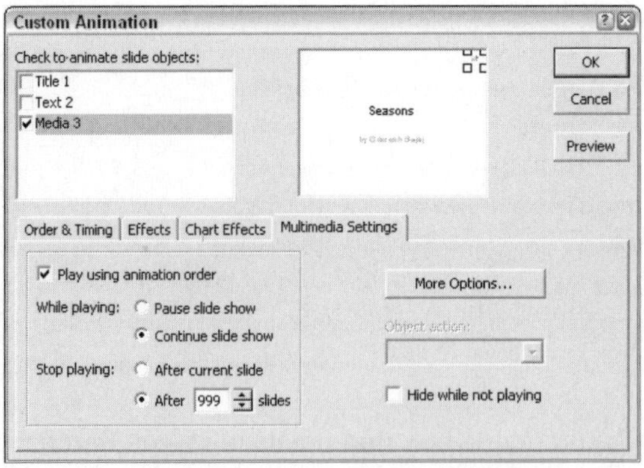

**Figure 10-11:**
Playing CD
tracks
across
slides
involves
tweaking
some
settings.

2. **In the Multimedia Settings tab, match your settings with these:**

   • *While Playing:* Continue Slide Show

   • *Stop Playing:* After 999 Slides

3. **Click OK.**

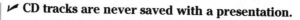

## Playing CD tracks: Guidelines

Follow these guidelines to avoid problems with CD tracks playing in PowerPoint:

✔ **CD tracks are never saved with a presentation.**

PowerPoint refers to tracks via track numbers — so if you choose to play tracks 2 through 5 using a particular CD and then replace that CD with another, PowerPoint plays tracks 2 through 5 from the new CD. This can be a blessing or a curse — whichever way you want to look at it!

✔ **Use the same CD drive to place your audio CD while presenting if your computer has more than one CD drive.** While your audio CD is in one drive, PowerPoint might be looking for it on the other drive!

✔ **Rip the tracks off the CD as WAV, MP3, or WMA files** (use MP3 if you're working between both the Mac and Windows versions of PowerPoint) that can be inserted as normal sounds in the presentation.

Later in this chapter, I show you how to rip CD audio tracks.

✔ **Be aware of copyright regulations, especially if you're distributing presentations.** More or less, all music is copyrighted, and the music business has an extremely negative opinion of illegal copying and sharing of its work.

# Converting Sound Formats

Many times, the sound you need isn't in a format you need. At other times, the *sampling rate* of a sound needs to be changed.

Sounds that have higher sampling rates have a higher fidelity. They can also be huge — and putting those high-fidelity sounds inside a PowerPoint slide may make the presentation unresponsive.

Fortunately, converting between sound formats and sampling rates is easy. In this section, you find out more about tools and procedures for conversion.

## Converting CD tracks

*Ripping* is the process of converting CD audio tracks to other formats like WAV, MP3, and WMA. Several shareware and freeware CD-ripping programs are available. You can also use Windows Media Player, an application that's part of Microsoft Windows.

Follow these steps to rip a CD audio track with Windows Media Player:

1. **Make sure that you have an audio CD in your CD drive.**

2. **Launch Windows Media Player and choose Tools⇨Options.**

   This summons the multitabbed Options dialog box, shown in Figure 10-12.

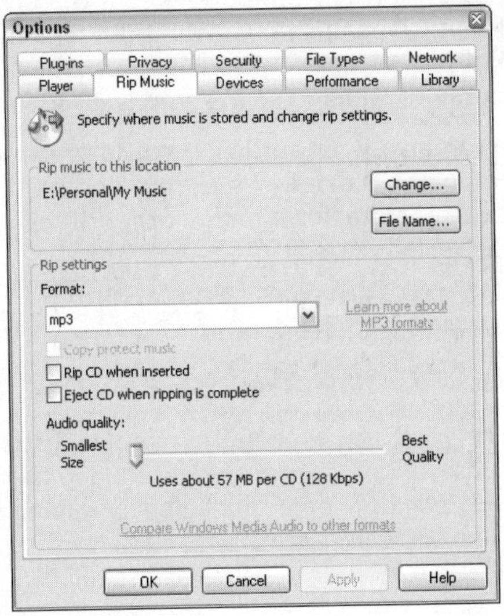

**Figure 10-12:** Options in Windows Media Player.

Options dialog box:

Tabs: Plug-ins | Privacy | Security | File Types | Network
Player | Rip Music | Devices | Performance | Library

Specify where music is stored and change rip settings.

Rip music to this location
E:\Personal\My Music            [Change...]
                                [File Name...]

Rip settings
Format:
mp3                      ▼        Learn more about MP3 formats

☐ Copy protect music
☐ Rip CD when inserted
☐ Eject CD when ripping is complete

Audio quality:
Smallest Size ——————————— Best Quality
Uses about 57 MB per CD (128 Kbps)

Compare Windows Media Audio to other formats

[OK]  [Cancel]  [Apply]  [Help]

3. **Click the Rip tab to find several options:**

   • Change the location of the folder where all your ripped music is saved.

   • Choose the format for ripping — options include MP3 and WMA.

4. **When you have chosen your options, click OK to exit this dialog box.**

   This gets you back to Windows Media Player.

   Click the Rip tab in the Player to see all your CD tracks listed.

5. **Click the Rip Music icon to start the ripping process.**

   Be patient. Ripping might take some time depending upon your computer speed and processor.

# Converting between MP3, WMA, and WAV

Converting between MP3, WMA, and WAV formats is something you might want to do often. For instance, you might want to

✔ **Use an MP3 track as a transition sound.** You'll have to convert it to a WAV because only WAVs can be used as transition sounds.

✔ **Convert a WAV to MP3 so that it takes less space.** This is even more important if you need to e-mail your presentation.

✔ **Convert WAV or MP3 to WMA to take advantage of the superior compression so that the sounds take even less space.**

The people at Illustrate offer a freeware program called dBpowerAMP Music Converter to help you convert sound files. You can download dBpowerAMP from

```
www.cuttingedgeppt.com/dbpoweramp
```

dBpowerAMP also lets you rip CDs to WAV files.

Follow these guidelines to convert between file formats with dBpowerAMP:

1. **Start dBpowerAMP Music Converter.**

   An Open dialog box (see Figure 10-13) appears.

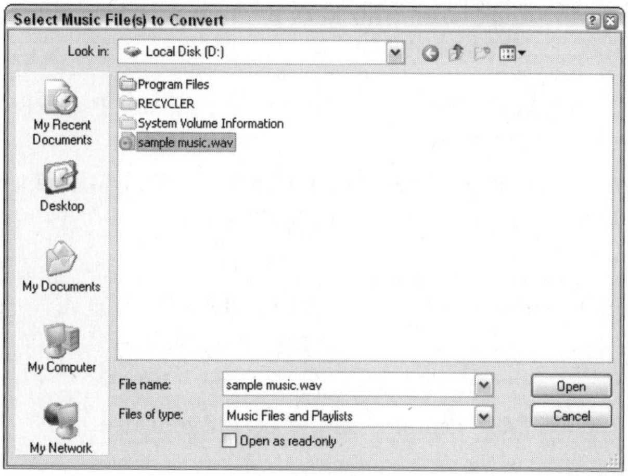

**Figure 10-13:**
Convert
sound
formats with
dBpower-
AMP.

2. **Choose a file you want to convert.**

   You see the dialog box shown in Figure 10-14.

   This dialog box lets you choose the destination format and save location for the converted file.

3. **Choose these options as required.**

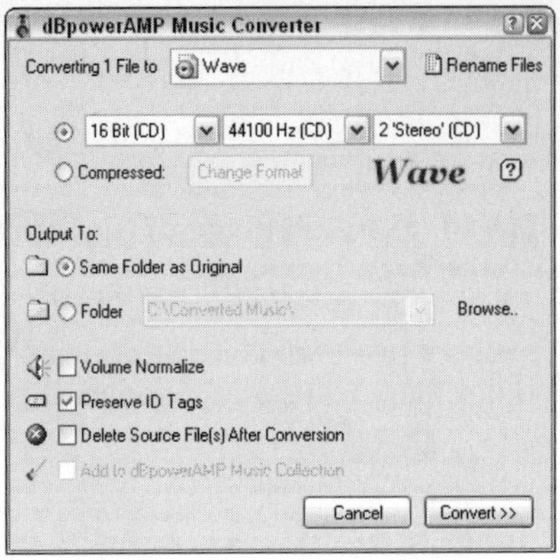

**Figure 10-14:**
Choose the
sound
format and
other
attributes.

4. **Click the Convert button and you're done!**

## Converting MIDI to WAV

MIDI files need a fairly high-level sound card to play with full fidelity. Thus, depending on your sound card, your MIDI might sound heavenly or clunky inside your PowerPoint presentation.

✔ If you're happy with the way the MIDI sounds inside PowerPoint, don't bother with the conversion.

✔ If you aren't sure of your delivery machine, or if the MIDI doesn't sound too good on your system, consider converting it to a WAV sound.

Several programs can do the conversion — this book's companion site has more details and download links to such programs:

www.cuttingedgeppt.com/midi2wav

You can find 100 free MIDI samples on the CD for your use.

## Converting sampling rates

The *sampling rate* loosely translates to the fidelity of the sound. The following instructions show you how to convert the sampling rate for a WAV file by using the Sound Recorder applet:

1. **Launch Sound Recorder by choosing Start⇨Run and typing** sndrec32 **in the resultant dialog box.**

2. **In Sound Recorder, choose File➪Open.**

3. **Select a high-quality WAV file and click Open.**

4. **Choose File➪Properties to summon the Properties dialog box, shown in Figure 10-15.**

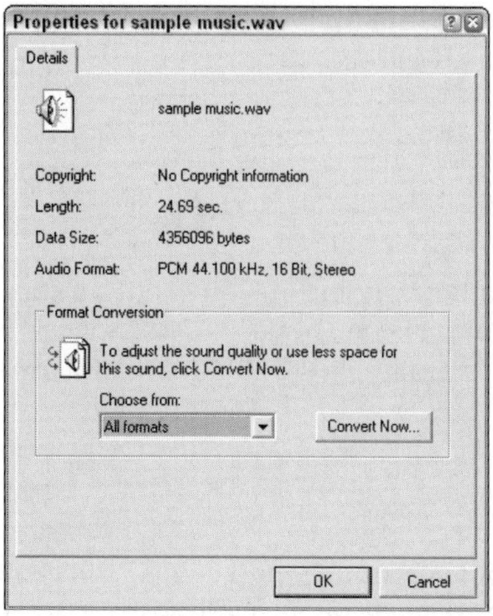

**Figure 10-15:**
Sound
properties.

Within the Properties dialog box, you find the *Format Conversion* option.

5. **Click the Convert Now button to view the Sound Selection dialog box, shown in Figure 10-16.**

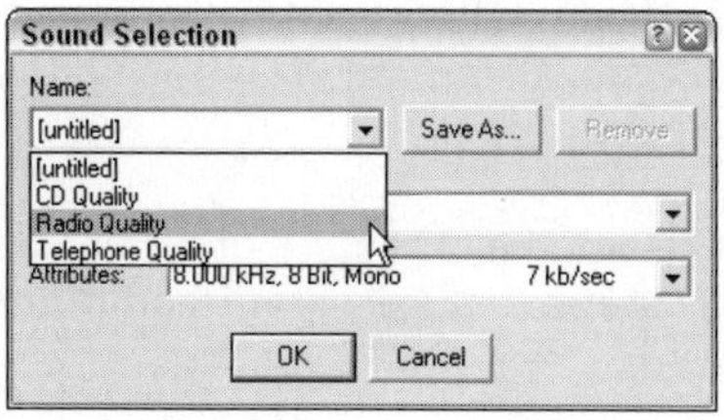

**Figure 10-16:**
Converting
sampling
rates.

You can choose your own format and attributes or just make it a whole lot simpler and choose any of the three default options available in the Name drop-down list:

- CD Quality

- Radio Quality

- Telephone Quality

For most PowerPoint work, Radio Quality offers a nice balance between file size and sound quality.

6. **Click OK to begin the conversion.**

   If this is a large file, Sound Recorder might take a while.

7. **Click OK again to exit the Properties dialog box.**

8. **Choose File⇨Save As and save the file under a new name so that the original file doesn't get overwritten.**

# Narration

To record narration from within PowerPoint, all you need is a sound card and a decent microphone. Yet, narration is one of PowerPoint's least used and most misunderstood aspects. Many people get frustrated and give up.

## Microphone setup

Most PowerPoint narration problems stem from outside PowerPoint — from incompatible sound cards to loose microphone cables to messed-up multi-media settings.

Before you start recording, install your microphone and test it. The following sections show you how.

### Installation

If your microphone isn't already installed, follow the instructions included with your microphone. Most of the time, all you need to do is plug your microphone into a sound card or a USB port.

Make sure that the microphone is selected as the default recording device in Microsoft Windows. Follow these steps to access your computer's audio settings:

1. **Open the Control Panel.**

   Depending on your Windows configuration, choose either

   - Start⇨Control Panel
   - Start⇨Settings⇨Control Panel

2. **In the Control Panel, click the audio icon.**

Depending on your Windows version, it's called either

- Sound and Audio Devices
- Sound, Speech, and Audio Devices

This opens the audio properties, shown in Figure 10-17.

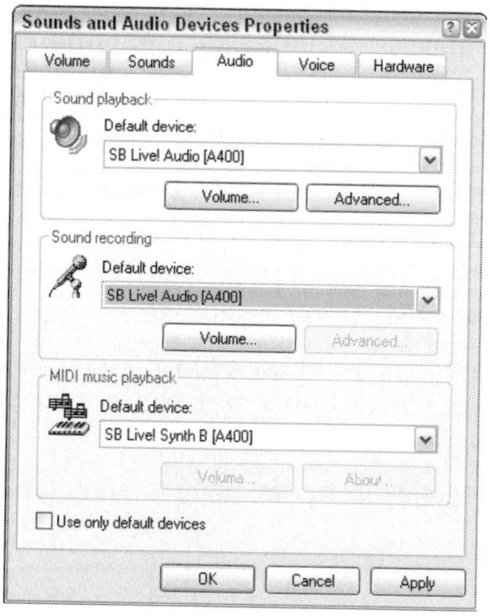

**Figure 10-17:**
Sound and
Audio
Devices
properties.

3. **Set these properties on the Audio tab:**

- Select your microphone as the default sound recording device.
- Select the option to present the Volume button to access the Record volume slider.
- Make sure the volume slider is around ¾ of the way up.

## Testing

If Sound Recorder can record your voice, you shouldn't have any problems recording your narrations in PowerPoint.

Follow these steps to do a test recording in Sound Recorder:

1. **Choose Start➪Run, type** sndrec32, **and click OK.**

   This launches the Sound Recorder applet, shown in Figure 10-18. This is a very simple, intuitive applet that looks and functions like a tape recorder.

2. **Click the rightmost (red) button to begin recording narration through the microphone.**

**Figure 10-18:**
Sound
Recorder.

3. **Speak a sentence or two before clicking the second button from the right to stop recording.**

4. **Play the recorded narration by clicking the Play button.**

   If Sound Recorder doesn't record, you may need to adjust your Play/Record Control properties:

   a. Double-click the small speaker icon to the right of your Windows taskbar. This opens your Play Control settings.

      If you can't see the speaker icon, choose Start⇨Run in the Windows taskbar and type **sndvol32.exe**. Either way you end up with the Play Control dialog box.

   b. Choose Options⇨Properties from the menu to summon the Properties dialog box.

   c. Select the Recording radio button and click OK.

      This causes the Play Control dialog box to change to the Recording Control dialog box.

   d. If the Microphone option in this dialog box is unchecked, check that option.

## Preparation

Your PowerPoint narration depends on

✔ **A good script**

   Make sure your script is ready — practice it aloud several times.

   In your script, avoid words with these sounds:

   • *Popping P,* such as *pack* and *topped*

   • *Hissing S,* such as *send* and *central*

✔ **Confidence**

   • Try for the exact nuance you need and experiment with speaking slowly in the parts where you want to provide more impact.

• Run the presentation in Slide Show mode and narrate along with the slides without recording anything.

At the end of this practice, you might want to make some changes in your script.

Be sure that you have enough light so that you can read your script clearly.

## Recording

When your microphone is connected and the script is ready, you can record your narration. Follow these steps:

1. **In PowerPoint, go to Slide Sorter view.**
2. **Select the slide where you would like to begin narration.**
3. **Choose Slide Show⇨Record Narration.**

   This opens the Record Narration dialog box, shown in Figure 10-19.

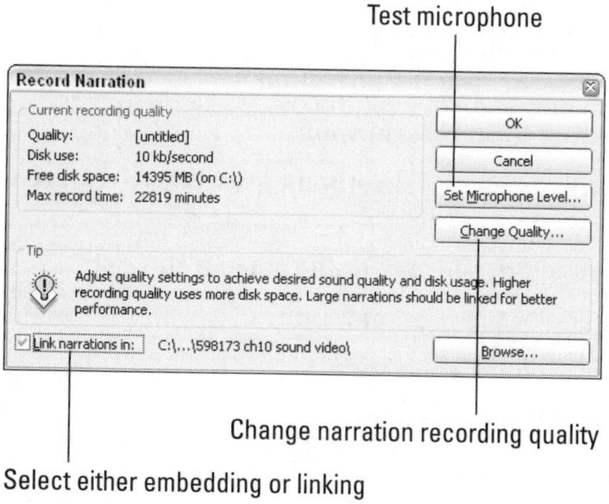

Test microphone

**Figure 10-19:**
Record
narration.

**Record Narration**

Current recording quality

| | |
|---|---|
| Quality: | [untitled] |
| Disk use: | 10 kb/second |
| Free disk space: | 14395 MB (on C:\) |
| Max record time: | 22819 minutes |

OK
Cancel
Set Microphone Level...
Change Quality...

Tip
Adjust quality settings to achieve desired sound quality and disk usage. Higher recording quality uses more disk space. Large narrations should be linked for better performance.

☑ Link narrations in:  C:\...\598173 ch10 sound video\    Browse...

Change narration recording quality

Select either embedding or linking

Before you click OK to start the recording, check out some options:

• *Set Microphone Level:* Click the Set Microphone Level button and you're presented with a Microphone Check dialog box. Use this dialog box to ensure that your microphone is working properly.

• *Change Quality:* This option lets you change the quality of the sound recorded. The three preset options, from highest to lowest quality, are CD, Radio, and Telephone.

## Sounding super!

Sound quality itself is influenced by many very subtle properties. Follow these guidelines to record great narration:

✔ Position the microphone close to yourself but slightly away from your mouth and nose.

✔ Speak normally, while not being overly loud.

✔ Start by placing the microphone around 4 inches away from your mouth and then adjust the distance to prevent breathing noises, hissing, and popping in the recording, so words with an *s* sound have no elongated "sss" sound, and *p* sounds don't pop.

Radio Quality provides the best balance between quality and file size in PowerPoint.

- *Link Narrations:* Check this box if you want to link your sound files instead of embedding them as part of the presentation. Enabling this option also lets you later directly open the recorded sound files and edit them in a sound-editing application like Sony Sound Forge, Adobe Audition, or Audacity.

4. **Click OK to start recording the narration.**

5. **Choose the starting location you want.**

   Before the recording begins, PowerPoint asks you to choose whether to begin narration from

   - The present slide (selected at the start of this list)
   - The first slide of the presentation

6. **Record the narration for each slide.**

   When you finish recording a slide:

   a. Leave a two-second pause.

   b. Either *click your mouse button* or *press the spacebar* on your keyboard to go to the next slide.

7. **Press Esc when you finish recording the narration for all your slides.**

   PowerPoint asks you if you want to save the *timing* with each slide (the duration of time that you spent narrating each slide).

8. **Click Yes to save the timing of your narration.**

## Editing

You don't have to use your narration exactly as you record it. PowerPoint lets you edit your recordings.

### Rough cuts

Often, you can just record your narration into PowerPoint as a "rough cut," choosing an option to link instead of embedding the narration sequences. Save these linked files in the same folder as the actual presentation because keeping all elements of the presentation in a single folder is very helpful when you want to transport the presentation to another system.

### Replacing narrations

If you're unhappy with the way your narration sounds, or if you used your narration as a stop-gap or temporary measure, you can replace the narration files with edited or new sound files:

- ✔ If you opted to link the narrations in the same folder as the presentation, you'll find them as a bunch of WAV files. These WAV files can be opened in a sound editor, where you can clean all the hiss and click sounds. Or you might want to hand over these WAV files to a sound technician to get them *cleaned.* Good sound technicians can also add reverb to your narration so that it sounds more impressive. They can also *normalize* your narrations so that all narrations play at the same volume.

- ✔ After you have edited or cleaned the narrations, just place them in the same folder as the original narrations. This will overwrite your old narrations, and PowerPoint won't even know that you have worked all that magic into the voices.

- ✔ You must be certain that the new narration files aren't longer than the original ones. Also, the new files must have the same names as the original files.

Other significant aspects are related to narration. Take a look at the "Sounding super!" sidebar to find out about them.

# Inserting Video

Normally, you insert video clips into PowerPoint by using the Insert menu options, as illustrated in the following steps. This works best for video files in the formats that PowerPoint understands, such as AVI, MPEG, and WMV. For other, unsupported formats, take a look at the "Link videos" section, later in this chapter.

Follow these steps to insert a video on a PowerPoint slide:

1. **Navigate to the slide where you want the video inserted in a new or existing presentation.**

2. **Choose Insert➪Movies and Sounds➪Movie from File.**

   This brings up the Insert Movie dialog box, shown in Figure 10-20.

3. **Select a video in any of the file formats that PowerPoint accepts.**

4. **PowerPoint asks you whether you want the movie to play automatically or only when clicked — choose your option.**

   The automatic option is a good idea if you aren't sure because

   • *Removing* that behavior later is a simple, one-click operation.

   • *Adding* that behavior later takes several steps.

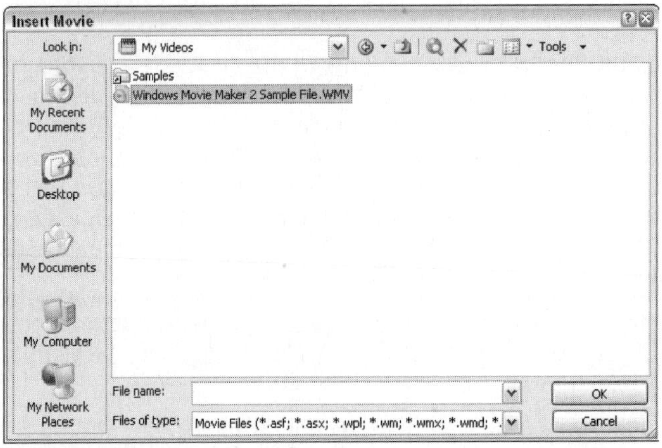

**Figure 10-20:**
Inserting
video.

## Resize the video

You can resize your video after it's inserted in a slide. If you select the video, you see eight handles around it — four on the corners and four between the corners (on the sides).

   ✔ Drag a corner handle to resize it in the same proportion on all sides.

   ✔ Drag a side handle to resize it without maintaining proportions.

   ✔ Drag the corner or sides with both the Ctrl and Shift keys pressed to resize it from the center.

## Add a border

You can also add a nice border to your video clip in PowerPoint. This ends up often looking like a frame.

1. **Right-click the video clip on the slide and choose Format Picture from the resultant flyout menu.**

   This opens the Format Picture dialog box.

2. **Within the Colors and Lines tab, choose a color from the Line Color drop-down list.**

   You can also alter the line weight, style, and dashed attributes of the line (border).

3. **Click OK.**

For a different effect, choose a weight of at least 10 points and then choose the Patterned Lines option in the Color drop-down menu. A striped or checked border that's somewhat thick can provide a very elegant look. Use light colors for patterned line borders so the border isn't more attractive than the video itself! You can find out more about Patterned Lines in Chapter 5.

## Link videos

For unsupported video formats, like RealVideo and QuickTime (newer versions), the only route open is to link the videos to a hyperlink on a slide. Such hyperlinks can then be clicked in Slide Show mode to play the video.

Follow these steps to link a video file from a PowerPoint slide:

1. **Create an anchor.**

   To link a video file, you need an *anchor* to link from. This can be any PowerPoint object, such as text or an AutoShape.

   Type something like **Click here to play video** or something descriptive within the text box or the AutoShape.

2. **Right-click the anchor and choose Action Settings from the resultant context menu.**

   The Action Settings dialog box opens (see Figure 10-21).

3. **In the Mouse Click tab, choose Other File from the drop-down menu in the Hyperlink section.**

4. **Navigate to and select the video file that you want to play and then click OK.**

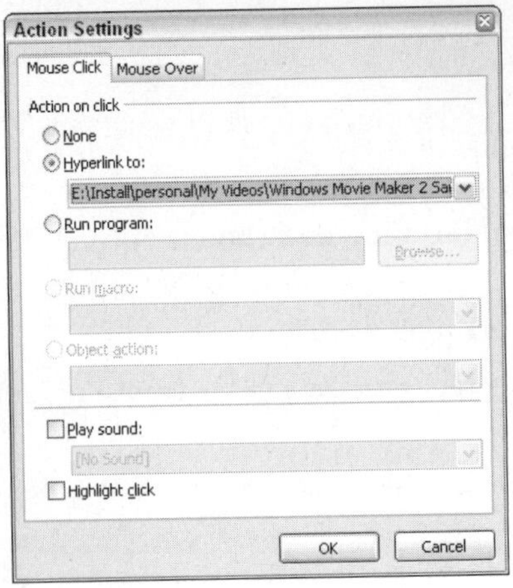

**Figure 10-21:**
Anchor a
hyperlink to
a video.

If you link to a RealVideo movie, clicking the hyperlink initiates RealPlayer; the QuickTime player opens if you link to a QuickTime movie. In all cases, you must close the video clip independently outside of PowerPoint after it finishes playing.

You can use the linking technique to initiate any associated program from within PowerPoint — even nonvideo files.

## Video with a controller

PowerPoint also lets you insert video objects within a slide. The advantage of inserting video objects is that you get a video controller along with the video itself while PowerPoint is in Slide Show mode. Thus, you can stop, pause, and play the video right within PowerPoint.

When you insert video using the conventional Insert⇨Movies and Sounds⇨ Movie from File command, you don't get a play controller. The play controller is available only if you insert the video as an object, as explained in this section.

Follow these steps to insert video objects with controllers on a slide:

1. **Navigate to the slide where you want your video inserted in a new or existing presentation.**

2. **Choose Insert⇨Object.**

    This summons the Insert Object dialog box, shown in Figure 10-22.

3. **In the Insert Object dialog box, make sure that the Create New radio button is selected and choose the Media Clip option.**

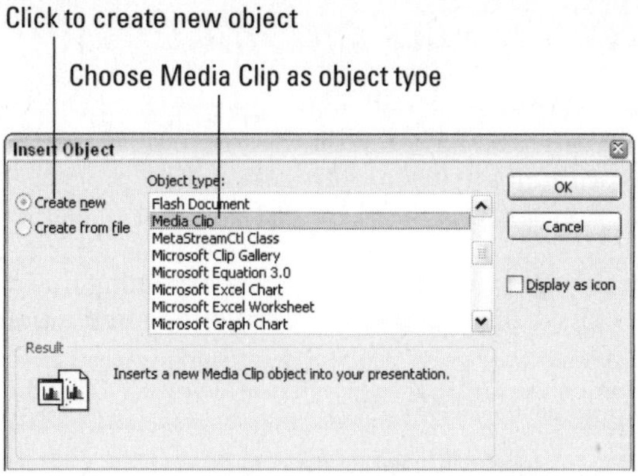

Click to create new object

Choose Media Clip as object type

**Figure 10-22:**
Inserting
video as a
Media Clip
object.

4. **PowerPoint's menus metamorphose into Media Player's menu options — choose the Insert Clip option on the menu.**

   This provides several options:

   - Video for Windows (for AVI videos)

   - DirectShow (for MPG, WMV, and ASF movies)

   - Other options for inserting sound objects

5. **Choose Edit⇨Options to view the Options dialog box, shown in Figure 10-23.**

6. **Select the Auto Rewind option.**

   You can also choose whether you want a control bar to be visible while the video plays. By default, this option is selected.

7. **Click OK when you're done.**

**Figure 10-23:**
Edit Media
Clip options.

8. **Click outside the object to get back to PowerPoint.**

Thereafter, you can reposition and resize your video as required.

# Playing video objects automatically

By default, all videos inserted as objects play on a mouse click. If you want them to play automatically, you have to edit the Custom Animation properties so that they play without any user intervention. The process to do that differs depending upon which version of PowerPoint you're using.

Whichever version you might be working with, I'm assuming that you have already inserted the video object as per the instructions in the preceding section.

### PowerPoint 2002 and 2003

Follow these steps to activate your video objects so that they play automatically:

1. **Select the video object and choose Slide Show⇨Custom Animation to activate the Custom Animation task pane toward the right of the PowerPoint interface.**

2. **In this task pane, choose Add Effect⇨Object Actions⇨Play, as shown in Figure 10-24.**

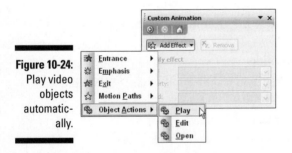

**Figure 10-24:** Play video objects automatically.

This adds a listing called Object in the task pane.

3. **With the Object listing selected, change the Start option to either With Previous or After Previous.**

### PowerPoint 2000

Follow these steps to activate your video objects so that they play automatically:

1. **Select the video object and choose Slide Show⇨Custom Animation to bring up the Custom Animation dialog box, shown in Figure 10-25.**

2. **In the Multimedia tab, change the Object Action to Play.**

3. **In the Order & Timing tab, change the Start Animation option to Automatically.**

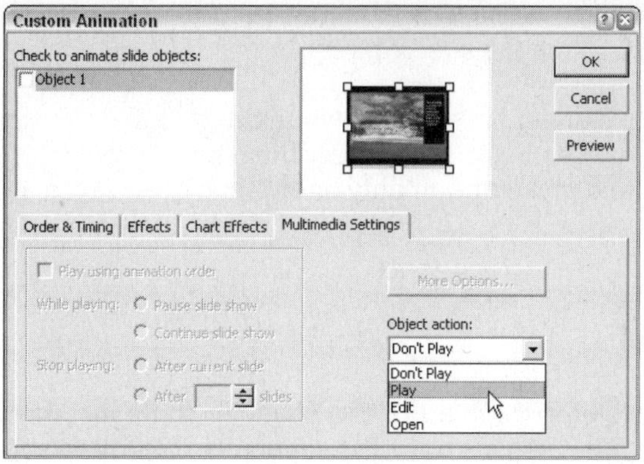

**Figure 10-25:** Activate video objects in PowerPoint 2000.

4. **In the Effects tab, make sure that the Entry Animation is set to No Effect.**

5. **Click OK to apply the changes or click Cancel to exit without changes.**

## Full-screen videos

Only PowerPoint 2003 allows playing of full-screen videos in a presentation. After you place a video in a presentation (see the previous "Inserting Video" section), follow these steps to make it a full-screen presentation:

1. **Right-click the video object and choose Edit Movie Object.**

   The Movie Options dialog box appears.

2. **Check the Zoom to Full Screen option.**

3. **Click OK.**

You also find options in the Movie Options dialog box to loop the movie or rewind it after playing.

## Links and link problems

Whenever you insert a movie (or a movie as an object) within PowerPoint, it's invariably linked to the presentation. In fact, PowerPoint can't embed any movies within the presentation — sound reasoning considering how embedded movies would balloon PowerPoint file sizes like nothing else!

Now for the bad news — PowerPoint isn't too good at remembering link locations. If the presentation and the video files are on the same system, you shouldn't face any problems. However, if you decide to move or copy the presentation to another system, PowerPoint can't locate the video files — it won't even offer to find the links for you.

The solution is quite simple: Assemble all your video files in the same folder as your presentation, even before you insert them into PowerPoint. And yes, insert the videos into a presentation only after it has been saved at least once.

# Sourcing Video

Finding good sources of video is more of a challenge than just inserting them in PowerPoint. The following sections list some possible video sources.

## Digital camcorders and cameras

Digital camcorders record straight to a digital video format that can be transferred to your computer through a special cable and saved to a PowerPoint-friendly video format like AVI, MPG, or WMV. Many digital cameras (as opposed to digital *video* cameras) also let you shoot short video clips. Digital camcorders start at around $500, and a good digital camera that can also record video costs less than that.

## Webcams

Webcams attached to your computer allow recording of live video while you sit in front of your PC. Most Webcams include a built-in microphone. Webcams cost between $100 and $200.

## Video stock libraries

Many a time, you want to add video to the beginning of a presentation to create a splash. For instance, you might want to show a collage of medical video clips before you speak to an audience about medicine. Luckily, locating stock video footage for most subjects is easy nowadays. Stock video footage is indeed more expensive than stock images, but prices are coming down.

Most clips are usually available in both WMV and MOV formats for use in PowerPoint for Windows and Mac, respectively.

A few royalty-free video clips can be found on the *Cutting Edge PowerPoint For Dummies* CD.

## Video capture devices

Various video capture devices let you digitize existing VHS or analog camcorder content to a format that PowerPoint can understand. Costs vary between $200 and $1,000, depending upon the video capture quality and features.

# Video Playlists in PowerPoint 2003

You can create a playlist of your videos in Windows Media Player and get PowerPoint to play the entire sequence of videos — an invaluable technique if you want to play a series of videos within a presentation seamlessly and don't have the time to get the videos rendered together in a video-editing package.

This feature is available only in PowerPoint 2003.

## Creating a video playlist

You can create a video playlist with Windows Media Player. To start with, you need some videos in the type of formats that Windows Media Player can play — these include AVI, WMV, and MPEG files.

You also need a copy of Windows Media Player 10 or higher — you can download a free copy of Windows Media Player from

`www.microsoft.com/windows/windowsmedia/download`

Follow these steps to create a video playlist in Windows Media Player:

1. **Place all the video files in the same folder and select them all.**

2. **With all of them selected, right-click and choose the Add to Now Playing List option.**

    This opens all the videos as part of a new playlist in Windows Media Player.

3. **Save this playlist by choosing File⇨Save Now Playing List As and save the playlist to a Windows Media Playlist file (*.WPL) in the same folder as the videos.**

## Inserting a video playlist

Follow these steps to insert your video playlist on a PowerPoint 2003 slide:

1. **In PowerPoint, create or open an existing presentation and go to the slide where you want to begin playing the videos.**

2. **Choose Insert⇨Movies and Sounds⇨Movie from File.**

   This summons the Insert dialog box.

3. **Navigate to the folder that contains the playlist (*.WPL) file.**

   You might need to change the Files of Type option to All Files (*.*).

4. **Select the WPL playlist and click OK.**

   PowerPoint asks you whether you want the movie to start automatically. Accept this option.

   PowerPoint places a rectangular shape representing the playlist on the slide. This rectangular shape is the same area where the videos will actually be played.

5. **Resize the playlist rectangle as required.**

You can also create a playlist that contains both videos and sound. In such a case, the videos play normally and the sounds display Windows Media visualizations. Try this; it looks cool.

## The DVD Factor

Lots of people want to play DVD clips inside PowerPoint, but most commercial DVDs are encrypted, and the studios and companies that own rights to these DVDs aren't too happy to allow their DVDs to be played within your presentation.

Another issue is entirely hardware-based — you probably don't want to play the clip straight off of a DVD because you might not have the same DVD spinning in your drive all the time. That translates to saving a part of the DVD as a movie clip within your hard drive. Again, that won't make too many of those movie studios happy.

Not surprisingly, Microsoft has steered away from directly supporting the playing of DVDs in PowerPoint. But lots of people nowadays create home DVDs with their camcorder footage. Such DVDs aren't encrypted, and clips from these sources can be easily inserted into a PowerPoint slide by using third-party products.

A company called Visible Light creates a product called Onstage DVD ($89) for PowerPoint that lets you insert and play DVD content within PowerPoint. It's available for download at

```
www.cuttingedgeppt.com/onstage
```

PFCMedia ($50) is another product that converts all your DVD content into playable movie clips. It also inserts the clips inside PowerPoint for you. You can find it at

A trial version of PFCMedia is available on the CD attached to this book.

One factor can never be stressed enough: copyright. Never assume that you can use a video or sound clip in a presentation if it's neither yours nor licensed to you. To use a video clip that is or contains copyrighted work, you need explicit permission in writing from the owner of that content.

This site has more info:

```
www.indezine.com/ideas/copyright.html
```

# Running Smooth Videos

What do you do if your video clips don't run well within PowerPoint?

Video requires more system resources than most other media, and some steps can go a long way in helping you run smoother videos. Here's some help:

- ✔ **Don't run any programs in the background that can be avoided.** These include instant messengers, camera or Webcam software, and your PDA connectivity application, among others. Also, it's a good idea to disable your screen saver.
- ✔ **Close all open programs except PowerPoint.**
- ✔ **Defragment your hard drive often so that it can function optimally.**
- ✔ **Upgrade your video RAM.** Also upgrade your system RAM if possible.

# Getting Friendly with Codecs

Codecs can be scary — unless you make friends with them. After you've broken the ice, you'll wonder why you were ever scared of codecs. If you're already convinced that codecs are a piece of cake, then you have enough time to go for a swim and become really cool! For everyone else, I have answers for two questions:

- ✔ Why should I know more about codecs?
- ✔ So, what's a codec, anyway?

And here are the answers!

Sound and video files can be huge — a dozen songs can fill an entire audio CD. There has always been a need for some technology that can squeeze the size of such files without deteriorating the quality. This entails both coding and decoding. Codecs take care of the coding and decoding — if that sounded too geeky, let me give you an example.

I just recorded a five-minute video clip with my digital camcorder. Its size leaves a lot to be desired, so I use a coding algorithm to compress it. Later, when I want to play it back, I use a similar decoding algorithm. Now, what I am essentially doing is coding and decoding — in other words, I am using a codec. The term *codec* is an abbreviation for *coder/decoder*.

Most multimedia problems in PowerPoint stem from *codecs.* Changing the codec or format of a multimedia file can provide a solution.

Different codecs use different coding and decoding algorithms. At last count, there were more than 100 unique codecs for the AVI video format alone!

## Which codecs are installed?

You can convert only between the codecs that are installed on your system.

Although you can view which codecs are installed on your system by using the options in the Windows Control Panel, specialized applications like AVICodec and GSpot provide much more information more easily. Both are freeware and can be downloaded from

```
www.cuttingedgeppt.com/codecapp
```

## Converting the codecs

Converting codecs is almost like converting a file format. I provide detailed instructions on converting codecs on my site:

```
www.indezine.com/products/video/virtualdub.html
```

# Export Your Presentation to a Movie

This is among the most often-requested features for PowerPoint. Maybe Microsoft will include it in a future version. Until then, you must use third-party software to create a movie from a PowerPoint presentation. Nothing is as easy and straightforward as a solution called Camtasia Studio, from TechSmith Corporation.

Actually, Camtasia Studio is a full-blown application that can capture all your on-screen activity and save it as a movie. These captured movies can then be further enriched with hot spots, narrations, and transitions. In addition, Camtasia Studio installs a new toolbar within your PowerPoint interface, as you can see in Figure 10-26.

Record audio (on/off)

**Figure 10-26:**
Camtasia
toolbar in
PowerPoint.

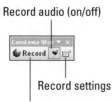

Record settings

Start presentation
and record to video

Just click the Record icon and Camtasia Studio starts capturing the entire live presentation to a video. Apart from the presentation, Camtasia Studio also captures your voice-over if you simultaneously narrate with a microphone. You'll have to set these options before you begin capturing.

Captured videos can be output to a multitude of video formats, including AVI, WMV, and QuickTime. In addition, you can also convert to Flash-based online rich content or record the captured video to create VCDs and DVDs.

More information can be found on this book's companion site:

```
www.cuttingedgeppt.com/camtasia
```

A full version of Camtasia 3 (the precursor of Camtasia Studio) can be found gratis on the CD attached to this book!

# Chapter 11

# Moving On with Animations and Transitions

**M**ovement beckons vision like nothing else can. Movement also takes PowerPoint presentations to a level that can never be attained by mere paper handouts.

Unfortunately, the rule of limits applies more to movements inside PowerPoint presentations than to anything else. If you have seen, presented, or created your share of PowerPoint presentations, you know what I'm talking about — those classic "too much" presentations in which every line of text flies onto the slide with a swishy sound. I'm talking about presentations in which special effects are so common that you spend your time wondering what new effect will turn the text upside down in the next slide instead of paying any attention to the actual content of the presentation. Who can be bothered when you have this circus to watch?!

PowerPoint allows two types of movement:

✔ **Custom animations:** Slide elements like text, AutoShapes, and pictures are animated via the Custom Animation feature.

✔ **Slide transitions:** Slides themselves use slide transitions to move and flow from one slide to the next.

The biggest changes from PowerPoint 2000 to PowerPoint 2002 and 2003 happened in the areas of animations and transitions:

- ✔ Wherever the versions behave differently, I explain the procedures for all versions.
- ✔ I mention when a feature isn't available in an older version.

# Animation Terms

Every element on a PowerPoint slide can be animated — yet there are different underlying animation attributes and ideas. Most of these may be familiar to you if you have used a multimedia or animation program. If you have never used an animation program before, don't worry: I explain all the concepts relevant to PowerPoint here.

Animation has its own terminology. Knowing these terms can help you understand and grasp the animation concepts.

## Build and sequence

_Builds_ are series of animations played one after the other to portray a logical _sequence_ of happenings. For example, the charts for the previous year animate before the charts of the present year. These builds are created using _animation events_.

## Animation events

PowerPoint gives you three types of animation events that determine the _happening_ (or starting) of an animation in relation to any other animation or event:

- ✔ **On Click** is the default animation event that occurs on a mouse click. Although it's called On Click, it also activates when the spacebar is pressed or when a specific button on a presentation remote control is pressed.

  On Click events need some user input like a mouse click or a key press.
- ✔ No mouse click or user intervention is required with either of these events:
  - **With Previous** (PowerPoint 2002 and 2003 only) is an animation event that plays simultaneously with the previous animation.

Think of this as two or more animations happening at the same time on a slide.

- **After Previous** events begin automatically after the previous animation has concluded.

Think of this as one animation waiting to play automatically after the previous animation has ended.

Both With Previous and After Previous events happen without any user interaction.

## Animation speed

PowerPoint 2002 and 2003 introduced the concept of *animation speed*. This feature isn't available in PowerPoint 2000.

PowerPoint includes a few speed presets that determine how long an animation takes to complete:

- **Very Slow** (5 seconds)
- **Slow** (3 seconds)
- **Medium** (2 seconds)
- **Fast** (1 second)
- **Very Fast** (0.5 seconds)

In addition, you can change the time to any duration you want by using the *Timeline*. You find out more about the Timeline later in this chapter.

## Animation types

PowerPoint 2002 and 2003 have new animation types. All types of animations in PowerPoint 2000 translate to the Entry animations in later versions of PowerPoint. Other animation options aren't available for PowerPoint 2000 users.

PowerPoint 2002 and 2003 let you insert four types of animations via the Custom Animation task pane:

- **Entry** animations are used when an object appears for the first time on a slide.
- **Emphasis** animations influence the animation of an object while it's on the slide between its entry and exit.

- ✔ **Exit** animations are associated with an object's departure from the slide area.

- ✔ **Motion Paths** let you move an object along a path set either by PowerPoint defaults or by a path that you draw on the slide.

PowerPoint 2002 and 2003 support *trigger animations.* An example of a trigger animation is a click on one object resulting in the animation of another object on the same slide. Trigger animations are discussed in more detail later in this chapter.

# Adding an Animation

In PowerPoint, you can add animation to any object on a slide. The steps and possibilities depend on the version of PowerPoint you're using.

This book's CD has sample presentations that show every single PowerPoint animation. It's a great reference to use when you want to look for that wonderful animation you saw last week (but you don't know the name of the animation!).

### PowerPoint 2002 and 2003

Follow these steps to animate an object in PowerPoint 2002 or 2003:

1. **Select an object and choose Slide Show⇨Custom Animation.**

   This opens the Custom Animation task pane, shown in Figure 11-1.

2. **Click the Add Effect button to reveal a flyout menu with four options (shown in Figure 11-1).**

   The four options are Entrance, Emphasis, Exit, and Motion Paths — these are covered in the preceding section.

3. **Select one of the options from the flyout menu.**

   You'll find another flyout menu that lets you choose one of the more frequently used animation styles, as shown in Figure 11-2.

4. **If you want to see more choices or preview the animations, click the More Effects option in the same flyout menu to summon a dialog box similar to the one shown in Figure 11-3.**

   This figure shows you the options for the Entrance animations, but the choices for Emphasis and Exit animations work in the same way.

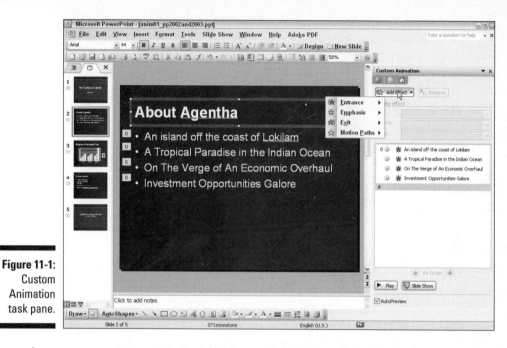

**Figure 11-1:**
Custom
Animation
task pane.

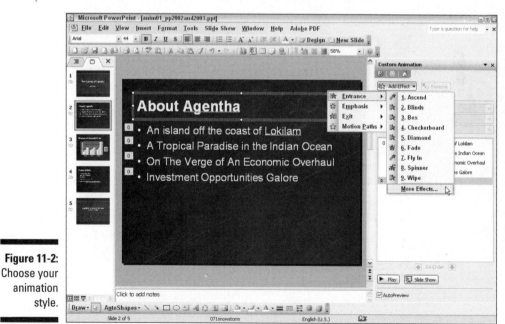

**Figure 11-2:**
Choose your
animation
style.

**Figure 11-3:**
More
animation
choices.

**Add Entrance Effect**

**Basic**

| | |
|---|---|
| ✯ Appear | ✯ Blinds |
| ✯ Box | ✯ Checkerboard |
| ✯ Circle | ✯ Crawl In |
| ✯ Diamond | ✯ Dissolve In |
| ✯ Flash Once | ✯ Fly In |
| ✯ Peek In | ✯ Plus |
| ✯ Random Bars | ✯ Random Effects |
| ✯ Split | ✯ Strips |
| ✯ Wedge | ✯ Wheel |
| ✯ Wipe | |

**Subtle**

| | |
|---|---|
| ✯ Expand | ✯ Fade |
| ✯ Faded Swivel | ✯ Faded Zoom |

**Moderate**

☑ Preview Effect   OK   Cancel

5. **Move this dialog box off the slide area and make sure that the Preview Effect option is enabled.**

6. **Click an effect to preview it on the slide with the selected object.**

7. **When you decide which effect you want, click OK to accept.**

Click Cancel to exit the dialog box without any changes.

A single object can have all animation types — Entrance, Emphasis, Exit, and Motion Paths — applied. You can also apply multiple animations of the same type. You discover how to fade and move text at the same time in Chapter 16.

### PowerPoint 2000

Follow these steps to animate an object in PowerPoint 2000:

1. **Select an object on the slide.**

2. **Choose Slide Show➪Custom Animation to summon the Custom Animation dialog box, shown in Figure 11-4.**

3. **Select the Effects tab.**

4. **In the Entry Animation and Sound area, choose any of the available animations.**

If you select an animation style that has more possibilities, a second drop-down list is enabled. For example, Wipe animations can move down, up, left, or right; Random Bars can be Horizontal or Vertical.

5. **Click the Preview button to preview your animation.**

6. **After you make your choices, click OK to accept the changes.**

   If you want to exit without changes, click Cancel.

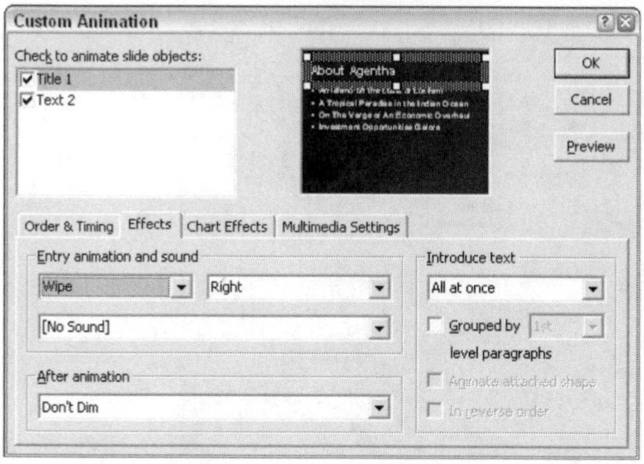

**Figure 11-4:**
Custom
Animation
dialog box.

# *Managing Animations*

PowerPoint provides numerous options for controlling the appearance and behavior of animations.

## *More movement in the Custom Animation task pane*

This section is only for users of PowerPoint 2002 and 2003 because many of the options in the Custom Animation task pane aren't available in PowerPoint 2000.

After you have added an animation to an object, you can change the timing and speed of the animation.

The Custom Animation task pane is the nerve center of all animation activity in a presentation. Follow these steps to view this task pane and make any changes:

1. **Select the object with animation already applied.**

   If the animation attribute hasn't been applied yet, read the "Adding an Animation" section, earlier in this chapter, to apply an animation.

2. **Choose Slide Show➪Custom Animation to reveal the Custom Animation task pane, shown in Figure 11-5.**

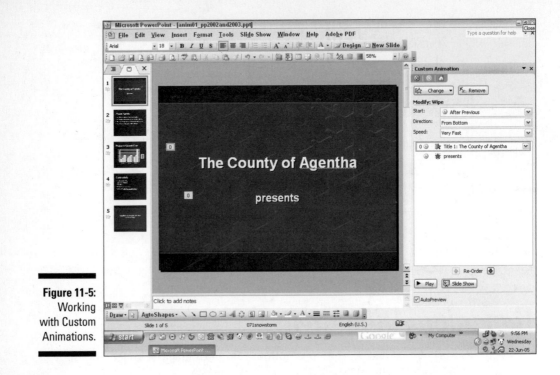

**Figure 11-5:**
Working
with Custom
Animations.

3. **The animation for the selected object is highlighted within the task
   pane (see Figure 11-5).**

   The task pane lets you change several attributes of the animation:

   - **Start:** You can change the animation event to On Click, With
     Previous, or After Previous. For an explanation of these terms,
     refer to the "Animation events" section, earlier in this chapter.

   - **Direction:** If you're using an animation that has no Direction
     attribute, this part might be grayed out. For an animation like Wipe
     that supports direction of the animation, you find choices like Up,
     Down, Left, and Right. Experiment with what works best for your
     presentation.

   - **Speed:** This is the time taken for the animation to play — predefined
     choices range from Very Slow to Very Fast, but these can be tweaked
     in the Timeline. The Timeline is covered later in this chapter.

4. **When you're done tweaking the settings, click Play to preview the
   slide with the animations.**

# Changing, removing, and reordering animations

At times, you might want to do some housekeeping with the animations already applied — for instance, you might want to change an animation. The process to change, remove, and reorder animations depends on the version of PowerPoint that you're using.

## PowerPoint 2002 and 2003

Follow these steps to change an existing animation in PowerPoint 2002 or 2003:

1. **If the Custom Animation task pane isn't visible, select any object on the slide and choose Slide Show⇨Custom Animation.**

2. **In the Custom Animation task pane, select the animation to be changed.**

   This causes the Add button to metamorphose into the Change button, as you can see in Figure 11-6.

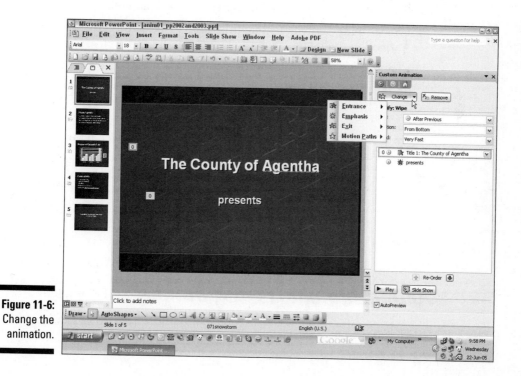

**Figure 11-6:** Change the animation.

3. **Change, remove, or reorder the animation.**

   • Click the Change button to open a flyout menu with Entry, Emphasis, Exit, and Motion Paths options. Choose any of the animations within these categories as explained in the preceding section.

   • To remove an existing animation, just select it in the Custom Animation task pane and click Remove.

   • To reorder the sequence of animations on a slide, select any of the animations in the Custom Animation task pane and then click either the Above or Below arrow buttons placed below the animation listing. Of course, this works only if you have more than one animated object on a slide.

4. **When you're done with all the changes, click Play to preview the slide with the animations.**

### PowerPoint 2000

Follow these steps to change, remove, or reorder your existing animations in PowerPoint 2000:

1. **Select the animated object that needs to be changed.**

2. **Choose Slide Show⇨Custom Animation to summon the Custom Animation dialog box (refer to Figure 11-4).**

3. **Change, remove, or reorder the animation.**

   • To change the animation type, choose the Effects tab and then change the animation type in the Entry Animation and Sound dialog box.

   • To remove the animation, just uncheck the object in the Check to Animate Slide Objects box.

   • To reorder the animation, choose the Order and Timing tab and click either the Above or Below arrow button to change the animation sequence. Of course, this works only if you have more than one animated object on a slide.

4. **Click OK when you're done.**

## Animating charts and bullets

PowerPoint provides options for animating charts and bulleted text — for example, you can have the series of the chart animate in sequence, and bullets can appear one at a time.

The steps to enable these special features depend upon your version of PowerPoint.

### Text animation

PowerPoint provides umpteen text animation possibilities — you can animate by words, by letters, and by paragraphs.

#### PowerPoint 2002 and 2003

Follow these steps to tweak the text animation options in PowerPoint 2002 or 2003:

1. **Select part of the text or the entire placeholder with bulleted text.**

2. **Choose Slide Show➪Custom Animation to activate the Custom Animation task pane (refer to Figure 11-1).**

3. **Add an Entry animation to the text if it isn't already done.**

   There are detailed instructions in the "Adding an Animation" section, earlier in this chapter.

4. **Double-click the animation within the task pane to summon the dialog box shown in Figure 11-7.**

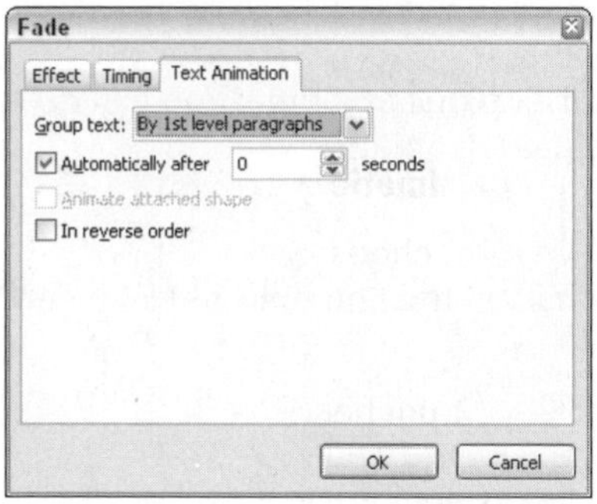

**Figure 11-7:**
Text
animation.

5. **Select the Text Animation tab and change settings as required:**

   • The Group Text option lets you animate the bulleted text in consecutive builds.

   • The By 1st Level Paragraphs option is selected by default; you can experiment with other options.

   • If you want to sync the time more evenly, select the time span after which the next bullet animation occurs.

   • If required, change the sequence of bullets to In Reverse Order.

6. **Click OK to apply the animation.**

### PowerPoint 2000

Follow these steps to tweak the text animation options in PowerPoint 2000:

1. **Select the bulleted text that you want to animate.**

2. **Choose Slide Show⇨Custom Animation to summon the Custom Animation dialog box (refer to Figure 11-4).**

3. **Add an animation to the text if it isn't already applied.**

   You can find detailed instructions in the "Adding an Animation" section, earlier in this chapter.

4. **Click the Effects tab in the Custom Animation dialog box and change the settings in the Introduce Text area.**

   By default, this is set to All at Once, but you can also choose By Word or By Letter. For most purposes, All at Once works best.

5. **If you want to animate individual bullets in sequence, place a check mark next to the Grouped by 1st Level Paragraphs option.**

6. **If you want to reverse the animation sequence, select In Reverse Order.**

## Chart animation

It's nice to see all your columns rise up one at a time. You can do this and more with PowerPoint's chart animation abilities.

### PowerPoint 2002 and 2003

Follow these steps to tweak the chart animation options in PowerPoint 2002 or 2003:

1. **Select the chart.**

   Don't double-click the chart; just select it.

2. **Choose Slide Show⇨Custom Animation to activate the Custom Animation task pane (refer to Figure 11-1).**

3. **Add an animation to the chart if it isn't already applied.**

   You can find detailed instructions in the "Adding an Animation" section, earlier in this chapter.

4. **Double-click the animation listed for the chart within the task pane to summon the dialog box shown in Figure 11-8.**

5. **Click the Chart Animation tab.**

6. **Click the Group Chart drop-down list, which provides you with several animation options.**

   By default, the By Series option works best, but you might want to experiment with the other alternatives. Whatever alternative you use depends on the type of chart and data being animated.

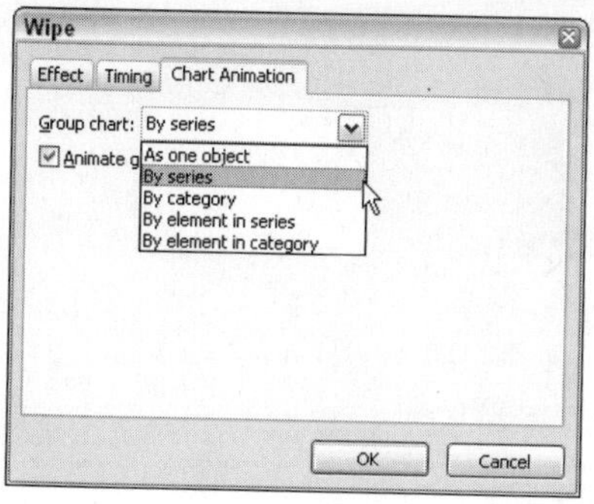

Figure 11-8:
Chart
animation.

7. **Select the Animate Grid and Legend option as required.**

   You can find out more about chart terminology in Chapter 9.

8. **After you finish tweaking the animations for the charts and bulleted text placeholders, preview them by clicking the Play button on the Custom Animation task pane.**

   If you aren't happy with the animations, return to the Custom Animation task pane and change the settings.

## PowerPoint 2000

Follow these steps to tweak the chart options in PowerPoint 2000:

1. **Select the chart that you want to animate.**

   Don't double-click the chart; just select it.

2. **Choose Slide Show⇨Custom Animation to summon the Custom Animation dialog box (refer to Figure 11-4).**

3. **Add an animation to the chart if it isn't already applied.**

   You can find detailed instructions in the "Adding an Animation" section, earlier in this chapter.

4. **In the Custom Animation dialog box, select the Chart Effects tab, as shown in Figure 11-9.**

5. **In the Introduce Chart Elements area, select an option to animate the chart by either** series, categories, or elements.

6. **Select or deselect the Animate Grid and Legend option.**

7. **Click Preview to view the animation; then click OK to apply the chart animation.**

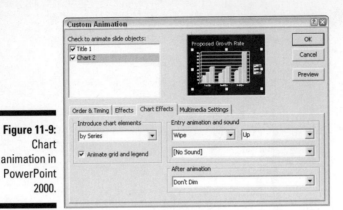

**Figure 11-9:**
Chart
animation in
PowerPoint
2000.

# Motion paths

Motion path animations let objects move along a preset or custom path. These animations are available only in PowerPoint 2002 and 2003.

A presentation that shows all motion path preset animations in PowerPoint is included on this book's CD.

Follow these steps to create motion path animations:

1. **Select an object on a slide that you want to animate on a motion path.**

   You can open one of the sample presentations on the CD attached to this book and select an object on one of the slides.

2. **Choose Slide Show⇨Custom Animation to activate the Custom Animation task pane (refer to Figure 11-1).**

3. **Click Add Effect on the task pane to reveal a flyout menu.**

4. **Choose Motion Paths to reveal another flyout menu, shown in Figure 11-10.**

5. **Choose any Motion Path.** You can

   • Choose any of the Motion Paths offered.

   • Select More Motion Paths to access the dialog box shown in Figure 11-11.

   You can find 64 motion path presets — choose any of them and you see a preview of the effect on the slide if the Preview Effect option is checked. All of these motion paths are previewed on a sample presentation on the *Cutting Edge PowerPoint For Dummies* CD.

6. **Click OK when you're done.**

**Figure 11-10:**
Motion
Paths get
your objects
moving.

**Figure 11-11:**
How do I
move you?
Choose
from 64
options.

If none of the 64 preset motion paths appeals to you, choose the Draw Custom Path option. You can use any of PowerPoint's line tools (like Line, Curve, Freeform, and Scribble) to draw your own motion path. You can find more coverage of these line tools in Chapter 6.

You can find more information and resources for motion paths on this book's companion Web site:

```
www.cuttingedgeppt.com/motionpaths
```

## Trigger animations

Trigger animations are available to PowerPoint 2002 and 2003 users only.

Trigger animations work with On Click animation events. In this case, the object being clicked doesn't animate; instead, another object on the slide is triggered to animate — hence the name *trigger animation*.

Follow these steps to create a simple trigger animation sequence. Make sure you have two images available to use in this tutorial — several sample images are available on the CD attached to this book.

1. **Create a new presentation and insert a blank slide.**

2. **Insert two images of the same size within this slide.**

    To insert an image, choose Insert⇨Picture⇨From File. Place the images in different areas of the slide.

3. **Select one of the images and choose Slide Show⇨Custom Animation.**

    This activates the Custom Animation task pane (refer to Figure 11-1).

4. **Click the Add Effect button in the Custom Animation task pane and then choose an Entrance animation.**

    I like the Appear animation because it happens almost instantly — that seems like a trigger. By default, PowerPoint chooses an On Click animation event for the Start options, which is what you should use for this example.

5. **Select the animation in the Custom Animation task pane.**

6. **Click the downward-pointing arrow to reveal a drop-down menu.**

7. **Click the Timing option in that menu, as shown in Figure 11-12.**

    This opens the Timing tab of the Appear dialog box, as shown in Figure 11-13.

**Figure 11-12:**
Timing
triggers.

8. **Click the Triggers button to reveal more options. Then**

    a. Choose Start Effect on Click Of.

    b. Choose the name of the second image you inserted on the slide.

    c. Click OK.

**Figure 11-13:**
Set the
trigger
action.

9. **Play the presentation. Clicking on the visible image triggers the visibility of the other image.**

A sample trigger presentation can be found on the CD.

You can find more resources on trigger animations on the companion Web site:

www.cuttingedgeppt.com/triggeranimations

When choosing which type of animation you want to use in PowerPoint 2002 or 2003, remember that the animation effects that aren't commonly used are listed under the More Effects option.

# Animation Timeline

Let me start with these questions:

- ✔ What happens when you want the speed of your animation to be a little faster or slower, and the speed presets don't work for you?
- ✔ What do you do when you want two animations to start at the same time, but maybe one of them should end two seconds before the other?

That sort of ultimate animation control in PowerPoint is possible through the *Advanced Timeline*. Like many of the advanced animation features covered in this chapter, this feature is available only in PowerPoint 2002 and 2003.

Follow these steps to access the Advanced Timeline:

1. **Add an animation to any object on a slide.**

   You can either

   - Follow the instructions provided in the "Adding an Animation" section, earlier in this chapter.
   - Open any sample presentation from the CD and select an animated object.

2. **With the object selected, choose Slide Show⇨Custom Animation.**

   This activates the Custom Animation task pane.

3. **Select any object in the task pane and click the downward-pointing arrow next to it to reveal a flyout menu.**

4. **Choose the Show Advanced Timeline option in the flyout menu, as shown in Figure 11-14.**

   The task pane changes to show the Timeline.

5. **To work more effectively with the Timeline, move it below the slide by dragging its title bar to the bottom of the screen, as shown in Figure 11-15.**

6. **Edit the animation by using the guidelines mentioned in the following section, "Using the Timeline."**

**Figure 11-14:**
Accessing
the Timeline.

**Figure 11-15:**
Relocate
the Timeline.

When you're done editing timings in the Timeline, you can get back to the normal Custom Animation task pane by following these steps:

1. **Select any object in the Timeline.**
2. **Click the downward-pointing arrow to the right of the object listing to reveal a flyout menu.**
3. **Choose Hide Advanced Timeline.**

## Using the Timeline

The Advanced Timeline is fairly easy to use, and these guidelines ensure that you get it right the first time:

✔ The main advantage of using the Advanced Timeline is in being able to control the time factor to the most minute level — you aren't limited to the time/speed presets that PowerPoint provides. Thus you can create a very, very slow animation that spans a whole minute or more by just dragging the start and end points for any animation in the Timeline.

✔ The Timeline provides a more intuitive look at which events happen at the same time or overlap — again, changing those timings is as easy as pulling the start and end points.

✔ You can zoom in and out of the Timeline. Just click the Seconds button below the Timeline to open a flyout menu with the Zoom In and Zoom Out options.

✔ After you select an animation in the Timeline, right-click it to access several logical options. These are the same options that are visible when you aren't viewing the Advanced Timeline, apart from one difference — you now find a Hide Advanced Timeline option that lets you get back to the normal Custom Animation task pane.

## Animation guidelines

Here are some guidelines to help you use animation more optimally in your presentations:

✔ **Emphasize, don't distract.**

You probably see presentations that flout this rule all the time. You might have seen some of those include-everything-except-the-kitchen-sink presentations — they use every animation option available in PowerPoint and needlessly bury the actual message in a slurry of effects.

If you're working on a presentation, I have a simple suggestion: Use one or two common animation styles like fades and wipes. And then, when you need to emphasize something on a few slides, use something that grabs attention and sets that slide apart from the others. Using this technique, you can ensure that your audience focuses on the important points. More importantly, your presentation appears professional and elegant — the fades and wipes ensure that your content flows smoothly from one concept to the next.

✔ **Use builds to get the message across.**

*Animation builds* are the result of playing one animation after the other in a logical sequence so that the audience can grasp the content more easily. For instance, you might want the figures for the last year to be visible entirely in a chart before the present year's figures appear, and then follow them with next year's forecasts. Because all these figures are animated (and thus become visible) one at a time in sequence, the audience has a better understanding of both the figures and their relation to the previous year's figures. This technique is even more effective when a narrative accompanies the slide: The builds appear along with the relevant voice-over.

✔ **Think of animation from the beginning.**

Animation can be an aid to delivering content right from the conceptualization stage of the presentation. Presentation creators often use animation as an afterthought after the presentation has been created. This lessens the creative opportunities in the use of animation because animation is relegated to the mere introduction of bullets on a slide instead of being used for more interesting output. For instance, you can use animation to

- Create builds in charts and graphs effectively.

- Show part of a diagram and then follow that up with builds to show remaining parts of the same diagram.

- Create info-graphics with PowerPoint's AutoShapes and text boxes and then reveal each part of the info-graphic sequentially.

- Create a timeline using PowerPoint's AutoShapes and then show logical parts of the timeline one after the other.

Animation is best used to emphasize content — this translates to sparing use. If you use too much animation, the audience quickly becomes distracted from the primary focus of your presentation — something you should avoid at all costs.

## Saving and sharing animations

Imagine that you just spent the greater part of an hour fine-tuning an animation sequence for a single object. Your boss likes it so much that he expects you to use that style on all the slides. The only problem is that those animation settings take so long to apply. PowerPoint can't save the animation sequences you so painstakingly created.

Thankfully, two PowerPoint add-ins let you reuse your animations:

- **Animation Carbon,** from Shyam Pillai, lets you save your animation styles in libraries. Thereafter, you can apply the same animations to other objects on the same presentation or even in other presentations. You can also share your animation libraries with friends and colleagues if they have a copy of Animation Carbon.

  `www.cuttingedgeppt.com/animationcarbon`

- **Effects Library,** from pptXTREME, lets you work in the same way as Animation Carbon but uses menus and submenus to organize your animation sequences into easily accessed libraries.

  `www.cuttingedgeppt.com/effectslibrary`

Both of these add-ins work only within PowerPoint 2002 and 2003.

# Making the Transition

*Transitions* are the movement (or lack of movement) that changes one slide to another. Movement in the transition period can add interest and flow to a presentation, and you should explore these options instead of accepting PowerPoint's default, boring, movement-free transition in which one slide just rudely disappears to allow another slide to be visible.

However, don't go crazy with the numerous transitions that newer versions of PowerPoint include. Try to use the same transition style for all the slides in a presentation. If that sounds like a punishment, I'll let you use one or two of those showy transitions for the really important parts of the presentation. But please don't expect any more concessions from me; the People for the Ethical Treatment of Transitions will be very angry if I let you use a zillion transition styles in one presentation!

## Transition concepts

Not surprisingly, transitions have their own terminology. Here are some of the secrets of transitioning in PowerPoint:

- **Transition Type:** PowerPoint ships with several built-in transitions.

  Wipes, Fades, Cut, Comb, and Dissolve are all types of transitions. PowerPoint 2000 includes several transition types; PowerPoint 2002 and 2003 include many more.

✔ **Transition Speed:** Transitions happen at three speeds: Slow, Medium, and Fast.

✔ **Transition Sound:** You can play a sound along with a transition. If the sound is longer than the transition, it continues playing on a slide after the transition is over.

Read Chapter 10 to find out how to use this to your advantage.

✔ **Advance Slide:** You can advance slides either by using the mouse click event or automatically after a given period of time.

## Adding transitions to slides

How you add transitions differs depending upon the version of PowerPoint you're using.

### PowerPoint 2002 and 2003

Follow these steps to add transitions to your slides in PowerPoint 2002 or 2003:

1. **To view the slides in Slide Sorter view, choose View▷Slide Sorter.**

   Viewing the slides in Slide Sorter view makes it easier to add transitions, especially if you want to add the same transition to multiple slides.

2. **Select one or more slides to apply the animation to.**

3. **Choose Slide Show▷Slide Transition to activate the Slide Transition task pane, shown in Figure 11-16.**

4. **Choose the transition type you want to apply and modify the transition speed to Slow, Medium, or Fast.**

   With the AutoPreview option at the bottom of the task pane checked, you can see previews of the transitions in real time.

5. **Choose a transition sound — or don't.**

   This option is best left unused unless you want to use transition sounds to play or loop across slides, as explained in Chapter 10.

6. **Choose an Advance Slide option.**

   Depending on the type of presentation intended, you can either

   • Transition the slide on a mouse click event.

   • Type in a time in the Automatically After box.

7. **If you want to apply the animation to all slides in the presentation, click the Apply to All Slides button.**

   To apply the animation only to the selected slides, do nothing.

**Figure 11-16:**
Slide
Transition
task pane.

### PowerPoint 2000

Follow these steps to add transitions to your slides in PowerPoint 2000:

1. **To view the slides in Slide Sorter view, choose View⇨Slide Sorter.**

   Viewing the slides in Slide Sorter view makes it easier to add transitions, especially if you want to add the same transition to multiple slides.

2. **Select one or more slides to apply the animation to.**

3. **Choose Slide Show⇨Slide Transition to summon the Slide Transition dialog box, shown in Figure 11-17.**

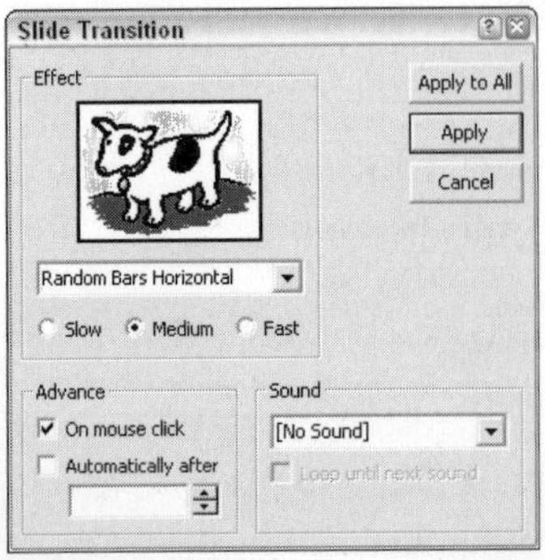

**Figure 11-17:**
Slide
Transition
dialog box.

4. **Choose the transition effect in the Effect area.**

    A thumbnail preview of the effect is shown as soon as you select a transition effect from the drop-down list box.

5. **Choose a transition speed option: Slow, Medium, or Fast.**

6. **Select one or both of the Advance options:**

    • The On Mouse Click option advances the slide and transition after clicking the mouse, pressing the spacebar, or clicking a specific button on a presentation remote control.

    • The Automatically After option lets you type a time for the delay in playing the transition and moving to the next slide.

7. **Add a transition sound — or don't.**

    This option is best left unexplored unless you want to use transition sounds to play or loop across slides, as explained in Chapter 10.

8. **Click Apply to add the transition to the selected slides or click Apply to All to add the transition to all slides in a presentation.**

## Transition guidelines

Follow these transition guidelines to ensure that your transitions serve your presentation well:

✔ Restrict your presentation to one or two transitions. If you use more transition types, you might end up interrupting the flow of the presentation.

✔ Think of transitions as a complement to your presentation instead of a distraction. Use simple transitions like fades and wipes if your slides differ in look and color. If all the slides follow the same visual pattern, you can be a little more adventurous — but don't overdo it.

✔ Transitions are resource hogs. Make sure that all computers that will deliver the presentations you create can cope with them. Fancier transitions are more resource-hungry than the simpler ones.

✔ Remember, rules are meant to be broken — even the rules in this book. If you believe that a particular transition effect is apt for a particular presentation, go ahead and use it.

So what do you do if you inherit a presentation of a hundred slides that contains 16 transition styles? Here's help:

1. **Replace all the transitions in your presentation with fades or wipes.**

2. **Add those special transitions to one or more slides.**

3. **Play the presentation to make sure that the presentation flow isn't interrupted.**

## PowerPlugs: Transitions

If PowerPoint's arsenal of transitions doesn't meet your expectations, and you want to play with fancier TV-style transitions, look to CrystalGraphics' PowerPlugs: Transitions, a set of third-party transitions that plug into PowerPoint. The full set includes all sorts of transitions, ranging from page flips to rotating screens.

You can find a free copy of PowerPlugs: Transitions LE on the CD included with this book.

PowerPlugs: Transitions effects aren't embedded as part of the presentation, so you can't really add those groovy transitions and save them to a disc hoping that it will work on a computer that doesn't have PowerPlugs: Transitions installed. However, the product includes a workaround — it renders movies of all the transitions and places it between slides so that they appear like transitions! This can be distributed and works quite well, although it isn't nearly as good as the real thing.

# Part IV
# Communicating Beyond the PowerPoint Program

The 5th Wave     By Rich Tennant

"Someone want to look at this manuscript I received on email called, 'The Embedded Virus That Destroyed the Publisher's Servers When the Manuscript was Rejected.'?"

# In this part . . .

This part is about doing more with your created presentations. From interactivity and quizzes to sharing and delivering, this part has it all.

# Chapter 12

# Interactivity and Linking

● ● ● ● ● ● ● ● ● ● ● ● ● ● ● ● ● ● ● ● ● ● ● ● ● ● ● ● ● ● ● ● ● ● ● ● ● ● ●

### In This Chapter

▶ Discovering anchors, hyperlinks, and targets

▶ Putting Action Buttons into action

▶ Creating links that bind you everywhere

▶ Getting rid of link problems

▶ So you want to become a quiz master?

● ● ● ● ● ● ● ● ● ● ● ● ● ● ● ● ● ● ● ● ● ● ● ● ● ● ● ● ● ● ● ● ● ● ● ● ● ● ●

*L*inking (or *hyperlinking*) is connecting one object to another object or an action. In PowerPoint, linking is much like networking a few computers — the value of the whole is always greater than the sum of the parts.

*Interactivity* is the result of linking and raises PowerPoint presentations to a whole new level. With interactivity, you can link to slides on the same presentation or to slides on another presentation. In fact, you can even link to another document on your computer or on the Internet. Take interactivity to its extremes and you can even create an interactive quiz inside PowerPoint, as I show you later in this chapter. And yes, you can link an object to an action as well, such as ending a presentation.

All this interactivity might lead you to believe that PowerPoint is a great tool for creating multimedia demos and CBTs (Computer Based Training). However, that's not the entire truth: Although there are instances of multimedia demos and CBTs being created in PowerPoint, they tend to be fairly basic.

## Linking All the Stuff

The hot pot of linking has three distinct ingredients:

> ✔ **Anchor:** Any object on a PowerPoint slide can be an anchor. In simple terms, an anchor is the object that contains the hyperlink. Typical anchors include Action Buttons or other AutoShapes, images, and text. (I tell you more about Action Buttons later in this chapter.)

✔ **Hyperlink:** A hyperlink is the address of the target contained within the anchor — for example, the path to a document on your computer or a Web URL. It's the functionality that links the anchor to the target.

✔ **Target:** A target launches as the result of clicking the anchor and causing the hyperlink to activate. Such targets can be another slide within the same presentation or a Web site that opens in your browser.

## All about Action Buttons

Action Buttons are special types of AutoShapes that are meant to be used as anchors for links. Action Buttons are used exclusively for linking. They contain overlaid symbols (such as home, before, and after) so that users understand what action clicking an Action Button will cause.

Action Buttons share almost all of the same attributes as other AutoShapes, such as PowerPoint's versatile fills and lines. To learn more about fills and lines for AutoShapes, refer to Chapter 5.

Figure 12-1 shows a sample of the Action Button types that PowerPoint provides.

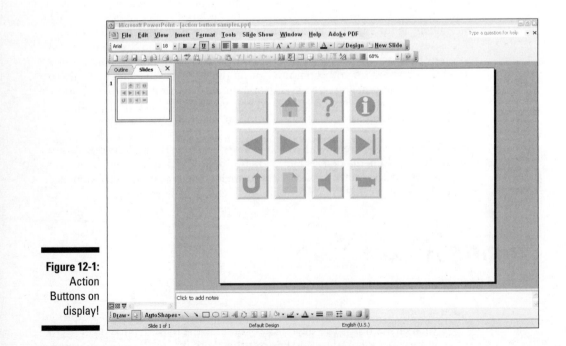

**Figure 12-1:**
Action
Buttons on
display!

Follow these steps to insert an Action Button on your slide:

1. **If the Drawing toolbar isn't visible, choose View⇨Toolbars⇨Drawing to make that toolbar visible.**
2. **In the Drawing toolbar, choose AutoShapes⇨Action Buttons to reveal the Action Buttons flyout menu.**

   You can drag this menu off its handle to spawn an Action Button toolbar, as you can see in Figure 12-2.

**Figure 12-2:** The Action Buttons toolbar makes life simpler.

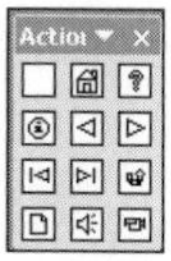

3. **Select any of the Action Buttons and click once on the slide to create an instance of the Action Button.**

   When you create an Action Button, PowerPoint brings up the two-tabbed Action Settings dialog box, shown in Figure 12-3.

**Figure 12-3:** The Action Settings dialog box.

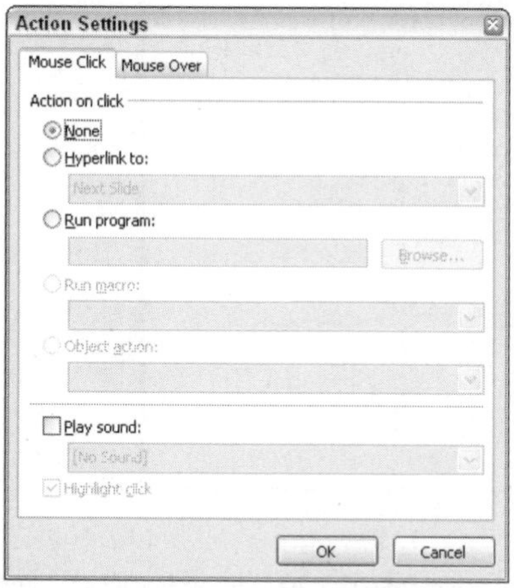

If you want to create a hyperlink now, you can use any of the options available in the Mouse Click tab to link to a slide in an existing presentation or to another presentation, document, or Web URL. I explain these options in the upcoming sections of this chapter.

After you close the Action Settings dialog box, you can resize the Action Button to your liking by dragging one of its corners.

You can summon the Action Settings dialog box for any object on a slide by right-clicking the object and choosing Action Settings from the context menu. Another way to do the same thing is to first select the object and then choose the Slide Show⇨Action Settings option.

## Linking within the same presentation

Follow these steps to link any PowerPoint object to a slide in the same presentation:

1. **Select the anchor.**

   This could be any PowerPoint object, such as text, an Action Button, another AutoShape, or an image.

2. **Right-click the object and select Action Settings from the context menu, as shown in Figure 12-4.**

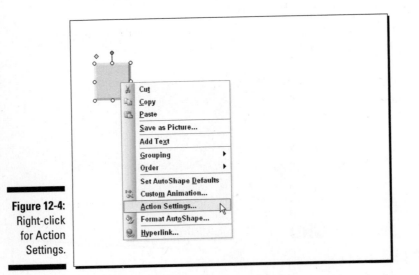

**Figure 12-4:**
Right-click
for Action
Settings.

This brings up the Action Settings dialog box that you saw in Figure 12-3. Make sure you select the Mouse Click tab of the dialog box.

3. **Click the Hyperlink To drop-down list to find several options.**

   The following are some of the options that let you link to another slide within the same presentation:

- *Next Slide* links to the next slide in the presentation.

- *Previous Slide* links to the previous slide in the presentation.

- *First Slide* links to the first slide of the presentation.

- *Last Slide* links to the last slide of the presentation.

- *Last Slide Viewed* links to the slide viewed before the current slide. For instance, if you moved from slide 7 to the first slide of the presentation, the Last Slide Viewed option takes you back to slide 7.

- *Slide* summons the Hyperlink to Slide dialog box, shown in Figure 12-5, which lets you link to any specific slide in the presentation.

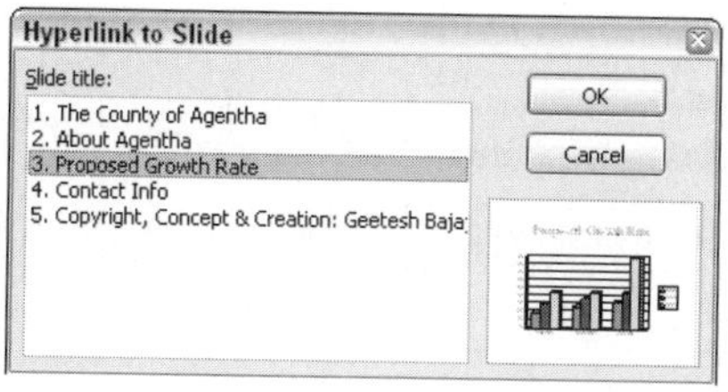

**Figure 12-5:**
Hyperlink to
any slide
you fancy!

4. **After you have chosen which slide you want to link to, click OK to apply this interactivity option.**

## Linking to other presentations

Instead of creating presentations with hundreds of slides that are such a mess to navigate, you might prefer to create multiple presentations with fewer slides and then link between slides of different presentations.

---

## Mouse Click and Mouse Over

The Action Settings dialog box has two tabs:

- **Mouse Click:** By default, the active tab is always Mouse Click. Any action that you choose in this tab happens on a mouse click.

- **Mouse Over:** On this tab, the actions work in the same way, but merely moving the cursor over the anchor object triggers these actions. Be careful about using this or you'll wonder why mysterious things happen while your presentation plays!

Presentations with fewer slides play more smoothly and are snappier with animation timings in comparison with presentations with more slides.

Follow these steps to link to another presentation:

1. **Navigate to the slide from which you want to link to another PowerPoint presentation and select the anchor.**

   This could be any PowerPoint object, such as text, an Action Button, another AutoShape, or an image.

2. **Choose Slide Show⇨Action Settings to come face-to-face with the Action Settings dialog box shown earlier in Figure 12-3.**

3. **Choose the Mouse Click tab of the Action Settings dialog box.**

4. **Click the Hyperlink To drop-down list to reveal several options; choose Other PowerPoint Presentation.**

   This opens the common dialog box shown in Figure 12-6.

5. **Choose the presentation that you want to link to, then click OK.**

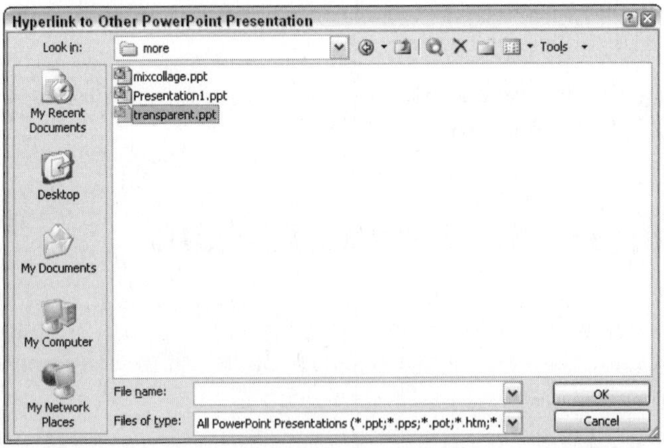

**Figure 12-6:** Link to another presentation.

6. **Click OK again to apply the link to the anchor.**

You can create a menu slide presentation that links to all of your other presentations. Just place all presentations in a single folder and then create a new single-slide presentation in that folder with links to all the presentations. If you need to share these presentations along with the menu presentation, just copy the entire folder!

Always place all linked presentations within the same folder. This advice is invaluable if you need to move the presentations to another computer.

# Linking to other documents and Web URLs

PowerPoint's linking capabilities let you link an object on a slide to almost any document on your computer — and even on the Internet. Follow these steps to link to other documents and Web URLs:

1. **Select any object on a slide that you want to use as an anchor for your link.**

2. **Choose Slide Show➪Action Settings to come face-to-face with the Action Settings dialog box shown in Figure 12-3.**

3. **Choose the Mouse Click tab of the Action Settings dialog box.**

4. **Click the Hyperlink To drop-down list and select one of these options:**

   - *Other File* lets you link to any other file or document on your computer.

     This options spawns the Hyperlink to Other File dialog box. You navigate to and select the file or document that needs to be linked.

   - *URL* lets you link to any *Web URL* or *e-mail address.*

     For a *Web URL,* just type the address in the Hyperlink To URL dialog box (see Figure 12-7).

     If you want to link to an *e-mail address,* type **mailto:** and the e-mail address in the Hyperlink To URL dialog box, like this:

     ```
     mailto:name@domain.com
     ```

     When you click a live e-mail link, your default e-mail application opens to a new, blank e-mail with the address that follows `mailto:` in the preceding code in the To box.

5. **Click OK to apply the link to the anchor.**

**Figure 12-7:**
Connect
your
presenta-
tions to Web
URLs!

You can find more information on linking to specific bookmarks in Microsoft Word files or to specific cells of Microsoft Excel spreadsheets in the next chapter.

## Transparent hot spots make great links

When you create a link anchor from text, you normally end up with underlined text that looks like a conventional hyperlink, as shown in Figure 12-8.

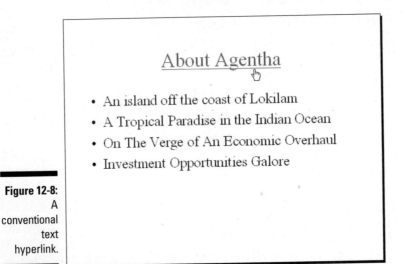

**Figure 12-8:** A conventional text hyperlink.

About Agentha

- An island off the coast of Lokilam
- A Tropical Paradise in the Indian Ocean
- On The Verge of An Economic Overhaul
- Investment Opportunities Galore

Most of the time, this doesn't bother you. But there may be times when you don't want the text to be underlined. This can be especially useful if you want the slide to have a clean look, or maybe you want to click that hyperlink only if necessary and you prefer that the audience not be aware of the hyperlink.

Follow these steps to create transparent hyperlinks without the underlines:

1. **Type some text in a text placeholder or text box and position it exactly as you want it on the slide.**

2. **If the Drawing toolbar isn't visible, choose View⇨Toolbars⇨Drawing to display the toolbar.**

3. **In the Drawing toolbar, select the Rectangle tool and draw a rectangle over the text you want to hyperlink.**

   Make sure that the rectangle covers the entire hyperlink area.

4. **With the rectangle selected, assign a hyperlink to the rectangle by choosing Slide Show⇨Action Settings.**

   This opens the Action Settings dialog box, shown in Figure 12-3.

5. **Hyperlink to wherever you want.**

   You can find more details about your linking options in previous sections of this chapter.

6. **After you have created the hyperlink, select the rectangle and choose Format⇨AutoShape.**

   This brings up the Format AutoShape dialog box.

7. **Set the Fill and Line attributes to No Fill and No Line, respectively.**

8. **Click OK.**

Another option for creating a transparent text link is to apply the Action Settings to the entire text box and not to just a part of the text. Select the entire text box (while making sure that no individual text is selected), then apply the links.

## Overcoming link problems

If you ever wondered why PowerPoint couldn't find the link to your spreadsheet or video file, you aren't alone.

These link problems happen because remembering links isn't PowerPoint's strong point. Perhaps you never knew that and just blamed yourself for what wasn't your fault!

The solution is actually simpler than the problem: PowerPoint isn't too good at remembering links, which saves you the trouble of learning the theory of *absolute* and *relative* links.

The easiest link option is to place all the content for a presentation in a single folder even before you create the presentation or start inserting links. Follow this rule and you'll be happy:

> *Think about folders that contain presentations and don't just think about presentations.*

If you flout this rule, you might run into all sorts of link problems.

If you don't have time for link problems, follow these guidelines:

✔ **Conceptualize your presentation.** *Conceptualize* is a very impressive-sounding verb, but you could make a nice start by creating an empty folder for any presentation that you will create.

✔ Before you link any sound or video files or other documents, copy them all to the same folder first and then link to them in your PowerPoint slide.

Don't even create subfolders within that folder — keep everything in the same folder!

✔ For other PowerPoint presentations that you need to link to, copy the presentation with all linked files to the same folder and then link them. Also ensure that all the links in the copied presentation are working!

✔ When you finish creating the presentation and all its links, just copy the entire folder to your laptop or anybody else's computer if required, and you will have no link problems.

✔ If you need to e-mail the folder, just archive the entire folder into a Zip file and e-mail it as an attachment.

You might have followed all precautions and still run into link problems. Or maybe you received someone else's presentations and that person was not half as good as you with links. I recommend that you download a copy of FixLinks Pro, a PowerPoint add-in that fixes or re-links missing links.

FixLinks Pro also copies all linked files to the same folder. This can be very helpful if you didn't place everything in the same folder before you linked them from within the presentation.

You can download a trial version of FixLinks Pro from

```
www.cuttingedgeppt.com/fixlinkspro
```

# Create a Simple Quiz

Quizzes are so much fun — especially if you win prizes for the right answers. I show you how to create a quiz in PowerPoint that you can

✔ Show after a business presentation as an excuse to give away corporate gifts.

✔ Use in a school environment after a lesson to ascertain how much the students understand.

✔ Use in a fund-raising event or anywhere else.

Regardless of why you need a quiz, creating it inside PowerPoint is easy and intuitive. In this tutorial, I show you how to create a multiple-choice quiz. The best part is that you don't need to use any programming at all!

You can find a sample quiz presentation on the CD attached to this book.

## Quiz material

Quiz slides require *questions* and *visuals*.

✔ Choose questions that can each have only one correct answer.

Five questions is a good number to start with.

✔ Use visuals to make the slides look interesting.

Defining *interesting* is up to you. Perfect quiz presentations can be created without pictures, too, but where's the fun in that?!

## Presentation steps

When you have your quiz material, you're ready to create a quiz presentation in PowerPoint. You need to create a new PowerPoint presentation, then *create* your question slides and *link* your questions into a quiz.

### Creating questions

Each question requires a set of three slides:

✔ The question slide

✔ The slide with the correct answer and a congratulatory note

✔ The slide that says that the answer is incorrect and prompts the participant to try again

Create a new PowerPoint presentation for your quiz, then follow these steps for each question to create three slides:

1. **Insert a new slide in the Title Only slide layout.**

   If you're using PowerPoint 2002 or 2003, follow these steps:

   a. Choose Insert➪New Slide.

   b. Choose Format➪Slide Layout to activate the Slide Layout task pane.

   c. Choose the Title Only layout.

   If you're using PowerPoint 2000, follow these steps:

   a. Choose Insert➪New Slide.

   b. Choose Format➪Slide Layout to summon the Slide Layout dialog box.

c. Choose the Title Only layout.

d. Click OK to get back to the presentation.

2. **Type your question in the Title placeholder.**

If you have any pictures, add them on the slide.

3. **Add the answers to the slide.**

a. Add a *text box* beneath the picture for each possible answer.

b. Type each possible answer into a separate text box, as shown in Figure 12-9.

Only one of the answers should be correct.

Three is a nice number of answers — one right answer and two wrong answers make a good combination.

4. **Create a "correct" slide.**

Type the correct answer on the "correct" slide, as I did in Figure 12-10.

You can also include inspirational quotations, words of wisdom, or embarrassing pictures of your coworkers on the slide. Be creative!

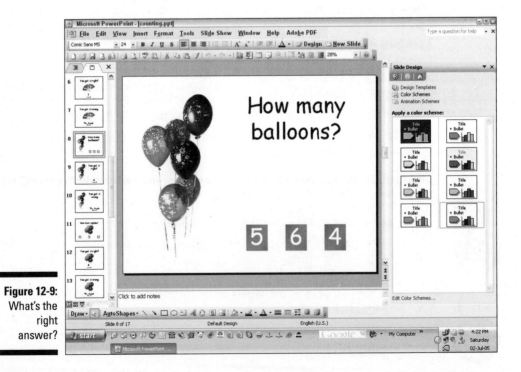

**Figure 12-9:**
What's the right answer?

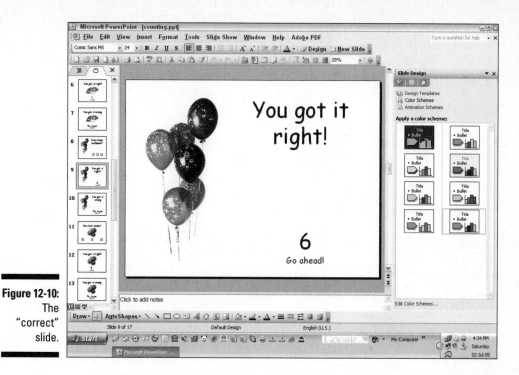

**Figure 12-10:**
The
"correct"
slide.

**5. Create an "incorrect" slide.**

On the "incorrect" slide, I suggested users go back to the question slide again and make another choice, as you can see in Figure 12-11.

You can also offer words of encouragement, silly pictures, or embarrassing pictures of your coworkers (especially if they are part of the audience!).

**6. Return to the question slide.**

**7. Link from each answer on the question slide to either the "correct" or "incorrect" slide:**

a. Select an answer text box on the question slide.

Select the text box, not the actual text.

b. Right-click the text box, then choose Action Settings to summon the Action Settings dialog box. (Refer to Figure 12-3.)

c. Select the Mouse Click tab of the Action Settings dialog box, then choose the Slide option in the Hyperlink To drop-down list.

This summons the Hyperlink to Slide dialog box (refer to Figure 12-5).

d. Create a hyperlink to the "correct" or "incorrect" answer slide.

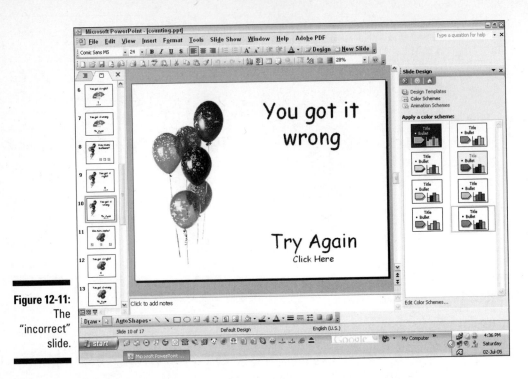

Figure 12-11:
The
"incorrect"
slide.

### Linking questions

When you have a presentation with all of the necessary slides, you're ready to link the questions into a quiz:

✔ For each "incorrect" answer slide, create a link to see the question again and attempt to answer it correctly. Add a link to the actual question slide so that users can attempt to answer the question again.

✔ On all the "correct" answer slides, provide a link to the next question slide.

Save your presentation!

# Chapter 13

# Exchanging Information

*P*owerPoint can create compelling content, but it can't do everything. Sometimes you need a better tool for a particular task. For instance, Microsoft Word creates better documents, and Excel's spreadsheets are far more capable than anything you can create with PowerPoint's tables. Acrobat PDFs are a standard in documentation these days for everything from fill-in forms to white papers, and you can't deny that Flash animations make PowerPoint's animation tools look primitive.

And I still haven't discussed CAD content from applications like AutoCAD, or bringing a live browser window into a PowerPoint slide.

And you can do everything I mentioned without leaving your PowerPoint slide! It's all explained in this chapter.

## Working with Word

Microsoft Word and PowerPoint work well as a team; Microsoft built the connections that bind them together rather nicely. There are some problem areas, though, but you'll find them addressed here.

If you want to learn how you can create a presentation from a Word document, head to Chapter 7. In this section, I show you how you can move your presentation from PowerPoint to Word. I also show you how you can link to a Word bookmark from a PowerPoint hyperlink.

## Converting presentations to Word documents

Why would anyone want to send a full presentation to Word? There are many answers to that question, but here are the most frequent reasons:

- ✔ To create handouts with more customized layouts.
- ✔ To use the advanced printing options in Word.
- ✔ To combine the presentation with more detailed content from elsewhere and create a report.
- ✔ To send a presentation-in-review document to your boss so that he can send it to his boss.
- ✔ To create training materials in Word from existing PowerPoint content.

Fortunately, this transfer is easy as long as you follow these steps:

1. **With your presentation open in PowerPoint, choose File➪Send To➪Microsoft (Office) Word.**

   This brings up the dialog box shown in Figure 13-1.

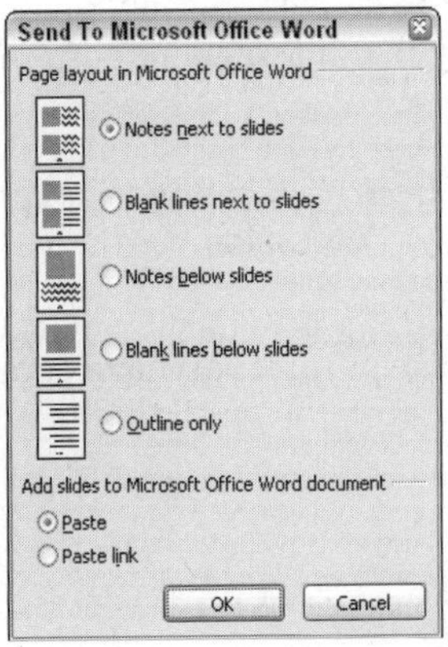

**Figure 13-1:** Your slides want to travel to Word?

2. **Select a page layout.**

   Various options allow you to choose the page layout that you want to use in Word. If what you need is not available, just choose the one closest to what you require; you can edit the layout later inside Word. Here's a brief description of the layout styles available:

   - **Notes Next to Slides** places the slide notes on the right side of the slide. This layout is best suited for presenters who like to have a printed copy of the slides and notes available to them while presenting. This layout places three slides on a single page in Word.

- **Blank Lines Next to Slides** places blank lines to the right of each slide. This layout is best suited for the audience because they can jot notes on the blank lines and save their "eureka!" moments. Again, this layout places three slides on a single page in Word.

- **Notes Below Slides** exports a single page for each slide and places the slide notes in the area below the slide. If the area under your slides is empty, that means that your slides had no notes!

- **Blank Lines Below Slides** is the same as Notes below Slides except that the notes are replaced by thoughtful blank lines so that your audience can scribble curses and acclaims within that space.

- **Outline Only** exports the entire presentation outline without any slides. If you end up with a blank document rather than the outline you expected, all your text in the presentation was not contained in PowerPoint's default placeholders. Refer to Chapter 7 to get updated about placeholders.

3. **Select either the Paste or Paste Link option.**

   The Paste option creates thumbnails of the slides inside Word, whereas the Paste Link option creates links to the actual slides. In either case, don't be too surprised if you end up with a bloated file — it's common for a 200KB presentation to balloon into a 10MB Word file!

   The Paste and Paste Link options are grayed out if you choose the Outline Only option.

4. **Click OK and PowerPoint fires up Word.**

   Word works for a while and then shows you a nicely formatted document that contains the slides or the outline.

   If you are transferring a very large presentation, you have enough time for a quick cup of coffee before Word can swallow all that information!

## Creating a smaller Word document

If you want to create a smaller Word document from a PowerPoint presentation, you need to break all links with the original presentation. Follow these steps to create smaller Word outputs:

1. **With your presentation open in PowerPoint, choose File⇨Send To⇨Microsoft (Office) Word.**

   This brings up the dialog box that you last saw in Figure 13-1.

2. **Choose any of the top four options, select the Paste Link option, and click OK.**

3. **When the presentation has been exported to Word, choose Edit⇨ Select All from within Word.**

4. **Now choose Edit⇨Links to bring up the Links dialog box, shown in Figure 13-2.**

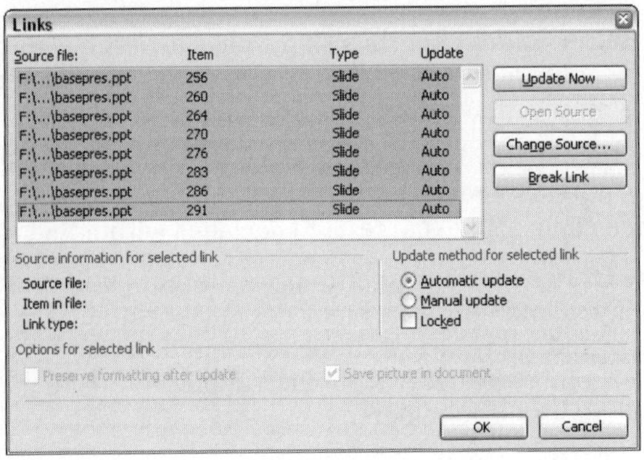

**Links**

| Source file: | Item | Type | Update |
|---|---|---|---|
| F:\...\basepres.ppt | 256 | Slide | Auto |
| F:\...\basepres.ppt | 260 | Slide | Auto |
| F:\...\basepres.ppt | 264 | Slide | Auto |
| F:\...\basepres.ppt | 270 | Slide | Auto |
| F:\...\basepres.ppt | 276 | Slide | Auto |
| F:\...\basepres.ppt | 283 | Slide | Auto |
| F:\...\basepres.ppt | 286 | Slide | Auto |
| F:\...\basepres.ppt | 291 | Slide | Auto |

Update Now
Open Source
Change Source...
Break Link

Source information for selected link
Source file:
Item in file:
Link type:

Update method for selected link
◉ Automatic update
○ Manual update
☐ Locked

Options for selected link
☐ Preserve formatting after update
☑ Save picture in document

OK    Cancel

**Figure 13-2:** Are you ready to break all that binds?

5. **Choose the Break Link option.**

   Word asks you to confirm whether you really want to break all links.

6. **Click Yes to break the links.**

7. **Now save your file and you'll end up with a more compact Word document.**

## Scrubbing your presentation with the Outline

A hidden use of the Outline Only option within the Send To Word feature is that you can use it to scrub your presentation clean. Suppose you want to get rid of all the images, the fancy fonts, and those dazzling animations in the presentation. Here's help:

1. **Send the outline to Word.**

   Choose File⇨Send To⇨Microsoft (Office) Word and opt for the Outline Only option within the dialog box that pops up. Then click OK.

2. **In Word, reverse the operation.**

   Choose File⇨Send To⇨Microsoft (Office) PowerPoint. This creates a new presentation in PowerPoint with a blank template.

This means you created a new presentation with your existing content — and in the process, you wiped out all the formatting, templates, animations, and transitions at one go! Of course, they aren't really wiped out — the original presentation is still intact with all that junk.

This trick works only with presentations that place all their text content inside default placeholders.

## Linking to Word bookmarks

Your boss just asked you to link from a PowerPoint slide to the second word in the third paragraph of page 16 in a 100-page Word document. She probably wanted to throw something impossible at you, but here's some help that will make you come out of the whole mess with flying colors:

1. **Open the Word document in Word — what else did you expect?**

2. **Select the word that your boss wants you to link to.**

   Find the second word in the third paragraph of page 16 in that epic of a document and select it.

3. **Choose Insert➪Bookmark to summon the Bookmark dialog box, shown in Figure 13-3.**

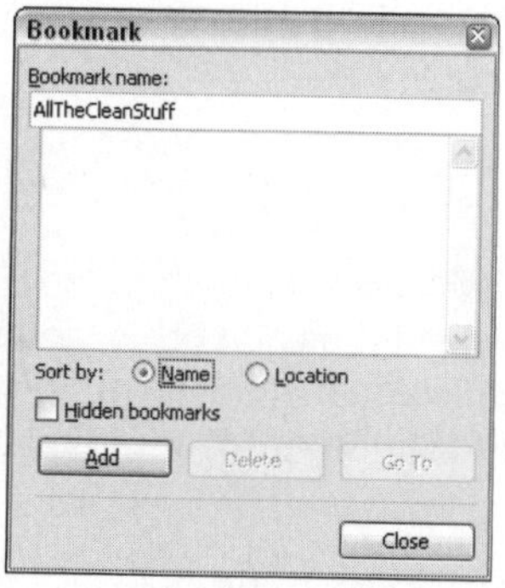

**Figure 13-3:** Bookmarks don't add marks — they just remember a location!

| Bookmark | ⊠ |
| --- | --- |
| Bookmark name: | |
| AllTheCleanStuff | |

Sort by: ⊙ Name   ○ Location
☐ Hidden bookmarks

[ Add ]   [ Delete ]   [ Go To ]

[ Close ]

4. **Give your bookmark a name and click Add.**

   I named my bookmark "AllTheCleanStuff."

5. **Save and close your Word document.**

6. **Inside PowerPoint, select an anchor to link from — this could be any PowerPoint object, such as text, an Action Button, an AutoShape, or an image.**

7. **Choose Insert➪Hyperlink to bring up either the Insert or the Edit Hyperlink dialog box, shown in Figure 13-4.**

8. **Click Existing File or Web Page on the left and navigate to the Word document that includes the bookmark.**

9. **When the path of the Word document is shown in the Address bar (see Figure 13-4), add a hash sign (#) followed by the bookmark name.**

   For example:

   ```
   C:/paste.doc#AllTheCleanStuff
   ```

10. **Click OK to accept. Now test your hyperlink!**

# Excellent Excel Stuff

Excel and PowerPoint are natural complements to each other, and many overlapping areas bring them together. This collision can have both pleasant results and terrible repercussions, and you explore ways to avoid the latter in this section.

In the following sections, I show you the best way to bring Excel data and charts into PowerPoint slides.

## Bringing in the Excel data sheets

The easiest way to bring in a range of Excel cells is to copy and paste — follow these steps to copy a range of Excel data inside PowerPoint.

Select a range of cells in Excel and choose Edit➪Copy (or press Ctrl+C). Launch PowerPoint if it is not already active. Click the slide where you want the data inserted and choose Edit➪Paste (or press Ctrl+V).

Depending on your versions of Excel and PowerPoint, your table might

- ✔ Be placed beyond the slide area
- ✔ Contain some truncated cells

### How do I see all the pasted Excel data?

If your Excel table ended up everywhere outside the slide area in PowerPoint, you probably pasted too much data from the Excel worksheet onto a PowerPoint slide. All that data would not fit on the slide and PowerPoint placed most of it outside the slide area.

Resizing won't help; it will result in smaller text, which means that your audience will have to squint to read the content. Really, you are faced with just two solutions:

- ✔ **Create a more abridged version of the entire data set in Excel and then paste it on a PowerPoint slide.**
- ✔ **Link to the Excel sheet from within PowerPoint.**

  Later in this chapter, I show you how you can link to a specific cell within an Excel worksheet.

### Why are some cells truncated?

If some of the cells in an Excel sheet end up truncated after being pasted in PowerPoint, the reasons might not be too obvious.

Would you believe that this has everything to do with which version of Windows you are using? If you use Windows 98, there is a limit to the amount of data that can be exchanged over the clipboard. This issue is more pronounced for users of Windows 98, whereas Windows XP users don't face such clipboard restrictions. The solution is to reduce text size and narrow the Excel columns before you copy and paste.

## Copying charts from Excel

To insert Excel charts inside PowerPoint, first select the chart that you want to copy in Excel and then choose Edit➪Copy (or press Ctrl+C). Switch to PowerPoint and choose Edit➪Paste (or press Ctrl+V) to bring in the chart.

This places an Excel chart inside PowerPoint that works almost in the same way as a native PowerPoint chart because both Excel and PowerPoint use the same graphing component. However, there are some caveats you need to be aware of, which I discuss next.

## Excel–PowerPoint caveats

Imagine that you have a 2MB Excel spreadsheet that includes many work-sheets and charts.

If you copy and paste an Excel chart from this spreadsheet to a PowerPoint slide, the presentation file size will increase substantially. When I tested this, the presentation size increased by 1MB!

This actually means that your entire Excel spreadsheet is embedded within each chart! Thankfully, this behavior is restricted to PowerPoint 2000 only. In PowerPoint 2002 and 2003, you can still paste the whole Excel spreadsheet, but that's not the default option.

Whatever you do, you must realize that pasting an entire spreadsheet has serious repercussions:

✔ Your PowerPoint file size keeps ballooning with each copy-paste sequence that you bring from Excel.

✔ Because you might end up distributing the presentation without being aware that a whole Excel spreadsheet is embedded, you might compromise the security of some discretionary content inside the spreadsheet. And you thought you were just showing them a chart!

The solution to these problems lies in using the Paste Special option in PowerPoint.

## Paste Special saves the day

The Paste Special option works for almost anything you paste into a PowerPoint slide. In the following example, I show you how you can use the Paste Special option to control exactly what you need pasted on a slide:

1. **In Excel, select a range or chart and choose Edit⇨Copy.**

2. **In PowerPoint, choose Edit⇨Paste Special to bring up the Paste Special dialog box shown in Figure 13-5.**

   Depending on whether you have chosen a chart or a range of cells, the options in the Paste Special dialog box might differ, as explained here:

   • **Microsoft Office Excel Chart Object** pastes the chart as an Excel object and includes all the spreadsheet content along with the chart.

- **Microsoft Office Excel Worksheet Object** pastes the cells as an Excel object and includes all the spreadsheet content within the presentation file.

- **Picture (Windows Metafile or Enhanced Metafile)** pastes a picture of the Excel chart or selected cells inside PowerPoint.

- **HTML Format** places all the cell data as a table inside PowerPoint.

- **RTF** and **Unformatted Text** place the cell content as text within the slide.

3. **Select any of the options and click OK.**

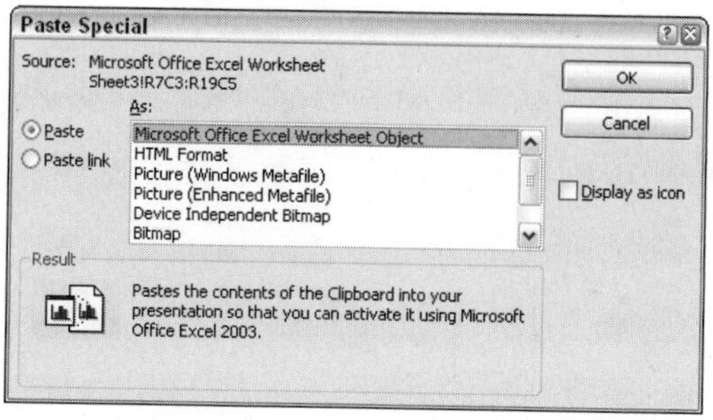

**Figure 13-5:** Paste Special options.

## Linking to Excel ranges

Maybe you want to make sure that your audience cannot see all the content on the first worksheet of your Excel spreadsheet — it might be best if a link within your PowerPoint presentation takes them directly to the wonderful forecasts in the third worksheet. Yes, that's possible — just follow these steps:

1. **In Excel, select a cell or a range of cells and choose Insert⇔Name⇔Define.**

   This brings up the Define Name dialog box, shown in Figure 13-6.

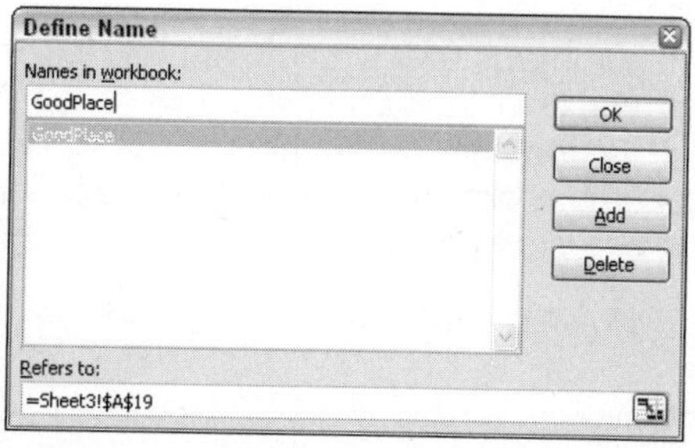

**Figure 13-6:** Give me a name.

2. **Type a name for the range and click OK.**

3. **Switch to PowerPoint and select an anchor to link from — this could be any PowerPoint object, such as text, an Action Button, an AutoShape, or an image.**

4. **Choose Insert⇨Hyperlink to bring up either the Insert or Edit Hyperlink dialog box, shown in Figure 13-7.**

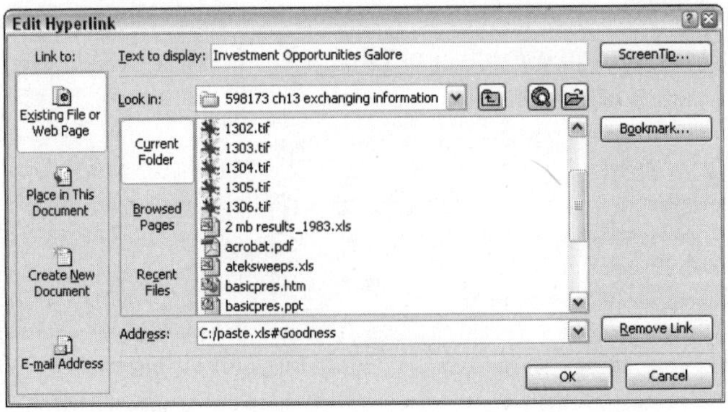

**Figure 13-7:**
Mark your
links with
ranges.

5. **Click Existing File or Web Page on the left and navigate to the Excel spreadsheet that includes the named range.**

6. **After the path of the Excel spreadsheet is shown in the Address bar (see Figure 13-7), add a hash sign (#) followed by the name you gave the range in Excel.**

For example:

```
C:/paste.xls#Goodness
```

7. **Click OK to accept. Now test your hyperlink!**

# PowerPoint and PDF

PowerPoint and PDF are both standards that were meant for distribution — so it's not out of the blue that you hear questions about ways to integrate both of them together. In this section, I show you how you can create better PDFs from PowerPoint presentations and also how to link to PDFs from PowerPoint.

# Creating PDFs from PowerPoint

If you have the full version of Adobe Acrobat or a similar PDF print driver product installed, you might have some icons on your PowerPoint toolbars that convert your presentations to PDFs with one click. Figure 13-8 shows the Acrobat toolbar inside PowerPoint.

**Figure 13-8:**
Acrobat
meets
PowerPoint.

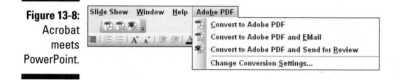

However, you'll notice that the PDFs created this way either lack all the transitions or don't include basic PowerPoint features, like interactivity and hyperlinks. That's very surprising considering that PDFs normally can cope with all these niceties. If you really are not too worried about these features, you can just click the magic Acrobat icon in PowerPoint and end up with a PDF that includes a reasonable amount of fidelity.

If you don't see any such icon, read the sidebar called "Where's the Acrobat in my PowerPoint?"

If creating PDFs with transitions and interactivity is important to you, take a look at PowerPoint MVP Steve Rindsberg's Prep4PDF product:

    www.cuttingedgeppt.com/prep4pdf

## Where's the Acrobat in my PowerPoint?

If you cannot see an Acrobat icon, toolbar, or menu within your PowerPoint interface, you probably don't have the full version of Adobe Acrobat installed on your system. Now, what do I mean by the full version? Acrobat is available in two versions:

✔ The free **Reader,** which allows you to read an Acrobat PDF file. It also works as a helper application that pops up when you try to read a PDF that's linked to a Web page.

✔ The full **Acrobat** software from Adobe, which allows you to create and edit your PDFs. Not surprisingly, this is not free, but several other free and low-cost alternatives are available. Just do an online search for "PDF Converter" and you'll find enough alternatives.

No, Prep4PDF doesn't create the PDFs for you; it just acts as an interpreter between PowerPoint and Acrobat. By inserting some clever code inside your presentation, Prep4PDF ensures that Acrobat retains all the bells and whistles that PowerPoint users expect.

Another area that is perfect for PDF creation is PowerPoint handouts. Nowadays, presenters commonly create PDF handouts from PowerPoint presentations that can be e-mailed before or after the presentation showing.

To create a PDF handout, just print handouts to the PDF printer driver. More information on handouts can be found in Chapter 14.

## Linking to PDFs

Linking to a PDF is almost like linking to any other file. Follow these steps to link to a PDF from within PowerPoint:

1. **Make sure that the PDF you want to link to is placed in the same folder as your PowerPoint presentation.**

2. **In PowerPoint, select an anchor to link from — this could be any PowerPoint object, such as text, an Action Button, an AutoShape, or an image.**

3. **Choose Slide Show⇨Action Settings to bring up the Action Settings dialog box, shown in Figure 13-9.**

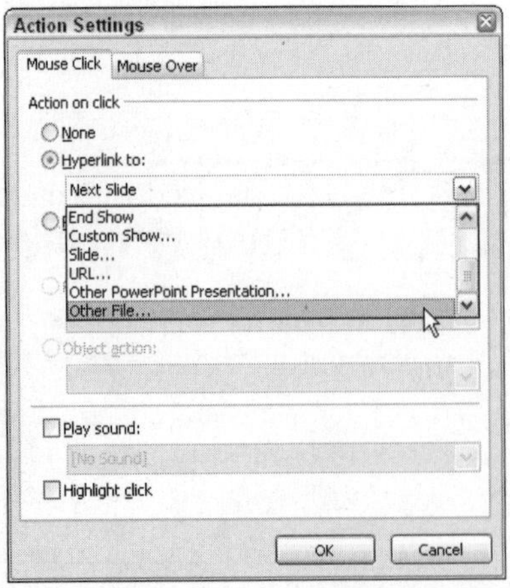

**Figure 13-9:** Access PDFs with one click.

4. **In the Mouse Click tab, click to open the Hyperlink To drop-down list and choose the Other File option to summon the Hyperlink to Other File dialog box, shown in Figure 13-10.**

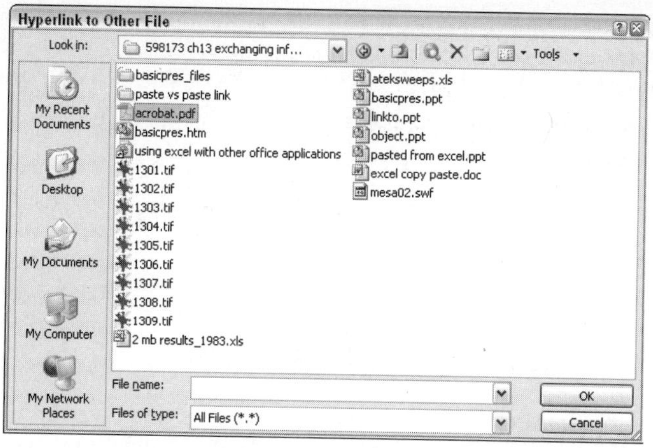

**Hyperlink to Other File**

Look in: 598173 ch13 exchanging inf...

My Recent Documents
Desktop
My Documents
My Computer
My Network Places

basicpres_files
paste vs paste link
acrobat.pdf
basicpres.htm
using excel with other office applications
1301.tif
1302.tif
1303.tif
1304.tif
1305.tif
1306.tif
1307.tif
1308.tif
1309.tif
2 mb results_1983.xls

ateksweeps.xls
basicpres.ppt
linkto.ppt
object.ppt
pasted from excel.ppt
excel copy paste.doc
mesa02.swf

File name:
Files of type: All Files (*.*)

OK
Cancel

**Figure 13-10:**
Hyperlink to PDFs and other files.

5. **Browse to the PDF (or any other document) and select it. Click OK to accept.**

6. **Make sure that you check your hyperlink!**

If you often need to distribute PowerPoint presentations linked to Excel spreadsheets, Word documents, or Acrobat PDFs, you should take a look at Sonia Coleman's Autorun CD Project Creator Pro product, which creates autorun CDs of linked presentations. PowerPoint, Excel, Word, and PDF viewers are included on the CDs!

www.cuttingedgeppt.com/acdpc

# Flash Comes to PowerPoint

If you've ever browsed online or been remotely involved with multimedia, you must be aware of Flash, the animation file format that creates amazingly compact, interactive movies.

Here's some more information on the Flash format:

✔ Flash is the name of an animation authoring program from Macromedia. It's also the name of the animation format that this program creates, which is commonly identified as SWF, the name of the file extension.

✔ Macromedia Flash is not the only program that outputs SWF files. A range of programs create everything from charts and maps to banners and 3-D art in the SWF format (see the sidebar, "Everything outputs Flash").

✔ PowerPoint has no direct support for Flash content. However, that hasn't stopped users from finding ways to insert Flash SWF content in PowerPoint slides.

- ✔ If you would rather not mess with the 11-step process that allows you to insert Flash content in PowerPoint, take a look at a range of free and commercial add-ins and companion products that will do it for you.

- ✔ You can go the other way around too, converting entire PowerPoint presentations to the Flash SWF format.

This book's CD contains a bunch of sample Flash SWFs that you can use for the tutorials in this section.

## Flash content in PowerPoint

If you want to insert or view Flash SWF content inside PowerPoint, there are some prerequisites. You should have these three applications installed on your computer:

- ✔ **A full version of PowerPoint:** The Flash movies cannot be seen using the free PowerPoint Viewer because it prohibits the running of ActiveX controls.

- ✔ **Microsoft Internet Explorer browser:** Most versions of Windows in the last several years come with this browser preinstalled.

- ✔ **Shockwave Flash ActiveX control:** Around 98 percent of the world's browsers already have this installed. This is a helper application that allows Microsoft Internet Explorer and other applications (including PowerPoint) to play back Flash SWF animations.

You can check whether the Shockwave Flash control is installed on your system by visiting the Flash Player site:

```
www.macromedia.com/shockwave/download/index.cgi?P1_Prod_
        Version=ShockwaveFlash
```

The site might ask you to install the Flash Player even if you have it already installed. Don't worry — just go ahead and install it. The page either updates your Flash Player or just redirects you to another page that informs you that the Flash Player was successfully installed.

## Inserting Flash content

Follow these steps to insert a Flash SWF inside PowerPoint:

1. **Copy your SWF file to the same folder as your saved presentation.**

2. **Open your presentation and navigate to the slide where you want to insert a Flash SWF movie.**

**3. If the Control Toolbox toolbar is not visible, choose View➪Toolbars➪ Control Toolbox to bring up the toolbar shown in Figure 13-11.**

Figure 13-11:
Control
Toolbox.

**4. On the Control Toolbox, click the bottom-right icon, called More Controls.**

This opens a drop-down menu with a list of controls installed on your system.

**5. Choose the Shockwave Flash Object option, as shown in Figure 13-12.**

Your mouse cursor transforms into a crosshair.

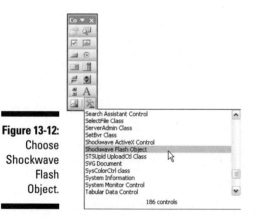

Figure 13-12:
Choose
Shockwave
Flash
Object.

**6. Drag a rectangle within the slide — don't bother too much about the rectangle dimensions because you can change that later.**

**7. Right-click the rectangle and then click Properties in the resultant flyout menu.**

This opens the Properties window, shown in Figure 13-13.

**8. Click the topmost listing, (Custom).**

This reveals an ellipsis (. . .) button toward the right, as you can see in Figure 13-13.

**Figure 13-13:**
Shockwave
Flash
properties.

9. **Click the ellipsis button to summon the Property Pages dialog box, shown in Figure 13-14.**

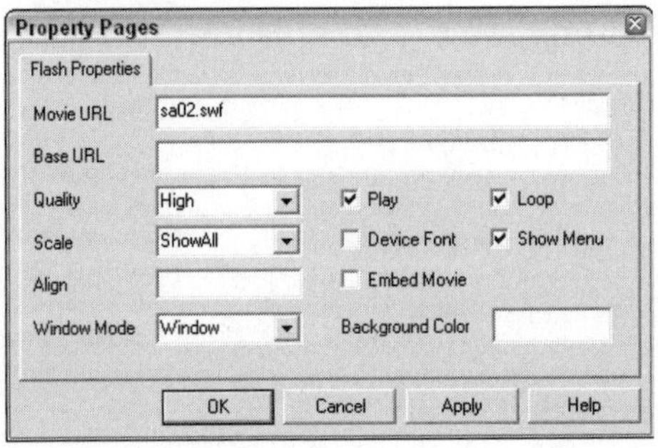

**Figure 13-14:**
The
Property
Pages
dialog box.

10. **Type the name of the Flash SWF file in the Movie URL box.**

No pathname is required because you already copied the SWF to the same folder as the presentation.

11. **Play the slide and the Flash SWF will play instantly. Press Esc to get back to editing mode and resize and reposition the movie on the slide as required.**

TIP

Now that you have successfully inserted a Flash SWF within PowerPoint, you might discover that the SWFs do not rewind after playing. Sometimes, they might even stall. To counter this error, you could either add some VBA code or download Flashback, a free add-in that automates the process:

www.cuttingedgeppt.com/flashback

## Everything outputs Flash

Nowadays, Macromedia Flash is no longer the only application that outputs Flash SWFs. Tons of other applications output SWFs. Here are a few of them; they can complement your PowerPoint presentation tools:

✔ **rChart** is a charting application that creates data-driven charts. It also automatically inserts Flash SWFs inside PowerPoint for you, including SWFs created by any other application.

✔ **Macromedia FlashPaper** converts any document to Flash SWF by using the FlashPaper printer driver.

✔ **Infommersion Xcelsius** does more than mere charting — it allows you to interactively analyze the data using dynamic charts that are exported as Flash SWF.

✔ **Wildform** creates several Flash output programs that create Flash banners and movies.

✔ **SWISHmax** is an easier Flash authoring environment for those who find Macromedia's environment intimidating.

You can find more links and resources at `www.cuttingedgeppt.com/moreflash`.

# *Flash from PowerPoint*

Now for the other way around. There are tons of applications that convert PowerPoint presentations to the Flash SWF format. Most applications that do the conversion fall into one of two categories:

✔ **Bare-bones PowerPoint-to-Flash conversion software.** These include products like

- PowerCONVERTER
- iMediaCONVERT
- TechSmith Camtasia

✔ **ORM (Online Rich Media) programs** that add more to the conversion by including hosting, sharing, collaborating, and Web-conferencing options into the product. Many of them add e-learning capabilities, too. Products in this category include

- Macromedia Breeze
- Articulate Presenter
- PointeCast

Naturally, the latter category of programs are considerably more expensive than the bare-bones converters. I discuss more about the ORM solutions in Chapter 15.

# Objects for Everything Else

Using objects in PowerPoint is a great way to integrate content that cannot be directly inserted on a PowerPoint slide.

So what is an object? An object is any document or file that can be embedded within a PowerPoint presentation. This can be just anything — a video, some music, documents, and so on.

To package such objects in PowerPoint, you use the suitably named Object Packager, a small application that has been part of Microsoft Windows for as long as I can remember.

In this example, I package a QuickTime video inside a PowerPoint slide, but you can use the same technique to make an object from any file. Follow these steps to insert an object inside PowerPoint:

1. **Navigate to the slide in which you want to insert the object.**

2. **Choose Insert⇨Object to bring up the Insert Object dialog box, shown in Figure 13-15.**

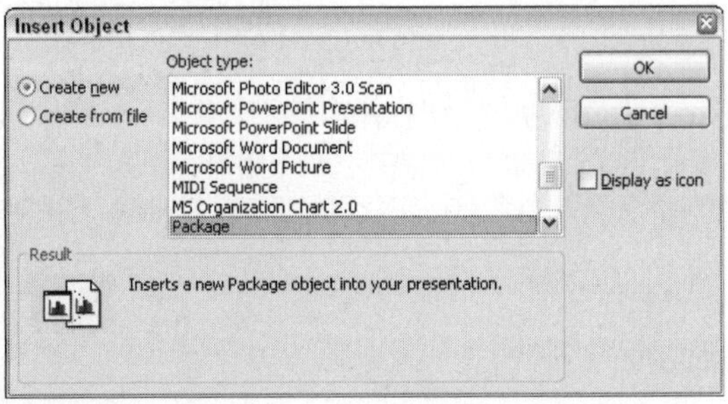

**Figure 13-15:** Inserting objects.

3. **In the Object Type list box, choose Package. Also make sure that the Create New radio button is selected.**

4. **Click OK, and you are presented with the Object Packager interface, shown in Figure 13-16.**

   If you think this window looks ancient, it is; it dates back to Windows 3.1 days!

5. **Choose File⇨Import, navigate to and select your video file, and click Open.**

   This brings you back to the Object Packager.

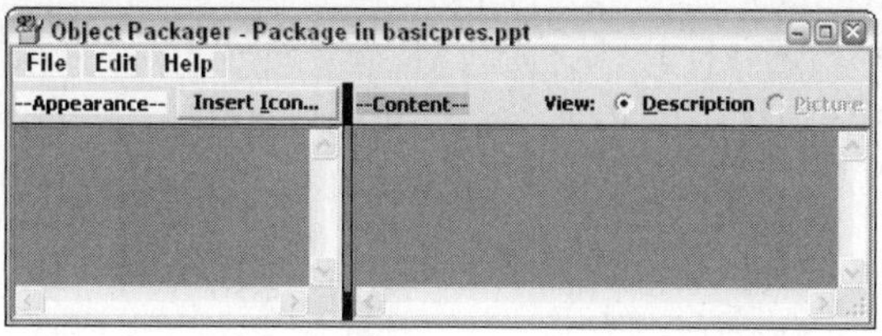

**Figure 13-16:**
Object
Packager is
a peep into
olde-world
Windows.

**Figure 13-16:**
Object
Packager is
a peep into
olde-world
Windows.

**6. Choose File➪Exit.**

Object Packager asks you whether you want to update your presentation file.

**7. Click Yes to accept.**

This brings you back to your PowerPoint slide, where you will find an icon of the object you just packaged.

**8. Right-click the object and choose Custom Animation from the flyout menu.**

In PowerPoint 2000, this opens the Custom Animation dialog box. In PowerPoint 2002 and 2003, this activates the Custom Animation task pane.

**9. Activate the contents of the object.**

Because of differences in the interfaces, how you activate the contents of the object is a bit different, depending on your version of PowerPoint:

- **In PowerPoint 2002 and 2003:** Choose Add Effect➪Object Animation➪Activate Contents within the Custom Animation task pane, as you can see in Figure 13-17.

- **In PowerPoint 2000:** Click the Multimedia Settings tab of the Custom Animation dialog box and set the Object Action to Activate Contents, as shown in Figure 13-18. Then click OK.

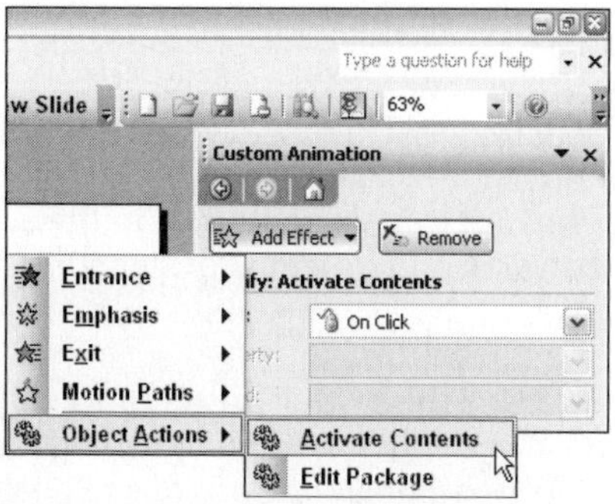

**Figure 13-17:**
Activate
your
objects!

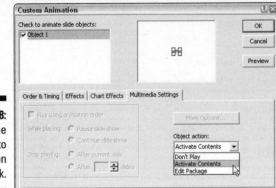

**Figure 13-18:**
Set the
movie to
activate on
a click.

10. **Position the package icon as required and save your presentation.**

11. **Test your object by playing the presentation.**

    You have to click the icon to activate the contents. PowerPoint might
    warn you of dire consequences, but if you are sure that the file is safe, go
    ahead and ignore the warning.

Packaging objects is certainly not as elegant as other options, but then if
you really need to connect a PowerPoint presentation to a file format that
PowerPoint doesn't directly support, using objects can be a life saver.

Even though the results might seem the same as linking, there's still a
crucial difference — the Object Packager contains the entire file within the
PowerPoint presentation. So if you find that your presentation size balloons
up enormously, that might be because of all those convenient packages it
contains!

# PowerPoint on the Web

Like almost every other application, PowerPoint has embraced the online
world. Unlike other applications, PowerPoint's Web outputs can be quite
large — often weighing several megabytes. The reasons are not difficult to
comprehend: PowerPoint's Web output needs to use sound and animations
apart from slide-by-slide navigation and visuals contained in the actual presentation. On top of that, most PowerPoint content is designed to play full
screen.

Leaving aside that file size grouse, publishing your presentation online with
PowerPoint can be painless, and I show you how. To make things easier, I
also explain more about alternative Web-publishing options available for
PowerPoint users.

Never consider PowerPoint as a Web page–creation tool. Rather, look at it as a creator of online presentations.

## PowerPoint's online presentations

As the Internet and browsing capabilities continue to evolve, newer PowerPoint versions offer more options than the earlier ones. Depending on your version of PowerPoint, the steps involved in creating online presentations may differ.

To see a preview of your presentation's Web output at any time, choose File➪ Web Page Preview.

### PowerPoint 2002 and 2003

Although PowerPoint 2002 and 2003 do output Web presentations that contain a fair amount of fidelity, you should fine-tune several options before doing an actual conversion.

Follow these steps to change the Web options:

**1. Choose Tools➪Options to bring up the multitabbed Options dialog box.**

**2. Click the General tab and then click Web Options.**

This summons the Web Options dialog box, shown in Figure 13-19.

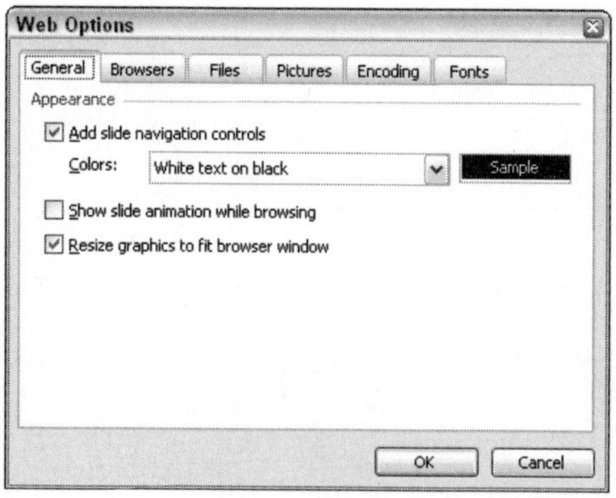

**Web Options**

General | Browsers | Files | Pictures | Encoding | Fonts

Appearance

☑ Add slide navigation controls

Colors: White text on black    Sample

☐ Show slide animation while browsing

☑ Resize graphics to fit browser window

OK    Cancel

**Figure 13-19:**
All those
Web options
are here.

**3. Change the settings in each of the six tabs as required:**

- The **General** tab allows you to enable slide navigation controls and choose a specific color combination for them. The default is white text over black. You can also show slide animations while browsing and choose to resize graphics to fit a browser window. All the options in this tab need to be checked to allow a faithful Web output.

- The **Browser** tab contains the most significant options related to PowerPoint's Web output. You configure your PowerPoint HTML output here in basically two ways — either you can choose one of the preset browser profiles or choose to create your own profile from the four options below the browser drop-down list.

- The **Files** tab has simple options. You can choose to organize supporting files in a subfolder, as opposed to storing them within the presentation folder itself. You can also opt to use long file names, as opposed to the earlier 8.3 Microsoft DOS convention.

- The **Pictures** tab allows you to configure your intended screen size and resolution. The default is 800 x 600 pixels.

- The **Encoding** and **Fonts** tabs can be left at the default values because the settings here are preconfigured according to your system's actual language encoding options.

4. **When you are done changing the options, click OK. Then click OK again in the Options dialog box to get back to your slides.**

Now that your Web settings are done, follow these steps to save your presentation as a Web page:

1. **Choose File➪Save as Web Page to bring up the Save As dialog box, shown in Figure 13-20.**

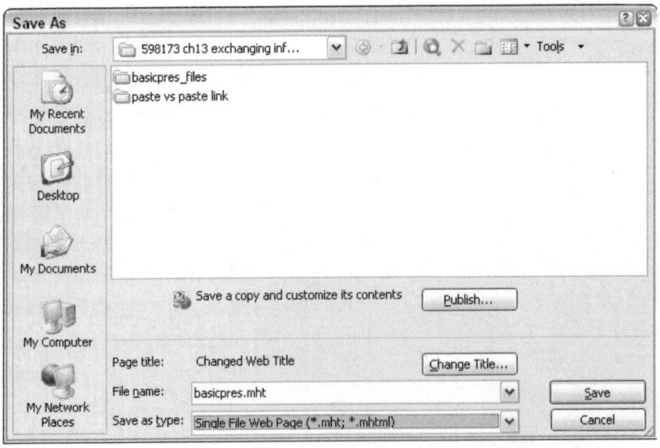

**Figure 13-20:** Create online presentations with PowerPoint.

2. **In the Save as Type drop-down list, choose from either of these output options:**

   - **Single File Web Page (*.mht; *.mhtml):** This option creates a single output file that contains all the slide pages and linked files.

- **Web Page (\*.htm; \*.html):** This option creates the conventional Web page with linked files and multiple pages.

3. **Provide a name for the output in the File Name box.**

4. **Change the title of the Web output by clicking the Change Title button.**

   This is the same title that appears on the title bar of the Web page when it is viewed.

   This step brings up the Set Page Title dialog box, shown in Figure 13-21.

**Figure 13-21:** Change the Web title.

5. **Type a new title in the dialog box and click OK.**

6. **Click the Publish button to summon the Publish as Web Page dialog box, shown in Figure 13-22.**

   This allows you to choose whether you want to publish some or all slides in the presentation as a Web page.

   Most of the other options are the same as the ones in the Web Options dialog box that I discuss earlier. Incidentally, you can bring up the Web Options dialog box again by clicking the Web Options button.

7. **Click the Publish button and PowerPoint outputs the presentation to a Web page or pages.**

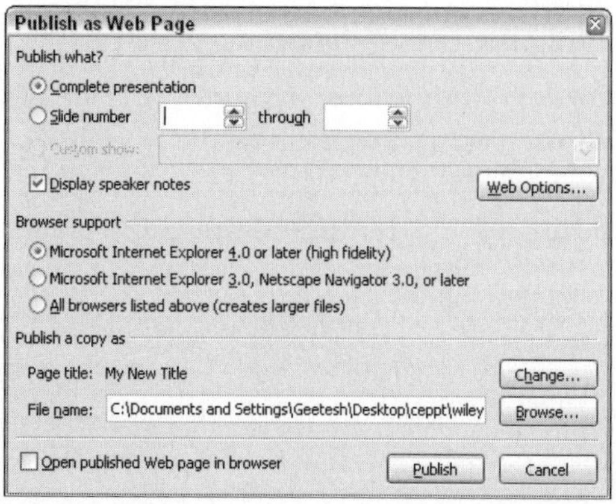

**Figure 13-22:** More publish options.

### PowerPoint 2000

Follow these steps to save your presentation as a Web page in PowerPoint 2000:

1. **Choose File⇨Save as Web Page to bring up the Save As dialog box, shown in Figure 13-23.**

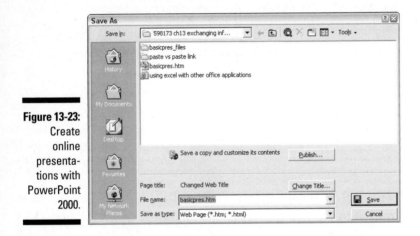

**Figure 13-23:**
Create online presentations with PowerPoint 2000.

2. **Provide a name for the output in the File Name box.**

3. **Change the title of the Web output by clicking the Change Title button.**

   This brings up the Set Page Title dialog box, where you can type a title name.

4. **Click the Publish button to open the Publish as Web Page dialog box, (shown earlier in Figure 13-22).**

   This allows you to choose whether you want to publish some or all of the slides in the presentation as a Web page.

   You can also click the Web Options button to open the Web Options dialog box, which allows you to change options related to navigation controls, animation, and encoding.

5. **Click the Publish button and PowerPoint outputs the presentation to Web pages.**

# More Web alternatives

PowerPoint's Web publishing options are quite extensive and customizable. Yet, sometimes you want even more control over the output. That's the time to look at third-party add-ins.

One such add-in is PPT2HTML, from Steve Rindsberg. This add-in allows you to use your own HTML templates for the Web output and creates cleaner and leaner Web pages with pure HTML output rather than PowerPoint's more proprietary output. PPT2HTML also creates more accessible HTML output that can be used by screen reader applications for people with disabilities. You can find it at

```
www.cuttingedgeppt.com/ppt2html
```

If you want to output the entire presentation to ORM (online rich media), check out Chapter 15 for more information.

# Roundtrip HTML

This is probably not the best place to mention the HTML roundtrip feature because it relates to both Web output and recovering corrupt presentations — those areas are as diverse as chalk and cheese. But this is still a great tip and will help you some day, although it works only in PowerPoint 2002 and 2003.

If you end up with a corrupt presentation that causes PowerPoint to crash, all hope is not lost. Follow these steps to roundtrip and salvage your presentation:

1. **Save the presentation to a Web page and accept the default values.**

2. **Launch PowerPoint and choose File➪Open.**

3. **Select the Web page that you created with PowerPoint and click Open.**

4. **Choose File➪Save As and save to the native PPT format.**

   You're done!

Because PowerPoint exports to a proprietary HTML format, you can bring the Web output back into PowerPoint with all your layouts and designs intact. Well, you do lose something in this roundtrip. Luckily, that might be some useless code that caused PowerPoint to crash your presentation!

# Chapter 14

# Preparing and Delivering Your Awesome Presentation

. . . . . . . . . . . . . . . . . . . . . . . . . . . . . . . . . . . . . . . . . . . . .

### In This Chapter

▶ Checking that presentation again

▶ Setting up a show

▶ Protecting your slides from prying eyes

▶ All about Custom Shows

▶ Printing thy presentation

▶ Handing something out

. . . . . . . . . . . . . . . . . . . . . . . . . . . . . . . . . . . . . . . . . . . . .

**Y**our presentation flows smoothly from slide to slide. Every slide is perfect, the animations enhance the concept and visualization of the presentation, and the message has been fine-tuned. When you have finished creating your presentation, it's show time! It's time to present.

Don't plug in the projectors just yet. It's time for testing and rethinking, subjects I discuss in this chapter.

I also discuss how to set up your shows and create custom presentations. Then I proceed to the holy grail of PowerPoint — password protection — and end with information about printing your presentation and making compelling and effective handouts to complement your presentation.

A bonus chapter on the CD shows how to repurpose and extend your presentation.

## Test, Test, and Test Your Presentation

Finding and correcting your own mistakes is one thing. It's an altogether different experience to see them in 32-point Arial with the rest of your audience. Mistakes happen, and it is far better to find and correct them *before* presenting. Follow these guidelines to iron out all the wrinkles in your presentation:

✔ **Practice your presentations out loud.** You don't need an audience for this testing. You can also speak out loud along with your slides and simultaneously record the narration on a voice recorder. Then, play the recorded voice and pay attention to any areas that require improvement in wording, delivery, or timing.

✔ **Show your slides to a colleague or family member and ask for an honest opinion.** You will be surprised to find several areas of improvement that can be discovered from another perspective.

✔ **Test your presentation at the venue a day or several hours before the showing.** Some projectors show colors in different values than the ones visible on your computer or laptop.

✔ **If you're working in a cross-platform environment, make sure that you test the presentation on both Windows and Mac computers.**

✔ **Make sure that the text is readable from a distance.** Try to read the text from as far as possible to make certain that the audience members seated in the last row can read the text.

✔ **Don't change your laptop at the last minute.** Software and hardware configurations differ from system to system and can wreak havoc with your carefully fine-tuned timings.

✔ **Keep a backup copy of your presentation on a USB drive or CD just in case.** For the same reason, keep a printed copy of your presentation with you at all times.

✔ Call me paranoid, but I suggest that you **e-mail a copy of the presentation to your Web e-mail account so that you can access it in an emergency.** It doesn't hurt to be safe!

# Awesome Delivery Ideas

After you have taken all precautions and tested your presentation a zillion times, it's time for the showing. Here are some awesome delivery ideas that will ensure that your presentation is a huge success:

✔ **Be sincere.** All the other tricks will come to naught if you don't follow the simple principle of being sincere.

So, what do I mean by *being sincere?* Being sincere means never discussing a topic that you don't know thoroughly. It also means that you aren't trying to mislead or divert the audience from the truth.

Audiences are very perceptive and can recognize a lack of sincerity within moments.

✔ **Wear understated clothing.** Restrain the urge to wear brightly colored clothes; your presentation, not you, should be the focus of attention.

Neither men nor women should wear too much jewelry. Try to achieve a clean, understated look.

✔ **Don't put everything in your pockets!**

I remember a presenter who had so much loose change in his trouser pockets that the constant jingling drowned out his presentation!

✔ **Identify with your audience.** Make sure that you know some people in the audience before you begin. This helps break the ice and involves the audience.

But don't just focus on those people you know all through the presentation — there are others in the audience too!

✔ **Weave some humor into your narrative.** However, don't carry this too far, and stay away from any humor that can be considered discriminatory or racist.

✔ **If you're using a remote control to move between your slides, make sure that you're comfortable with the controller.** Also make sure that the batteries in the controller are sufficiently charged to last through your presentation.

✔ **Encourage the audience to ask questions.** If you're discussing multiple topics, you might want to ask for questions often during the presentation. Alternatively, you might want to reserve some time for questions at the end of the presentation.

✔ **Try to weave in some audience activity, like a brief quiz or short game, during or after the presentation.** Audiences love interactivity.

There are more ways than one to set up your PowerPoint show — and most of these options stem from the fact that presenting situations differ all the time. For instance, you might want to present

✔ A conventional presentation in which you move from slide to slide and speak to the audience

✔ A slide show presentation that includes many pictures along with a background music score

✔ A pre-narrated presentation for those times when you can't make it to an event

✔ A kiosk-style presentation that runs unattended at exhibitions

✔ A touch screen–style presentation that moves to another slide only at the click of an Action Button.

Whichever type of show you present, your first stop has to be the Set Up Show dialog box, which is accessed by choosing Slide Show➪Set Up Show.

This dialog box provides different options depending upon your version of PowerPoint:

- Figure 14-1 shows how the dialog box looks in PowerPoint 2002 and 2003.
- Figure 14-2 shows the same dialog box options in PowerPoint 2000.

**Figure 14-1:**
Make your
PowerPoint
2002 and
2003 shows
behave
themselves!

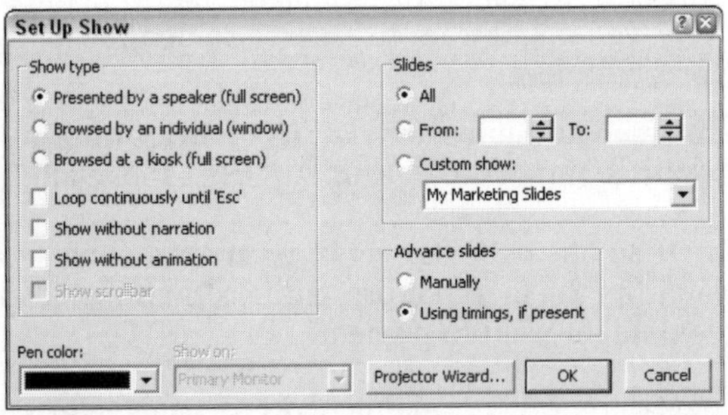

**Figure 14-2:**
And this is
how you
do it in
PowerPoint
2000.

## *Set Up Show settings*

You have many options in the Set Up Show dialog box. Just select or change the options to your liking and then click OK, and you're good to go.

- **Show Type:**

    - **Presented by a Speaker (Full Screen):** This is the default choice and relates to the conventional use of a live speaker in attendance during the presentation. The presentation plays full screen. All keyboard shortcuts work, and you can use either a mouse or a presentation remote control to navigate between slides.

- **Browsed by an Individual (Window):** This option (see Figure 14-3) doesn't play the presentation full screen. You can still view all the toolbars, although you won't see the outlines or any task pane. This mode is best suited for quick edits and reviews or for an in-house presentation.

  You can also select the Show Scrollbar option, which displays the scroll bar toward the right of the slide.

- **Browsed at a Kiosk (Full Screen):** Use this mode in a trade fair or exhibition. This mode automatically loops the entire presentation. The mouse cursor is also visible all the time so that the audience can move between slides easily.

✔ **Show Slides:** In PowerPoint 2000, this group is simply called **Slides.**

- **All** shows all the slides in your presentation except the *hidden slides.* See the section, "Slides behind Veils," later in this chapter, for the lowdown on hidden slides.

- **From** and **To** options allow you to choose a series of slide numbers that you want to display.

- **Custom Show** lets you play a custom show you've created within the active presentation. If this option is grayed out, you have no custom shows created. See the "Custom Shows" section, later in this chapter, for more information.

**Figure 14-3:**
Individual
browsing in
PowerPoint.

✔ **Show Options:** These options allow you to choose specific viewing options. Some of these might be grayed out depending on the Show type you choose.

In PowerPoint 2000, these options fall under the Show Type category.

- **Loop Continuously until 'Esc'** is selected by default if you change the show type to kiosk mode. For all show types, selecting this option loops the presentation continuously until you press the Esc key.

- **Show without Narration** plays the presentation without any added narration. This only works if you have used PowerPoint's own Record Narration feature — if you have inserted narratives through recordings made outside PowerPoint, this feature will not work.

- **Show without Animation** plays the presentation without animation — all slides that contain animated elements appear in the post-animation stage.

- **Pen Color** lets you choose a pen color from a convenient color swatch box.

  The *pen* annotates a slide while it is being shown (or projected).

✔ **Advance Slides:** Lets you choose how you want your slides to progress one after the other.

- **Manually** lets you advance slides manually — this overrides any set transition times within the slides.

- **Using Timings, If Present** is the default option — this follows the slide timings set in the Slide Transition properties.

✔ **Multiple monitors:** This option is available only in PowerPoint 2002 and 2003. If you don't have a multiple-monitor setup, this option is grayed out.

- **Display Slide Show On** lets you choose the primary monitor for the presentation.

- **Show Presenter View** enables the Presenter View, a special multi-monitor viewing mode that shows you thumbnails of slides and previews the next slide that's coming up after the one being shown. It also shows the elpased time since the presentation started and provides a convenient End Show button.

✔ **Performance:** These options are available only in PowerPoint 2002 and 2003.

- **Use Hardware Graphics Acceleration** turns on graphic acceleration if your computer has the capability. If you notice more sluggish performance with PowerPoint shows after you turn on this option, turn it off.

- **Slide Show Resolution** lets you change the resolution of the presentation playback — if your presentation is running smoothly, don't change the default settings.

TIP

If you're up to it, experiment with all the settings to figure out which works best for you.

✔ **Projector Wizard:** This button brings up the Projector Wizard (what else did you expect?), as shown in Figure 14-4. This option is available only in PowerPoint 2000.

The wizard includes profiles of well-known computer and projector manufacturers and explains which hot keys you need to press to enable projector and monitor output. (It also tests the sound levels in projectors that support this feature.)

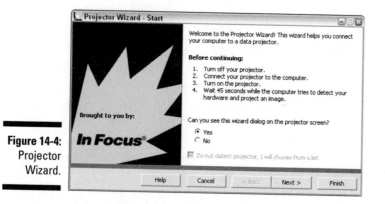

Figure 14-4:
Projector
Wizard.

# Slides behind Veils

PowerPoint slides can hide behind veils — but they can also decide to come out of hiding if the situation demands. No, this isn't some soap opera; PowerPoint provides an option to hide some slides that contain information not suitable for all eyes. These slides are visible in editing mode, they just decide to play the invisible game when the show is playing.

You'll want to use the "hidden slides" feature if

✔ You want to include some backup slides in the presentation, which you can unhide if the situation demands.

✔ You already have a presentation that's fairly suitable for a presentation that your boss just told you that you have to give in the next 15 minutes, and hiding a few unsuitable slides seems like a better idea than creating a new presentation.

✔ You need to remove some slides but you don't want to delete them because you might regret that later — so hiding them is a better idea!

If any of these tricks sound like something you want up your sleeve, let me show you how to proceed.

Follow these steps to hide one or more slides in your presentation:

1. **Choose View➪Slide Sorter to view thumbnails of all slides in the presentation.**

2. **Select one or more slides in the presentation.**

   You can select multiple consecutive slides by clicking the first slide and then Shift-clicking the last slide in the series.

   You can select multiple, nonconsecutive slides by clicking the first slide and then Ctrl-clicking each other slide you want to select.

3. **Choose Slide Show➪Hide Slide to hide the selected slides.**

   This is a toggle menu option — you need to select the same slides and choose Slide Show➪Hide Slide again to unhide the slides.

   You can also right-click a slide thumbnail in Slide Show view and choose the Hide Slide option from the context menu (see Figure 14-5).

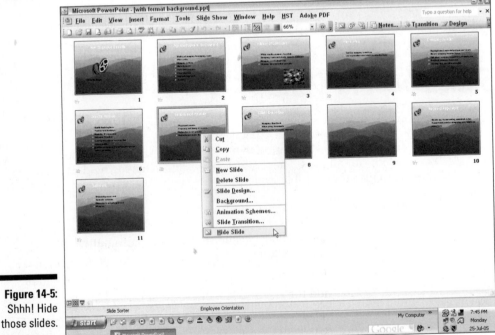

**Figure 14-5:** Shhh! Hide those slides.

# Custom Shows

A *custom show* is a set of slides chosen within a presentation that acts like another presentation. Why would you want your presentation to have a dual side of its existence?

✔ You need to create umpteen versions of the same presentation, each containing a subset of that hundred-slide presentation that was created many moons ago. Do you find yourself creating 25- and 40-slide abridged or specialized versions of the same presentation?

✔ You need to insert the same slide multiple times within the same presentation — for example, you might want the Agenda slide to show up after each section in a long presentation.

✔ Just for once you need to rearrange a few slides.

✔ You don't want to create multiple presentations that contain the same slides — it's such a blessing not to edit those charts in multiple presentations!

## Creating custom shows

Follow these steps to create a custom show:

1. **Choose Slide Show⇨Custom Shows to summon the Custom Shows dialog box, shown in Figure 14-6.**

2. **Click New to bring up the Define Custom Show dialog box, shown in Figure 14-7.**

3. **Give your custom show a name.**

   By default, PowerPoint just calls it *Custom Show 1,* but you can call it *My Marketing Slides* or *Employee Orientation* or something that you can remember easily.

4. **Add the slides you want to include in the custom show.**

   • To add a slide, select the slide in the Slides in Presentation box and click the **Add>>** button; the slide appears in the Slides in Custom Show box.

     You can add the same slide more than once.

   • To remove added slides, just select them in the Slides in Custom Show box and click **Remove**.

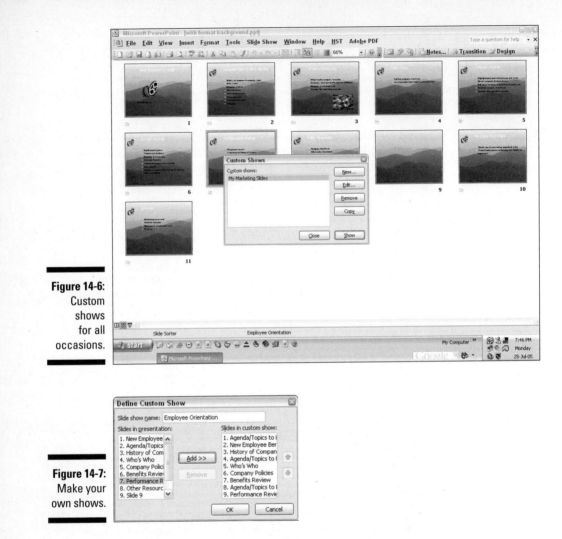

**Figure 14-6:**
Custom
shows
for all
occasions.

**Figure 14-7:**
Make your
own shows.

5. **Click OK to create the custom show or click Cancel to exit without changes.**

   This brings you back to the Custom Shows dialog box. If you have already created some custom shows, you'll find them all listed here.

   To view any of the custom shows, just select them in the list and click the Show button. You'll also find buttons that Remove, Edit, and Copy the custom shows.

   If you want one of your custom shows to run as the default presentation, just change the settings in the Set Up Show dialog box, accessed through the Slide Show⇨Set Up Show option. I discuss this in more detail earlier in this chapter.

You might change the default show to one of your custom shows and forget all about it. And you know what happens when you play that presentation six months later — you end up with an audience that isn't too amused. Go and change the settings in Slide Show⇨Set Up Show and breathe a sigh of relief! Even better, link to your custom shows rather than setting them as default shows — I show you how to do that next.

## Linking to custom shows

If you want an easier way to access your custom shows, follow these steps to create a link slide in your presentation:

1. **Create your custom shows as required by following the steps in the preceding section.**

   Test them all and give them nice, descriptive names.

2. **Choose Insert⇨New Slide to add a new slide in your presentation.**

   Change your slide layout if required by choosing Format⇨Slide Layout.

3. **Add anchors for links to custom shows.**

   These anchors could be any PowerPoint object, such as text boxes, AutoShapes (including Action Buttons), and pictures. Figure 14-8 shows a sample link slide I created.

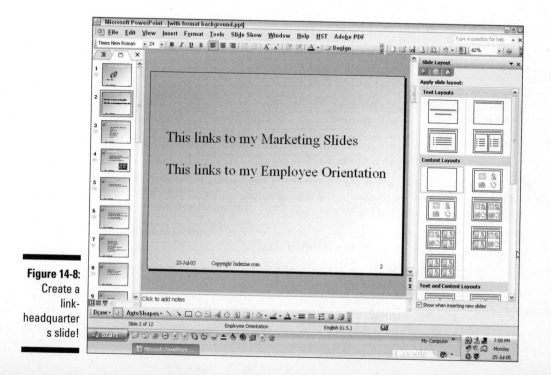

**Figure 14-8:** Create a link-headquarters slide!

4. **Select one of the anchors and choose Slide Show⇨Action Settings to bring up the Action Settings dialog box shown in Figure 14-9.**

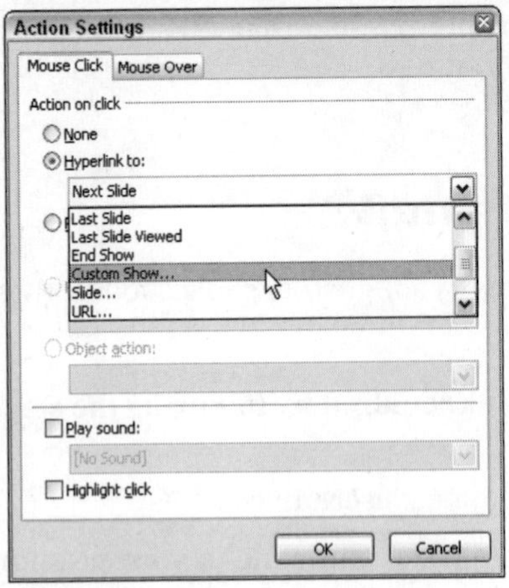

**Figure 14-9:**
Action
settings link
to custom
shows!

5. **In the Hyperlink To drop-down list box, choose the Custom Show option to summon the Link To Custom Show dialog box, revealed in Figure 14-10.**

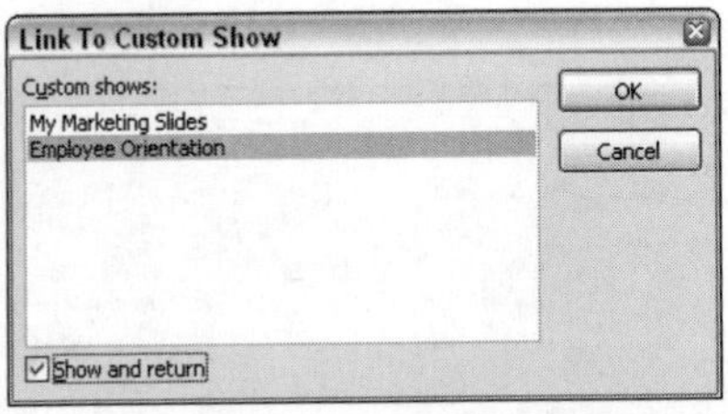

**Figure 14-10:**
Choose your
custom
show.

6. **All your custom shows are listed here — just select the one you want to link to and click OK.**

   If no custom shows are listed here, that means you haven't created any custom shows in the presentation — trek back to earlier in this chapter to discover how you can create custom shows.

   The Show and Return option lets you return to the link slide after the custom show has finished playing.

   Click OK in the Action Settings dialog box to get back to your presentation.

In today's world, it's perfectly acceptable to be paranoid and safe — so just go ahead and password protect your presentation.

This feature is supported only in PowerPoint 2002 and 2003. It is also not supported by Mac versions of PowerPoint.

Follow these steps to password protect your presentations:

1. **Choose Tools⇨Options to bring up the Options dialog box, shown in Figure 14-11, and then click the Security tab.**

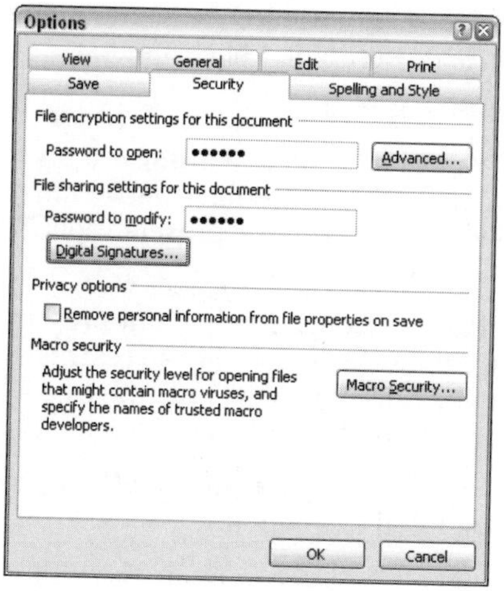

**Figure 14-11:**
Enter the
security
zone.

2. **You can set two different passwords here:**

   • *Password to Open* requires others to use a password to open and view your presentation.

   • *Password to Modify* requires a password to edit your presentation.

   You can enter both types of password for the same presentation; they're intended for different access permissions.

   You can also enter a password just for Modify and leave out the password for Open. This allows anyone to see your presentation, but nobody can do any edits.

   If your password options are grayed out on the Security tab, that means you have disabled new features on the Edit tab of the same dialog box.

3. **Click OK to apply the changes or click Cancel to dismiss the dialog box.**

If recipients of your password-protected presentation are using a version of PowerPoint that is older than PowerPoint 2002, they will be unable to open it, even if they know the password. They will see an error message that offers no explanation about the problem because older versions don't know what a password is! For the same reason, Mac versions of PowerPoint can't open password-protected presentations.

## More password options

The following options are for you if you don't have PowerPoint 2002 or 2003, or if you need to distribute your presentations to others who don't use these versions. Here are the options:

- PowerPoint MVP Shyam Pillai has created SecurePack, a product that converts any PowerPoint presentation to a password-protected EXE file — end users, however, need PowerPoint installed on their systems. This option leaves out Mac users of PowerPoint. Check it out at

  `www.cuttingedgeppt.com/securepack`

- You can zip up a PowerPoint presentation and password protect the zip archive. This, however, provides full edit permissions to anyone who can provide the unzip password and view the presentation. This solution works for both Windows and Mac users.

- You can create an Acrobat PDF file from a PowerPoint presentation. If you have the full version of Adobe Acrobat, you can restrict editing and printing of the PDF. Recipients, however, need only the free Acrobat Reader. Discover more information about PDFs in Chapter 13.

- Convert your presentation to rich media by using an Online Rich Media (ORM) product. ORM is covered in Chapter 15.

# PowerPoint Printing

Many PowerPoint presentations never travel the distance from the screen to the printer. But many other presentations make that trip and get their impressions marked on papyrus.

Whichever journey your presentation is destined to make, you can't deny that printing PowerPoint slides involves a hundred nuances — from color, black and white, and grayscale to handouts, slides, and outlines. If all those terms make you dizzy, rejoice in the fact that the following paragraphs present no new riddles, only solutions.

The headquarters of PowerPoint's print abilities is the multifaceted Print dialog box, shown in all its glory in Figure 14-12.

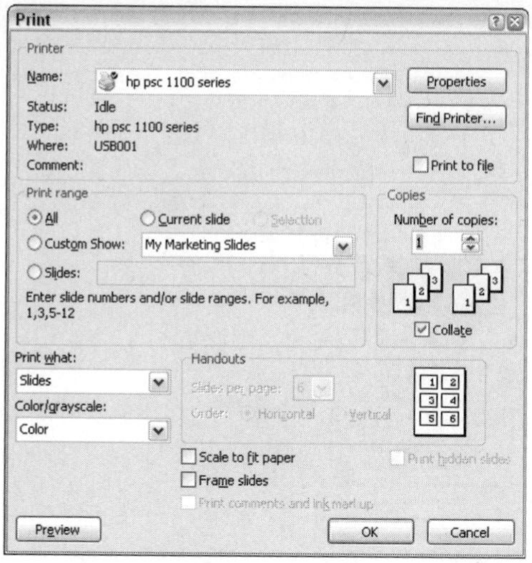

**Figure 14-12:**
The friendly
Print dialog
box.

Follow these steps to access and use the print options:

1. **If you made any last-minute edits, save your presentation so that all changes are committed.**

2. **Choose File⇨Print to bring up the Print dialog box (see Figure 14-12).**

3. **Change settings as required.**

   For more information on these settings, check out the next section in this chapter.

4. **Click Preview to bring up the Print Preview window, shown in Figure 14-13, and see how your presentation will look in its printed incarnation.**

   You need to have a local printer installed for the Print Preview function to work — head to Chapter 2 for more on this option.

5. **Click Print to get back to the Print dialog box.**

6. **Change settings again as required. When you're done, click OK to send the print command to the chosen printer.**

   You can also click Cancel to dismiss the dialog box and go back to the presentation without printing.

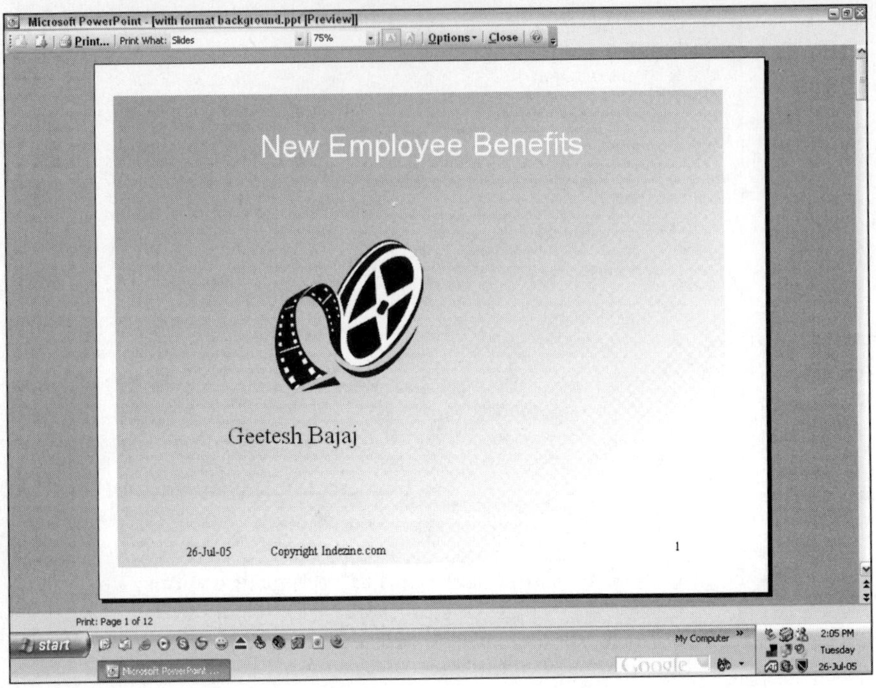

**Figure 14-13:**
The Print
Preview
mode.

## All the print stuff

Here's a rundown of all the printing options in the Print dialog box:

✔ **Printer:** The Printer Name drop-down list lets you choose from a list of physical and virtual printers installed on your system.

- *Physical printers* include normal inkjets, laser printers, and printing devices that are connected to your computer (or network).

- *Virtual printers* are actually printer drivers that output to file formats rather than to paper. Examples include Adobe PDF, Microsoft Office Document Image Writer, and the TechSmith SnagIt printer driver.

Whichever printer you choose, make sure that you click the Properties button next to the printer drop-down list. This presents you with options specific to your printer.

✔ **Print Range:** Choose All Slides or Current Slide, or type the slide numbers you want to print in the Slides box.

You can also choose to print all slides contained in a custom show — remember, if the Custom Show option is grayed out, that's because there are no custom shows in the presentation.

You also see a Selection option. This option is grayed out unless you select one or more slides in the Slide Sorter view (View⇨Slide Sorter) before clicking the Print option. The Selection option prints only the selected slides.

✔ **Copies:** Enter the number of copies you want to print in the Number of Copies text box or use the up and down arrows to select a number. Select the Collate check box if you want to collate your copies.

✔ **Print What:** This lets you choose from Slides, Handouts, Notes Pages, and Outline View. If you choose Handouts, you'll find even more options for the number of slides you want printed on each handout page. Handouts are covered in more detail later in this chapter.

✔ **Color/Grayscale:** This lets you choose between color, grayscale, and pure black and white.

Depending on your version of PowerPoint, the default color mode might be either color or grayscale — make sure you make the changes to the color mode before you print. Even better, print a test page to see which mode works best for you.

✔ **Include Animations** (only in PowerPoint 2000): This lets you print how the slide will look after each custom animation — thus a slide with three animations will print as four slides (three for animations and one for the pre-animated stage).

## Printing perils

Everyone has a few questions about printing — and here are workarounds for the most frequent printing perils:

### My slide backgrounds don't print!

Unless you print in color, most slides with photographic backgrounds print without any background.

This might be a blessing in disguise because you'll end up saving buckets of ink and toner. However, you might want to control what prints and what doesn't (and stop worrying about ink and toner for now!).

To overcome this problem, follow these guidelines:

✔ Make sure that your picture backgrounds are inserted through the Insert⇨Picture⇨From File option rather than the Format⇨Background option.

✔ After you insert the picture, resize it to fill the slide area. Also, right-click the inserted picture and choose Order⇨Send to Back from the context menu.

### Print proofs for free!

Depending on whether you're printing to an inkjet or laser printer, you might end up wasting tons of ink or toner if you don't create proofs before printing a hundred copies of hundred-slide presentations. If you do create a proof, one mistake might send a hundred sheets of paper to the waste bin, rather than a thousand.

If you love to save trees and protect the environment, print your slides to a PDF first. This gives you an accurate impression of how your slides will look when printed on paper.

If you don't have a full version of Adobe's Acrobat software to create the PDFs, you can still find several free and low-priced PDF-creation programs — a quick Google search will provide some options.

### Printing animations

With PowerPoint 2002 and 2003, Microsoft removed the ability to print your slides in different stages of animation. This was primarily because the new animation engine was so advanced, with the new motion paths and trigger animations, that most users would end up with flipbooks rather than three or four stages per slide if the ability to print animations was retained!

However, there's still hope. Shyam Pillai's free PowerPoint add-in, *Capture Show,* lets you print animated stages of a slide from PowerPoint 2002 and 2003. In addition, it can also output slide builds as images to a specified folder.

```
www.cuttingedgeppt.com/captureshow
```

### Printing for prepress

Are you asked to create posters from your PowerPoint slides? Do you need to send high-resolution slide images to a prepress agency?

If you need to output something suitable for prepress usage, PowerPoint probably isn't the right tool for the job.

But that's something your boss doesn't know much about, and there's no way he or she will understand this — all the praise you garnered for the wonderful pie chart you created has landed you in a situation that needs you to send a 300 dpi, poster-size image to the design agency!

To find out more about dpi and resolution, check out Chapter 8.

I could tell you about increasing the resolution output and other tedious image manipulations, but I normally just use a PowerPoint add-in from Steve Rindsberg called PPTools Image Exporter. You can download a demo version from this site:

www.cuttingedgeppt.com/imageexporter

Handouts are normally sent for review to those who matter before an actual presentation is shown to an audience. They can also be provided as takeaways after the presentation.

Normally, these sheets have thumbnails of slides, and the slide layouts can be customized to suit specific requirements. Figure 14-14 shows you a sample handout.

Depending on which version of PowerPoint you're using, you can include 1, 2, 3, 4, 6, or 9 slide thumbnails per handout page. Some layouts, such as the one for 3 thumbnails, also provide some space next to the thumbnail for notes.

## The Handout Master

Most of the layout options in handouts are directly influenced by the Handout Master. Thus, if you position any logo in the Handout Master, you can be reasonably sure that all handouts printed from that particular presentation will contain the logo.

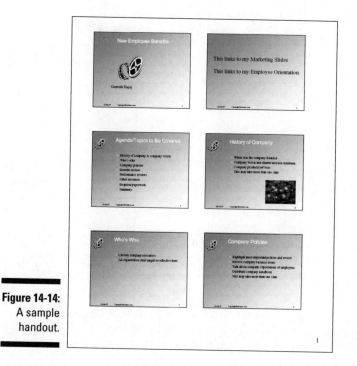

**Figure 14-14:**
A sample
handout.

Unlike slides, Handouts are almost always intended for print, so it might be a good idea to edit the Handout Master based on that assumption. You need to be sure to use content that prints well to both black-and-white and colored output.

Follow these steps to edit the Handout Master:

1. **Choose View➪Master➪Handout Master to get to the Handout Master View, shown in Figure 14-15.**

2. **Edit the four regions of the Handout Master.**

   These four regions are the header, footer, number, and date. You can edit all four of these regions as required, and because all edits are being done on the Handout Master, you will be able to see results in every printed handout.

3. **If you're printing color handouts, you can change the Handout background from the default white.**

   To change the background, choose Format➪Handout Background. This brings up the Handout Background dialog box, which works just like the Format Background dialog box. To find out more, refer to Chapter 4.

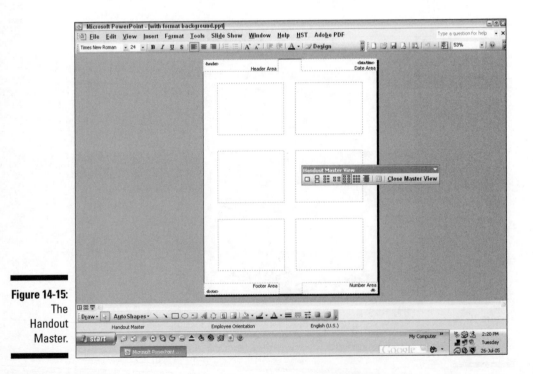

**Figure 14-15:** The Handout Master.

4. **Insert a logo or any other element that you want to be visible in all the handouts.**

   A logo with a light variation that blends well with the background works best because you don't want the recipients to focus more on the background than on the slide thumbnails themselves.

5. **When you're done, choose View⇨Normal to get back to Normal view.**

Printing handouts works in the same way as printing anything else in PowerPoint — refer to the section "PowerPoint Printing" for more information.

# Part V
# The Part of Tens

The 5th Wave          By Rich Tennant

"We need to pimp our storage system."

# In this part . . .

I've been reading the For Dummies books for a decade, and I always read this part first. May you enjoy these tips as much as I enjoyed compiling them for you!

# Chapter 15

# My Ten Favorite PowerPoint Tips

## In This Chapter

▶ Creating PowerPoint presentations in Notepad?

▶ Putting your picture in a star

▶ Creating timelines in PowerPoint

▶ Creating *Star Wars*–style credits

▶ Counting down

▶ Maximizing your presentations with other software

*T*his chapter is all about my favorite PowerPoint tips. I decided to include tips that are quick and easy so that you can get almost instant results.

I start with teaching you to create PowerPoint presentations without PowerPoint! Then, you learn to put a picture inside a star or any other shape. I also teach you how you can use PowerPoint's shapes to create a quick time-line that can be used for projects as diverse as product development and history homework. I then move on to helping you add pizzazz to your presentation titles in a *Star Wars*–style moving, fading crawl.

There's more — learn to create a countdown timer and add readymade frames to your pictures. And finish the chapter with a discussion on PowerPoint's glue-like abilities.

## Create a Presentation in Notepad

You really can create a PowerPoint presentation in Notepad! That statement renders so many people speechless, but the technique really isn't all that difficult:

1. **Choose Start➪(All) Programs➪Accessories➪Notepad to fire up the Notepad application.**

2. **Type some text — this might help you get started:**

   ```
   Indezine for PowerPoint
   Why, How and Everything Else
   The PowerPoint Blog
   What's New
   PowerPoint Tips
   Fresh Template Designs
   More Stuff
   PowerPoint Ezine
   Sample Presentations
   Interviews
   ```

   If you would rather not type all this stuff, just open the sample text file, `notepad.txt`, that I have included on the CD.

3. **Choose File➪Save to open the Save As dialog box.**

4. **Save the file with a `.ppt` extension by typing "notepad.ppt" in the File Name text box. (Make sure you type in everything, including the quotation marks.)**

   If you don't include the `.ppt` extension on the filename, Notepad saves the file with a `.txt` extension by default.

   If you forget to add the `.ppt` extension when you save your file, don't despair. Just right-click the file to open a contextual menu. Choose the Rename option and change the extension from `.txt` to `.ppt`. Windows pops up the dialog box shown in Figure 15-1, warning you that the file may become unusable. Click Yes to disregard the warning.

**Figure 15-1:** Disregard this warning and have your way!

| Rename | |
| --- | --- |
| ⚠ | If you change a file name extension, the file may become unusable. Are you sure you want to change it? |
| | [ Yes ]   [ No ] |

5. **Double-click the PPT file, and you'll find that each line in that file is now the title of a new slide.**

   But slide titles don't a presentation make. You add bullets next.

6. **Choose Start➪(All) Programs➪Accessories➪Notepad to fire up the Notepad application again.**

   Choose File➪Open to access the Open dialog box and make sure you select All Files from the Files of Type drop-down list box. Navigate to wherever you saved `notepad.ppt`, and double-click it to open the file.

7. **Add tabs wherever you need bulleted text. For instance, your text might now look like this:**

```
Indezine for PowerPoint
    Why, How and Everything Else
The PowerPoint Blog
    What's New
    PowerPoint Tips
    Fresh Template Designs
More Stuff
    PowerPoint Ezine
    Sample Presentations
    Interviews
```

8. **Save this again.**

9. **Double-click the file to open it in PowerPoint.**

   Every tabbed line becomes a bullet! You can see how this looks in Figure 15-2.

**Figure 15-2:**
Tabs
become
bullets!

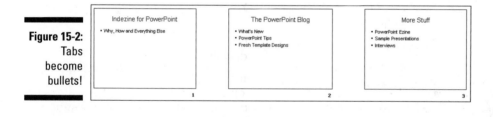

So what happens when you want a sub-bullet of a bullet? That's easy — just press Tab twice at the beginning of a line to create a second-level bullet. Similarly, press Tab three times to create a third-level bullet . . . you get the idea!

You can create presentations with only text like titles and bullets with this technique — no images, sound, or video can be added with this process.

This is a great way to create an outline of a presentation when you have some free time — most PDAs and even mobile phones nowadays allow you to create text files. The next time you're waiting for a doctor's appointment or to catch a plane, you could create the skeleton of your next presentation!

Such presentations normally end up as black text on white slides — you can instantly make over a presentation created this way by applying a template.

Templates are covered in Chapter 4, and you'll find tons of free templates on the companion CD.

# Picture in a Star

Imagine a rectangle on the slide — now imagine that this rectangle is actually a picture. Now, what's so imaginative about a picture that's a rectangle? Almost all pictures are rectangles, but they don't have to be! You just have to use a little imagination.

You can use any AutoShape as a container for a picture. The following steps show you how to put your image in a star, but you can use any of the AutoShapes available.

For the skinny on AutoShapes, refer to Chapter 5.

1. **If your Drawing toolbar isn't visible, choose View➪Toolbars➪Drawing.**

2. **In the Drawing toolbar, click the AutoShapes menu and open the Stars & Banners category.**

3. **Select any of the star types.**

   The 5-Point Star works best for this technique, but you can choose any AutoShape.

4. **Draw the AutoShape on the slide.**

5. **Select the AutoShape and choose Format➪AutoShape to open the Format AutoShape dialog box.**

6. **In the Format AutoShape dialog box, click the downward-pointing arrow next to Color and choose Fill Effects.**

   The Fill Effects dialog box appears.

7. **In the Fill Effects dialog box, click the Picture tab.**

8. **Click the Select Picture button and navigate to and select your picture on your hard drive.**

9. **Click OK twice to get back to your slide.**

   Figure 15-3 shows how your picture might look within the star.

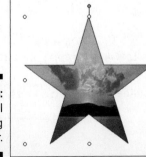

**Figure 15-3:**
A beautiful evening star.

Follow these ideas to do more with this technique:

✔ Even after you contain the picture in a star, you can change the star shape to something else. To change the shape, select the star and choose Draw⇨Change AutoShape from the Drawing toolbar and select the new AutoShape.

✔ If you need to draw a set of similar picture-filled AutoShapes, create the first one and then duplicate it any number of times. Thereafter, edit (resize) the duplicated shapes as required.

✔ In PowerPoint 2002 and 2003, picture fills in AutoShapes can be transparent, too — you can fill an AutoShape with a picture and apply a transparent value from 0 to 100 percent in the Colors and Lines tab of the Format AutoShape dialog box.

✔ Play with shadows to add more impact to picture-filled AutoShapes. The Shadow Style icon can be found in the Drawing toolbar.

✔ Use a slide with a dark blue background and draw a hundred stars on the slide. Fill them all with a blue-white picture fill. Then, set the stars to animate one after the other. Animation is covered in Chapter 11. This makes a great intermission slide.

You'll find a sample presentation (`starfield.ppt`) with the starry sky on the companion CD!

# Creating a Sequential Timeline

Although PowerPoint's AutoShapes can be combined to make effective visuals, they tend to look very uninspiring without the proper fills and animations. In this section, I show you how you can create a timeline using AutoShapes. To add pizzazz to the visual, I then add gradient fills to all the shapes.

To see the finished timeline, open the sample presentation (`timeline.ppt`) on the CD. You can also see the timeline on Color Plate 16-1.

The presentation was created for a fictitious pharmaceutical company that's working on a new, fictitious drug. In the presentation, you find three slides:

✔ The first slide shows you how the timeline has been constructed.

✔ The second slide is merely the first slide with gradient fills applied, as shown in Figure 16-4.

✔ The third slide is again the same timeline but with an animation build applied.

Animation is covered in Chapter 11.

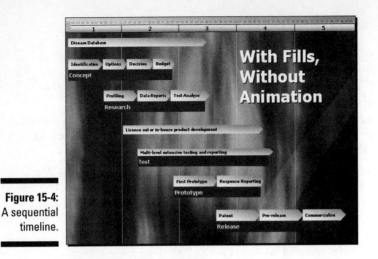

**Figure 15-4:**
A sequential
timeline.

# Before you begin

Sequential timelines are perfect for representing

- ✔ Product development
- ✔ History timelines
- ✔ Legal processes

A product development timeline typically illustrates the stage progression of a product from idea to release — with all types of research, tests, and proto-types represented in between. Using PowerPoint's AutoShapes, you can represent most of the tasks involved:

- ✔ Concept
- ✔ Research
- ✔ Licensing
- ✔ Testing
- ✔ Prototype
- ✔ Release

# Creating the timeline

Follow these steps to create your own timeline on a slide:

1. **Draw a small rectangle and then resize it so that it that covers the top part of your slide to create a time bar (see Figure 15-5).**

   Draw several small rectangles in a row below the top strip that span the slide from edge to edge, as shown in Figure 15-5, to create a time divider.

   Timelines need a way to represent time. This can be done by creating the time bar and time divider on the top portion of the slide.

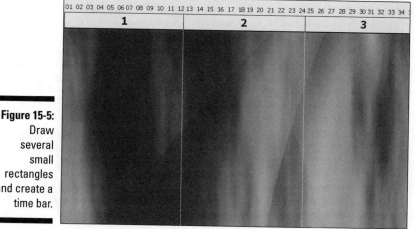

**Figure 15-5:**
Draw several small rectangles and create a time bar.

2. **Put numbers in the rectangles to represent a period of time. Add fills as required to the rectangles.**

3. **Position all the rectangles in a row and select them.**

4. **Choose Draw⇨Group in the Drawing toolbar to group them all.**

   Now you have to draw AutoShapes that represent the actual tasks within the timeline.

5. **In the Drawing toolbar, choose AutoShapes⇨Block Arrows, select the Pentagon shape, and draw one of them on the slide.**

6. **Resize the pentagon as required and drag the yellow diamond handle on the pentagon to taper the edge of the arrow.**

7. **Copy the pentagon and paste multiple times to duplicate the AutoShape. Position and resize all pentagons as required, as shown in Figure 15-6.**

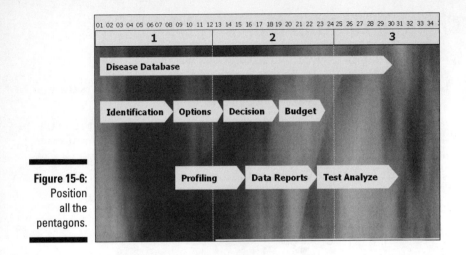

Figure 15-6:
Position
all the
pentagons.

8. **To add text within a pentagon, right-click one and choose Add Text. Then just type the text.**

   After you add the text, some of the pentagons may require some resizing. Scale them width-wise (never height-wise).

9. **Because all pentagons have been placed in clusters, you might want to identify each cluster of tasks. Draw a long, thin rectangle below a cluster of tasks and add text as required, as shown in Figure 15-7.**

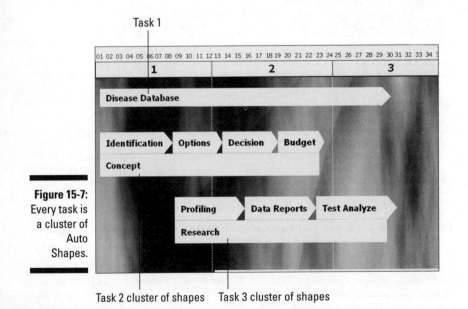

Figure 15-7:
Every task is
a cluster of
Auto
Shapes.

10. **At this point, you might want to arrange all your AutoShapes to achieve the relative position under the time bar. Your timeline will now look similar to what you see in Color Plate 16-1.**

If you followed the entire step-by-step procedure, you just created a product development timeline. The best part is that you aren't restricted to creating such timelines for product development alone — feel free to adapt it for your situation. Examples of use include historical timelines, progressive project status, event planning, training, and any other concept that evolves within a timeline frame.

## Design guidelines

Follow these guidelines to make your timelines travel that extra mile:

- ✔ Tasks can often be repetitive and overlapping with other tasks. Your timeline design has to accommodate such requirements.

- ✔ Because the timeline visual often takes an entire slide, use a clean background. Abstract backgrounds also work very well.

- ✔ Leave out the details. Just mention the tasks along with a representative period to show their duration.

- ✔ If you need to add more detail, create an individual slide for each task and link it from the main timeline slide. Linking is discussed in Chapter 12.

# Star Wars Credits

In PowerPoint 2002 and 2003, you can create a *Star Wars*–style credit screen, with your text moving up against a starry background and then tapering and fading into oblivion.

This technique works only in PowerPoint 2002 and 2003 because it uses the new animation options available in these more recent versions of PowerPoint.

The CD includes a single-slide PowerPoint presentation (starwarsempty.ppt) with a starry slide background that you can use for this presentation. I also included a finished presentation (starwarsstylecredits.ppt) based on this tutorial so that you can see how it looks.

## *Creating the credits*

Follow these steps to create your own *Star Wars*–style credits in PowerPoint 2002 or 2003:

1. **Open the `starwarsempty.ppt` single-slide presentation from the CD that contains the starry background.**

2. **Choose Insert➪New Slide to insert a new slide.**

3. **Choose Format➪Slide Layout to activate the Slide Layout task pane, as shown in Figure 15-8. Then choose the Blank layout option within the Content Layouts category so that you end up with a slide with no text placeholders.**

4. **If your Drawing toolbar isn't visible, choose View➪Toolbars➪Drawing.**

5. **In the Drawing toolbar, select the text box icon and click anywhere on the slide to place a text box.**

6. **Type a single- or two-line credit text in the text box.**

   For example, I typed this:

   ```
   Concept And Creation
   Geetesh Bajaj
   ```

7. **If your text isn't center justified, choose Format➪Alignment➪Center while the text box is still selected.**

   Also, you can change the color of your text, make the text bold, and increase the size of the font.

8. **To start adding the animation, move the text box to the bottom center of the slide.**

9. **Choose Slide Show⇨Custom Animation to activate the Custom Animation task pane.**

10. **In the task pane, click the Add Effect button and choose Motion Paths to open a flyout menu. In this flyout menu, choose the Up option.**

   If the Up option isn't available, choose the More Motion Paths option to open the Add Motion Path dialog box. Now choose the Up option within the Lines & Curves section and click OK.

11. **Change your settings for the Motion Path within the Custom Animation task pane to match these, as shown in Figure 15-9:**

   • **Start:** After Previous

   • **Path:** Unlocked

   • **Speed:** Slow

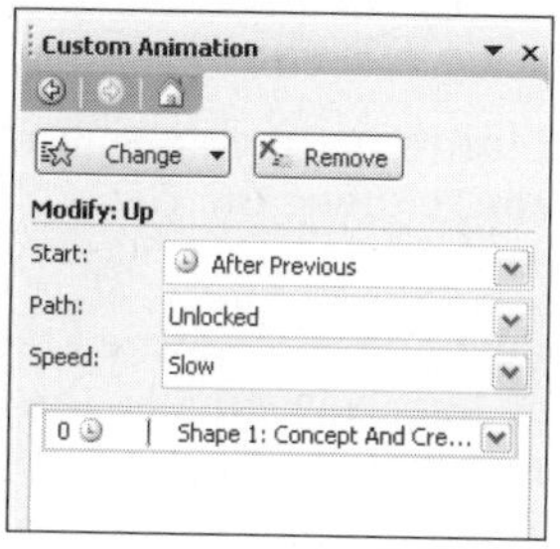

Figure 15-9: Match these custom animation settings.

With your text box and the motion path still selected on the slide, you will see green-arrow (play) and red-arrow (play until) indicators on either side of the motion path, as shown in Figure 15-10.

12. **Click the red arrow to select the path.**

   If you see two white handles on either side of the motion path, you know that the path is selected.

13. **Drag and pull the white handle on the peak of the path (above the red arrow) to the top of the slide to extend the motion path to the entire height of the slide.**

   If you hold the Shift key while pulling the white handle, you'll ensure that your path is extended in a straight line.

14. **Drag the bottom of the path by pulling the bottom white handle somewhere close to the bottom of your slide.**

   You might want to preview the animation to fine-tune it by clicking the Play button on the Custom animation task pane.

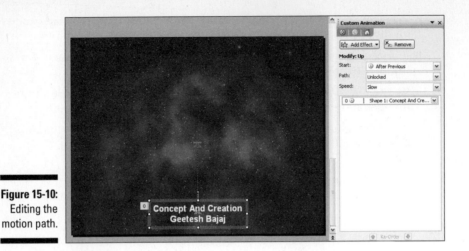

Custom Animation

Add Effect ▼   Remove

Modify: Up
Start:    After Previous
Path:     Unlocked
Speed:    Slow

0   Shape 1: Concept And Cre...

Re-Order

Concept And Creation
Geetesh Bajaj

**Figure 15-10:**
Editing the
motion path.

15. **With the text box still selected, add another animation by choosing Slide Show⇨Custom Animation to activate the Custom Animation task pane.**

16. **In the task pane, click the Add Effect button and choose Emphasis to open a flyout menu. In this flyout menu, choose the Grow/Shrink option.**

    If the Grow/Shrink option isn't available, choose the More Effects option to open the Add Emphasis Effect dialog box. Now choose the Grow/Shrink option within the Basic section and click OK.

17. **Change the animation settings.**

    Match your settings for the Grow/Shrink options with these in the Custom Animation task pane:

    - **Start:** With Previous

    - **Size:** Smaller (50%)

    - **Speed:** Slow

    Preview and fine-tune as required.

    At this point, this is what you've done:

    - The first motion path animation moved the text from the bottom of the slide to the top.

    - The second emphasis animation reduced the size of the text as it moved from bottom to top.

    Now, you need to ensure that the text fades into oblivion as it exits from the slide. This means we need to add a third animation to the same text box.

18. **With the text box still selected, choose Slide Show⇨Custom Animation to activate the Custom Animation task pane.**

19. **In the task pane, click the Add Effect button and choose Exit to open a flyout menu. In this flyout menu, choose the Fade option.**

    If the Fade option isn't available, choose the More Effects option to open the Add Exit Effect dialog box. Now choose the Fade option within the Subtle category and click OK.

20. **Fine-tune the Fade settings.**

    Match your settings for the Fade options with these in the Custom Animation task pane:

    • **Start:** With Previous

    • **Speed:** Slow

    Because all three animations happen simultaneously, you choose the Slow speed option for all three. If you want to choose a different speed (such as Very Slow), you need to change the speed of all three animation types — the Motion Path, the Emphasis, and the Exit.

21. **Drag the text box off the bottom of the slide.**

    Select the text box and keep pressing the bottom arrow key on your keyboard until the text box is just outside the slide area.

    Preview and fine-tune again. You might want to extend (drag and pull the top handle of) the motion path upward to compensate for the added downward distance of the text box.

22. **Duplicate the text box by copying and pasting — change the text credits as required and place the text box immediately over the earlier text box.**

    Repeat to create as many text boxes as required. Because all the text boxes overlap each other, it might be a little difficult to edit the text within them later. Use the Tab key to select each of these text boxes one at a time so that you don't make inadvertent changes to a text box.

23. **Preview your slide by clicking the Play button on the Custom Animation task pane, and save your slide.**

    You might want to check the sample presentation on the CD to check the settings I've used or to compare the presentations.

You just duplicated an animated text box within the same slide. You can carry this concept forward and duplicate text boxes across slides and even across presentations, thus making short work of an otherwise tedious job.

Experiment with adding a *Star Wars*–style soundtrack to the credits slide — you can search the Internet for a *Star Wars* theme sound in WAV or MP3 format. Whatever you do, make sure you respect copyrights.

# Countdown Timer

Creating a countdown timer in PowerPoint is so much fun — and countdown slides can be used to add impact to an announcement in an upcoming slide or just to give you another way to start a presentation.

Follow these steps to create your own countdown timer:

1. **Choose Insert⇨New Slide to add a new slide to a new or existing presentation.**

2. **Choose Format⇨Slide Layout to activate the Slide Layout task pane.**

3. **Choose the Blank layout option within the Content Layouts category so that you end up with a slide with no text placeholders (refer to Figure 15-8).**

4. **If your Drawing toolbar isn't visible, choose View⇨Toolbars⇨Drawing.**

5. **In the Drawing toolbar, select the text box icon and click anywhere on the slide to place a text box.**

6. **Type the number 1 or 01 or 001 depending on how many digits you want your counter to display, as shown in Figure 15-11.**

7. **With the text box still selected, choose Format⇨Alignment⇨Center to center align the text.**

8. **Change the font size to something large, like 200, and resize the text box so that all digits are placed and visible on the same line.**

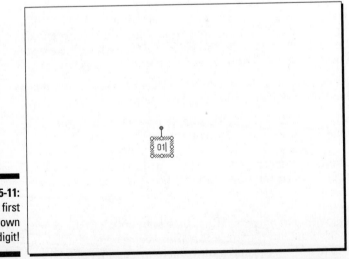

**Figure 15-11:**
Your first
countdown
digit!

9. **Change your font style as required and position the text box right in the center of the slide.**

10. **Choose Slide Show➪Slide Transition.**

    This activates the Slide Transition task pane in PowerPoint 2002 and 2003, or the Transition dialog box in PowerPoint 2000.

11. **Choose a simple transition.**

    For this example, I chose the Box Out transition effect. You can also choose the No Transition option if you prefer. I've also set the Speed to Fast and opted to automatically advance the slide after 10 seconds. You might want to choose a shorter or longer time delay for the transition.

    You can find out more about transitions in Chapter 11.

12. **Choose View➪Slide Sorter and click the formatted timer slide to select the slide.**

13. **Choose Edit➪Copy. Then choose Edit➪Paste to paste an identical slide.**

    Keep pasting that slide until you end up with the number of slides you want your countdown to contain. At this point, your Slide Sorter View might look like Figure 15-12.

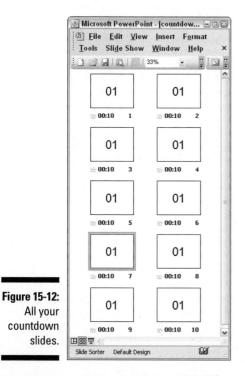

**Figure 15-12:**
All your
countdown
slides.

14. **Within each of the slides, change the countdown number in reverse order so that the last slide contains the number 1.**

Because my example presentation contains ten slides, it looks like Figure 15-13 after the number values have been edited.

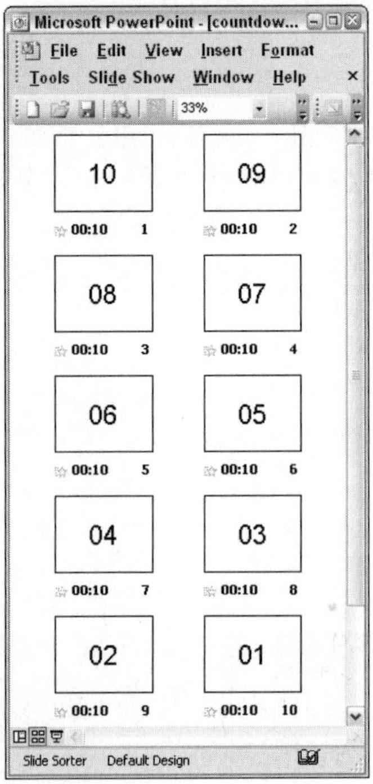

**Figure 15-13:** The slides in sequence.

15. **Choose View⇨Slide Show to run the presentation and see the countdown.**

A sample presentation with a countdown timer (`countdown.ppt`) can be found on the CD.

## Design guidelines

If you just finished creating your own countdown timer, you might want to experiment with slide backgrounds, transitions, animations, font color, and style to create a unique look. You might even want to experiment with calculator style digits (search online for a calculator font) or include seconds within the slides (for example 01:00).

Also consider adding some text, such as "minutes/seconds remaining," to each countdown slide.

# PowerPoint Is the Glue!

Here's my favorite PowerPoint tip — and this doesn't even include a tutorial!

Think of PowerPoint as the glue that binds all elements together — these elements often include pictures, sounds, movies, charts, diagrams, and more.

Many times, you'll find PowerPoint's editing options for these elements adequate. But if you're serious about creating cutting-edge PowerPoint presentations, you'll soon realize that you want that out-of-the-ordinary look that sets your style apart from what everyone else is doing.

To attain this objective, you'll want to create your own presentation paraphernalia box that contains much more than just PowerPoint. At the very basic level, you'll want image- and sound-editing applications.

## Image editor

At the very least, consider buying an image editor. In fact, all images you insert in PowerPoint should first be cleaned up and edited in an image-editing application like Adobe Photoshop. I know that's an expensive program, but Adobe also creates a cut-down version called Photoshop Elements that contains a surprisingly large amount of Photoshop's capabilities.

There are other alternatives, too, including Microsoft's Digital Image Pro and Corel's Paint Shop Pro.

## Sound editor

If you often need to add sound to your presentations, your choice of a sound-editing program depends upon how you will use the sounds:

  ✔ If you need musical background scores for presentations, you can get one of the sound libraries created for use with PowerPoint. These include CrystalGraphics' PowerPlugs: Music and Indigo Rose's Liquid Cabaret collection.

✔ If you would rather create all the music on your own, look at something like Sony's ACID program. This lets you create music scores using sound loops and is surprisingly easy to use. You could end up creating your first background score within an hour.

✔ If all you need to do is polish your narrations and remove some hiss or noise artifacts, look at Bias SoundSoap — this is an intuitive application that intelligently cleans up your narrations. A more capable Pro version is also available.

✔ If you need more advanced sound editing, use high-end professional programs like Adobe Audition or Sony Sound Forge.

# Chapter 16

# Ten PowerPoint Problems

*L*et me just start by saying that PowerPoint has no problems at all. All those linking problems and the presentation perils are just figments of an overworked imagination. And that red X that sits where your favorite image is supposed to be is just a bad dream — pinch yourself and it will go away.

It's also so easy to send a PowerPoint slide to prepress. What's Section 508 anyway? And certainly nobody needs to know about more PowerPoint resources after reading this book!

Well, the opening paragraphs were wishful thinking. Now let me welcome you to the real world, where problems happen. Fortunately, many problems have solutions and workarounds that make things simpler for you. That's precisely the reason for this chapter!

In this chapter, I show you how you can avoid getting a red X on your slide and how you could possibly recover corrupt presentations. I offer hard-to-come-by information on overcoming sound and video issues in PowerPoint and help if you cannot locate PowerPoint on the computer! And yes, the chapter ends with a listing of must-see PowerPoint resource sites.

# Where Is PowerPoint?

Yes, you read that right! This question has been asked so many times before that I knew it had to be the first thing in this chapter!

If you can't find PowerPoint, here's where you should start looking:

- ✔ Just because you have Microsoft Office installed doesn't mean you have PowerPoint as well. Several editions of Office do not include PowerPoint. These include the Small Business Editions of Office 2000 and 2002(XP) — the Small Business Edition of Office 2003, however, does include PowerPoint. But the Office 2003 Basic Edition, which is bundled by several OEMs (Original Equipment Manufacturers), does *not* include PowerPoint.

  Yes, you can upgrade by adding PowerPoint to a version of Office that does not include it, but you need to make sure that you have a qualifying product for the upgrade to a new version of PowerPoint. More information can be found at:

  ```
  www.cuttingedgeppt.com/ppupgrade
  ```

- ✔ Maybe you have PowerPoint installed, but the shortcut that used to launch the program got deleted. To find out if you really have PowerPoint, follow these steps:

  1. **Choose Start⇨Run.**

     This will bring up the Run dialog box.

  2. **Type** powerpnt.exe **in this dialog box and click OK.**

     If you have PowerPoint installed, the program's splash screen will appear. If that doesn't happen, Windows might complain that it can't find powerpnt.exe, which means you don't have PowerPoint.

- ✔ If you're using a computer at work, you might want to ask your system administrator whether PowerPoint is installed.

# Linking Problems

Nothing is as frustrating as PowerPoint refusing to find that linked narration or video, especially if this debacle happens in full view of an audience.

You can avoid link problems altogether by doing some housekeeping. If you still run into link problems, I also show you how to restore links.

## The housekeeping part

The secret is to stop thinking of your presentations as mere .ppt files. Instead, start thinking of them as folders. The minute you need to create a new presentation, just follow these steps:

1. **Start by creating an empty folder.**

2. **Create a single-slide presentation and save it within this folder.**

3. **Copy all the sounds and videos you want to insert in the presentation to this folder.**

   Copy all the other documents you want to hyperlink from the presentation, such as other PowerPoint presentations, Word and PDF documents, and Excel spreadsheets.

4. **After you finish copying these files into the same folder as the presentation, create your presentation and start inserting or linking them within the presentation.**

5. **If you want to link another sound, video, or document, copy it to the folder first and then insert it.**

6. **If you want to move the presentation to another computer, copy the entire folder (not just the presentation) and PowerPoint will have no problems finding those linked files!**

## The fixing part

You might be saying, "Thank you for the nice folder idea, but my presentations are already created! What do I do with all those gazillion missing links in existing presentations? Surely you don't expect me to recreate each of them again!"

No, I don't expect you to recreate those links again — I suggest you download a copy of Steve Rindsberg's FixLinks Pro product from

```
www.cuttingedgeppt.com/fixlinkspro
```

FixLinks Pro isn't free, but a demo version is available. The demo version doesn't fix the links, but it does let you know which links are missing, which is more than PowerPoint will tell you.

The full version restores missing links for you and also copies linked files to the same folder as the presentation.

# The Dreaded Red X

In PowerPointland, this is the worst thing to happen to any presentation. After a presentation shows that dreaded red X in place of that nice picture (see Figure 16-1), there's no known way to get back your picture.

**Figure 16-1:**
You're lucky
if you've
never seen
this red X.

The red X is PowerPoint's way of telling you that it doesn't know what to display — and it doesn't even know why! What's more, the folks at Microsoft have found no known cure for this problem. They haven't even really found the cause because it has been impossible to replicate causing a red X! There are no explanations, but some things are known to cause the red X more than others. Here that old adage holds good — "An ounce of prevention is worth a pound of cure."

Here are some guidelines to help you stay away from the red X:

✔ **Apply the latest Service Pack for your PowerPoint version, turn off Fast Saves, and reduce the number of undo levels.** I show you how to do all this in Chapter 2.

✔ **Don't open and then save files from removable media, especially floppy diskettes, or from network drives.** In all cases, copy the presentation to a local drive first. Then work on it and save it on the local drive itself. Copy it back to a removable drive or a network location if required.

✔ **Sometimes double-clicking a red X helps.** This is always the case when you see a red X on a PowerPoint presentation sourced from a Mac version of PowerPoint that contains an embedded Word or Excel document.

✔ **Avoid using CMYK images inside PowerPoint.** I explain about RGB and HSL color spectrums in Chapter 3. CMYK is a similar color spectrum used for images intended for prepress and print usage.

✔ **Don't run too many programs when PowerPoint is running.** Lack of sufficient system resources can also cause a red X.

As you can see, plenty of things can cause the red X. With no known cure and no way to replicate the cause of a red X, it's best to take precautions.

The best precaution is probably to save a backup copy of your file often. If you can't remember to do that, get a free copy of Shyam Pillai's Sequential Save add-in for PowerPoint at

`www.cuttingedgeppt.com/seqsave`

# Corrupt Presentations

Although I hope you never end up with a corrupt presentation, things don't always happen according to our wishes. Bad things happen — good people start acting wicked, and nice presentations become corrupted. Although I have no cure for the wickedness, you can do a few things about corrupt presentations. I first show you how you could possibly recover your corrupt presentation, and later I explain what steps you can take to avoid getting your presentations corrupted.

## Treating corrupt presentations

Whatever you do, first create a backup copy of your corrupted presentation and use these techniques on the backup copy. This ensures that your original presentation is safe, even though it is corrupted!

- **Don't send your PowerPoint presentations as e-mail attachments.** Instead, archive them by using a zipping utility so that the presentation doesn't get corrupted during its online journey.

- **If you try to open a PowerPoint 2002 or 2003 presentation in an older version and PowerPoint says it's corrupt, you could have compatibility problems.** This presentation might have been password protected, and the older version just throws a fit because it doesn't know anything about password protection! Try opening the presentation in a more recent version of PowerPoint if you can.

- **Get a free copy of OpenOffice.org, a suite of programs that includes a presentation component.** This program has a PowerPoint import feature that might open presentations that PowerPoint fails to open. Go to

`www.cuttingedpeppt.com/openoffice`

- **Create a new, blank presentation and then try to insert slides from the corrupted presentation:**

*1. Create a new presentation and choose the Insert➪Slides from Files option.*

The Slide Finder dialog box, as shown in Figure 16-2, appears.

*2. Click the Browse button.*

This opens the Browse dialog box that allows you to navigate and select your corrupted presentation. Click the Open button to get back to the Slide Finder dialog box.

*3. Insert your slides.*

If no error messages are displayed, select one, multiple, or all slides in the Select Slides area and then click the Insert (or Insert All) button to insert those slides in your presentation.

If you get an error message, you cannot continue with this process.

Sometimes this allows you to recover your slides.

✔ **Try opening the file in Microsoft Word:**

*1. Open Microsoft Word and then choose File➪Open.*

The Open dialog box appears.

*2. In the Files of Type drop-down list box, select Recover Text from Any Document.*

*3. Double-click your backup copy of the corrupt presentation.*

At the very least, you could end up retrieving the text content of the presentation!

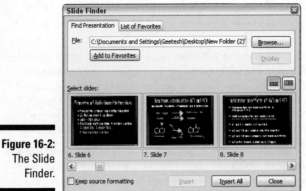

**Figure 16-2:**
The Slide
Finder.

## Precautions

Here are some precautions you should take so that your presentations don't get corrupted:

- **Set up PowerPoint in a way that minimizes corruption risks and maximizes productivity.** To do that, you'll want to turn on AutoRecover, disable Fast Saves, reduce your number of undo levels, and apply the latest Service Pack for your version of PowerPoint (and Microsoft Office).

  Chapter 2 details these techniques.

- **If you need to work with removable media, never open and save presentations directly from these media.** Instead, copy the presentation to a local drive and work on it. Save and copy the presentation back to the removable drive when you're done, if you need to. The same rule applies for network drives, too.

- **Make backups often.** In fact, you should create backups of all your presentations (and other files) at least once a week — or maybe even more often. With automated backup solutions available nowadays, you have no excuse to not backup your files.

  Shyam Pillai's Sequential Save add-in for PowerPoint saves sequential backups of your presentation as you work. Download a free copy from

  `www.cuttingedgeppt.com/seqsave`

## Sound and Video Problems

Sound and video problems aren't abundant in the land of PowerPoint. They come up rather infrequently, but always at times when you least expect them. And PowerPoint can't even help — even with all the best intentions in the world!

Why is PowerPoint so helpless? Simple: PowerPoint doesn't know how to play sound and video. Whenever it finds a multimedia file, it just passes on the control to the MCI Player. The *MCI Player* is the same archaic piece of software that's been playing sound and video files for more than a decade in Windows. In fact, it dates back to the Windows 3 era, when the norm for hard drives was 256MB and RAM standards were at a princely 4MB!

PowerPoint 2003 was the first version in a generation of PowerPoint releases to change this state of affairs. Nothing dramatic, though. This new version just passed the mantle of playing those multimedia files to the new Windows Media Player, but only if the MCI Player coughs and crackles over a particular file. To put it mildly, things on this front are not too elegant.

Solutions to this problem could fill a whole book, so I'll lead you to online resources rather than put everything in one paragraph!

Here's how you should approach sound and video problems — or rather a problem with a particular sound or video file:

✔ **Try to open the sound or video file in MCI Media Player:**

1. *Choose Start⇨Run.*

   The Run dialog box appears.

2. *Type each of the following commands:*

   ```
   mplayer
   mplay32
   mplayer32
   ```

   Depending on your version of Windows, one of these should successfully fire up the MCI Media Player shown in Figure 16-3.

3. *Within the MCI Media Player, choose File⇨Open and double-click your problem audio or video file.*

   If the file plays well in MCI Media Player, there's no reason why it shouldn't play inside PowerPoint.

✔ **Check your file's format.** The file might be in a format that PowerPoint doesn't recognize. As much as possible, use only .wav, .wma, and mp3 sound formats in PowerPoint. For video, use the .api, .mpg, and .wmv formats.

✔ **Try changing the codec of the file.** Codecs are covered in Chapter 10.

✔ **Visit this book's companion site for more information and links to sites that provide even more helpful tips:**

   www.cuttingedgeppt.com/troubleshoot

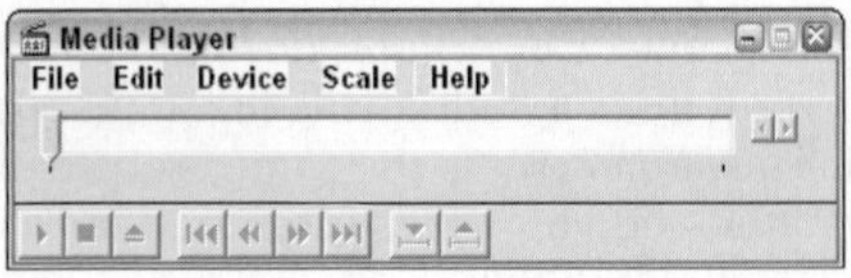

**Figure 16-3:**
The MCI
Media
Player.

# PowerPoint Problems and Solutions

The perils of PowerPoint stem ironically from the ease of use that PowerPoint provides. Microsoft made PowerPoint work so much like Word and Excel (as far as the logical interface and look were concerned) that more people than ever imagined are using PowerPoint!

To accommodate the growing number of novice users, Microsoft created PowerPoint's omnipresent AutoContent Wizard, which creates a 12-slide presentation for you in the blink of an eye — you just fill in the blanks! And that's why this book doesn't cover the AutoContent Wizard. If you use the AutoContent Wizard, you end up with a presentation that looks and feels strikingly similar in appearance and content to millions of other presentations!

And that's PowerPoint's biggest problem.

Here are some guidelines to combat this problem and help you create a truly cutting-edge presentation:

- **Start with the background.** Avoid shocking and fluorescent backgrounds. Stay away from bright photographs as backdrops. Whichever color or image you use as a background, make sure that all text and other content on the slides is readable and visible over it.

- **Color combinations are another important playing field.** Although this is too detailed a subject to discuss here, you should choose combinations that are both appealing and utilitarian. Also, use company-specific colors to further the corporate identity of your client or end user. For a subtle and sophisticated effect, try using black and white as your color combination!

- **Keep font sizes readable.** I've seen many great presentations marred by a 20-line paragraph that was never readable. Also, if you have to use a lot more text than you can afford to, make it a point to incorporate white text on a dark background, rather than the other way around. Make sure the audience does not have to squint to read!

- **Avoid long sentences.** Break your sentences into small points.

  Try different line-spacing options in your text boxes. Select Line Spacing from the Format menu and experiment with the options.

- **Avoid using ALL-UPPERCASE characters in a sentence unless it is indispensable.** Unless you're typing in a company or product name that you want to highlight, all-uppercase letters look like you're yelling.

- **Always cross-check any factual references in your presentation.** Nothing is more annoying for your audience than a blatant factual mistake.

Don't point out mistakes for which you can't offer any solutions.

- ✔ **Don't get carried away by the multitude of clip art available with PowerPoint.** Many excellent presentations have been made without using any clip art. In fact, the general professional trend nowadays is to use specific collages and subdued pictures instead of comic-style clip art.

- ✔ **Optimize your images outside PowerPoint.** Don't insert a full-screen picture into PowerPoint and then resize it to a quarter screen. Do all resizing in a specialized image editor before importing into PowerPoint.

# PowerPoint and DTP

This could be one of your worst nightmares! Your boss loved the flowchart you created so much that it has to be used in the company's annual report, and you have the privilege of exporting that flowchart to a format that can be sent straight to prepress.

First, let me congratulate you for the flowchart.

Now, as you must already be aware, there's no real way to export the graphic to a professional graphic format like EPS so that your prepress folks can use it. PowerPoint just declared a dead end — all roads ahead are closed!

All except one. You need to have Adobe Acrobat and Adobe Illustrator available on your system. Follow these steps to get the flowchart to prepress:

1. **Print the PowerPoint slide that contains your flowchart to an Acrobat PDF file using Adobe Acrobat's printer driver.**

2. **Open the PDF in Adobe Illustrator and delete everything but the flowchart.**

3. **Save (export) the flowchart as an EPS file using Illustrator's File⇨ Export or File⇨Save As option.**

# Section 508 and PowerPoint

Section 508 of the Rehabilitation Act was enacted by the U.S. Congress in 1998 so that people with disabilities could access information without barriers.

Under this Act, people with disabilities should get the same information as everyone else. That's easier said than done when it comes to PowerPoint because PowerPoint is not really designed to be very accessible. But you can still go a long way toward making your PowerPoint presentations more accessible:

✔ **Keep all the text content within PowerPoint's default text placeholders.** This means you should not use any text boxes in your presentation, just the text placeholders. All text in the default placeholders becomes part of the presentation's outline. This allows specialized screen-reading applications to access all the content from the PowerPoint presentation.

✔ **Download the Web Publishing Accessibility Wizard for Microsoft Office and read Glenna Shaw's amazing report on PowerPoint accessibility at**

```
www.cuttingedgeppt.com/accessibility
```

# PowerPoint Resources

Learning more about PowerPoint is a continuous process, and the Internet is a treasure trove of information related to this program. Here is a list of my favorite PowerPoint sites:

✔ I'll unashamedly lead you first to my own site, **Indezine,** which discusses almost every aspect of PowerPoint. There are tutorials, reviews, interviews, templates, backgrounds, add-ins, books, blogs, tips — and even a bi-weekly e-zine that gives away freebies all the time.

```
www.cuttingedgeppt.com/indezine
```

✔ Top of the heap is Microsoft MVP **Steve Rindsberg**'s celebrated PowerPoint FAQ. The site is bare of graphics, yet a mine of information. You'll find no tutorials, but when you are stuck with a problem, Steve's FAQ is the best place to go. The best way to use the FAQ is to enter your keywords into the search box at the site home page.

```
www.cuttingedgeppt.com/pptfaq
```

✔ **Microsoft's own PowerPoint home page** is definitely a must-see resource, with info on program updates and downloads. You can also order a 30-day trial CD of Microsoft Office (which includes PowerPoint) here. There are links to several tutorial pages on Microsoft's site and the PowerPoint knowledge base.

```
www.cuttingedgeppt.com/ppthome
```

✔ If you have a problem that remains unsolved, visit the **PowerPoint newsgroup archives at Google Groups.** This is your window to an almost unlimited store of info on any aspect of PowerPoint.

```
www.cuttingedgeppt.com/pptgoogle
```

✔ *Presentations* magazine discusses almost every aspect of presentations — both software- and hardware-related. Unsurprisingly, the software part is more often than not related to PowerPoint. A large part of its archives from printed issues is available online at its site.

```
www.cuttingedgeppt.com/presentations
```

✔ **Sonia Coleman,** PowerPoint MVP, runs her own site that has hundreds of free downloadable templates in addition to several detailed PowerPoint tutorials and a small PowerPoint FAQ.

```
www.cuttingedgeppt.com/sonia
```

✔ **Echo's Voice** is the site of Echo Swinford, a PowerPoint MVP whose site has detailed info on using Bézier curves, animation, masters, and color schemes in PowerPoint.

```
www.cuttingedgeppt.com/echo
```

✔ Shyam Pillai runs the **OfficeTips** site, where you can download tons of free add-ins for PowerPoint, in addition to some commercial ones. The PowerPoint section of the site also has a small FAQ section.

```
www.cuttingedgeppt.com/shyam
```

✔ You can find a wealth of PowerPoint information at **Kathy Jacobs'** site. A search facility is available onsite so you can quickly locate what you need.

```
www.cuttingedgeppt.com/kathy
```

✔ **Glen Millar**'s site has some nice tutorials on using PowerPoint's AutoShapes imaginatively — and on animation.

```
www.cuttingedgeppt.com/glen
```

# Appendix

# What's on the CD-ROM

## System Requirements

You need a working copy of Microsoft PowerPoint 2000, 2002, or 2003 on a Windows PC with a CD-ROM drive.

## Using the CD with Microsoft Windows

To install the items from the CD to your hard drive, follow these steps.

1. **Insert the CD into your computer's CD-ROM drive.**

2. **Click Start⇨Run.**

3. **In the dialog box that appears, type** D:\Start.EXE.

   Replace *D* with the proper drive letter if your CD-ROM drive uses a different letter. (If you don't know the letter, see how your CD-ROM drive is listed under My Computer.)

4. **Click OK.**

   A license agreement window appears.

5. **Read through the license agreement, nod your head, and then click the Accept button if you want to use the CD — after you click Accept, you'll never be bothered by the License Agreement window again.**

   The CD interface Welcome screen appears. The interface is a little program that shows you what's on the CD and coordinates installing the programs and running the demos. The interface basically enables you to click a button or two to make things happen.

6. **Click anywhere on the Welcome screen to enter the interface.**

   Now you are getting to the action. This next screen lists categories for the software on the CD.

7. **To view the items within a category, just click the category's name.**

   A list of programs in the category appears.

8. **For more information about a program, click the program's name.**

   Be sure to read the information that appears. Sometimes a program has it's own system requirements or requires you to do a few tricks on your computer before you can install or run the program, and this screen tells you what you might need to do, if necessary.

9. **If you don't want to install the program, click the Back button to return to the previous screen.**

   You can always return to the previous screen by clicking the Back button. This feature allows you to browse the different categories and products and decide what you want to install.

10. **To install a program, click the appropriate Install button.**

    The CD interface drops to the background while the CD installs the program you chose.

11. **To install other items, repeat Steps 7–10.**

12. **When you've finished installing programs, click the Quit button to close the interface.**

    You can eject the CD now. Carefully place it back in the plastic jacket of the book for safekeeping.

To run some of the programs on the CD, you may need to keep the disc inside your CD-ROM drive. This is a good thing. Otherwise, a very large chunk of the program would be installed to your hard drive, consuming valuable hard drive space and possibly keeping you from installing other software.

# What You'll Find on the CD

The following sections are arranged by category and provide a summary of the software and other goodies you'll find on the CD. If you need help with installing the items provided on the CD, refer back to the installation instructions in the preceding section.

*Shareware programs* are fully functional, free, trial versions of copyrighted programs. If you like particular programs, register with their authors for a nominal fee and receive licenses, enhanced versions, and technical support. *Freeware programs* are free, copyrighted games, applications, and utilities. You can copy them to as many PCs as you like — for free — but they offer no technical support. *GNU software* is governed by its own license, which is included inside the folder of the GNU software. There are no restrictions on distribution of GNU software. See the GNU license at the root of the CD for more details. *Trial, demo,* or *evaluation* versions of software are usually limited either by time or functionality (such as not letting you save a project after you create it).

## Author-created material

All the examples provided in this book are located in the Author directory on the CD. The folders contain files for Chapters 3, 5, 6, 7, 8, 11, 12 and 16, plus hundreds of backgrounds, templates, and Flash samples.

The CD-ROM also contains a bonus chapter in PDF format.

## Software

The *Cutting Edge PowerPoint For Dummies* CD-ROM contains these powerful software programs:

✔ **Neuxpower NXPowerLite**

   Compresses your presentation files as much as 90 percent.

   `www.Neuxpower.com`

✔ **SmartDraw 7**

   A terrific tool for creating tables and charts.

   `www.smartdraw.com`

✔ **TechSmith Camtasia**

   Commercial product records your presentation to video.

   `www.techsmith.com`

✔ **PowerCONVERTER Lite**

   Commercial product from Crystal Graphics converts your presentation to Flash.

   `www.crystalgraphics.com/powerpoint/powerconverter.main.lite.asp`

✔ **PCFMedia**

   Trial product from Austin Myers inserts multimedia into your presentations.

✔ **AutoShape Magic**

   A free add-in from the author to control and adjust shapes and gradients.

✔ **Xara 3D 3**

Trial version of this robust software for creating and editing 3D graphics

www.xara.com

✔ **Xcelsius**

Demonstration version of the tool that blends Excel spreadsheets into your presentations.

www.infommersion.com

# Media

The *Cutting Edge PowerPoint For Dummies* CD-ROM contains these third-party resources to improve your presentations:

✔ **Liquid Cabaret Music Samples**

Free music samples for your presentations from the royalty-free Liquid Cabaret music library.

www.liquidcabaret.com

✔ **ShutterStock**

Free still image samples for your presentations from the royalty-free ShutterStock library.

www.shutterstock.com

✔ **PowerFinish Templates**

Free background and document templates from the PowerFinish library of designs.

www.powerfinish.com

✔ **Style Workshop Sampler**

Sample of "Drag'n'Drop Ready" graphics from the Indigo Rose's Style Workshop.

www.styleworkshop.com

✔ **Cartoons from Ron Leishman**

Samples from Toon-A-Day to brighten up your presentations and your day.

www.toonaday.com

✔ **Movieclip.biz Video Clips**

A powerful sample of the broad range of Movieclip video for your presentations.

www.movieclip.biz

# *Troubleshooting*

I tried my best to compile programs that work on most computers with the minimum system requirements. Alas, your computer may differ, and some programs may not work properly for some reason.

The two likeliest problems are that you don't have enough memory (RAM) for the programs you want to use, or you have other programs running that are affecting installation or running of a program. If you get an error message such as Not enough memory or Setup cannot continue, try one or more of the following suggestions and then try using the software again:

- ✔ **Turn off any antivirus software running on your computer.** Installation programs sometimes mimic virus activity and may make your computer incorrectly believe that it's being infected by a virus.

- ✔ **Close all running programs.** The more programs you have running, the less memory is available to other programs. Installation programs typically update files and programs; so if you keep other programs running, installation may not work properly.

- ✔ **Have your local computer store add more RAM to your computer.** This is, admittedly, a drastic and somewhat expensive step. Howeveradding more memory can really help the speed of your computer and allow more programs to run at the same time. This may include closing the CD interface and running a product's installation program from Windows Explorer.

If you still have trouble with the CD, please call the Customer Care phone number: (800) 762-2974. Outside the United States, call 1 (317) 572-3994. You can also contact Customer Service by e-mail at techsupdum@wiley.com. Wiley Publishing Inc. will provide technical support only for installation and other general quality control items; for technical support on the applications themselves, consult the program's vendor or author.

# Index

### • B •

# Notes

# Notes

# NESS, CAREERS & PERSONAL FINANCE

0-7645-5307-0        0-7645-5331-3 *†

**Also available:**
- Accounting For Dummies †
  0-7645-5314-3
- Business Plans Kit For Dummies †
  0-7645-5365-8
- Cover Letters For Dummies
  0-7645-5224-4
- Frugal Living For Dummies
  0-7645-5403-4
- Leadership For Dummies
  0-7645-5176-0
- Managing For Dummies
  0-7645-1771-6

- Marketing For Dummies
  0-7645-5600-2
- Personal Finance For Dummies *
  0-7645-2590-5
- Project Management For Dummies
  0-7645-5283-X
- Resumes For Dummies †
  0-7645-5471-9
- Selling For Dummies
  0-7645-5363-1
- Small Business Kit For Dummies *†
  0-7645-5093-4

# ME & BUSINESS COMPUTER BASICS

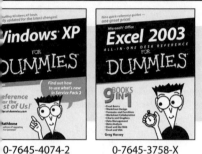

0-7645-4074-2        0-7645-3758-X

**Also available:**
- ACT! 6 For Dummies
  0-7645-2645-6
- iLife '04 All-in-One Desk Reference
  For Dummies
  0-7645-7347-0
- iPAQ For Dummies
  0-7645-6769-1
- Mac OS X Panther Timesaving
  Techniques For Dummies
  0-7645-5812-9
- Macs For Dummies
  0-7645-5656-8

- Microsoft Money 2004 For Dummies
  0-7645-4195-1
- Office 2003 All-in-One Desk Reference
  For Dummies
  0-7645-3883-7
- Outlook 2003 For Dummies
  0-7645-3759-8
- PCs For Dummies
  0-7645-4074-2
- TiVo For Dummies
  0-7645-6923-6
- Upgrading and Fixing PCs For Dummies
  0-7645-1665-5
- Windows XP Timesaving Techniques
  For Dummies
  0-7645-3748-2

# D, HOME, GARDEN, HOBBIES, MUSIC & PETS

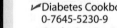

0-7645-5295-3        0-7645-5232-5

**Also available:**
- Bass Guitar For Dummies
  0-7645-2487-9
- Diabetes Cookbook For Dummies
  0-7645-5230-9
- Gardening For Dummies *
  0-7645-5130-2
- Guitar For Dummies
  0-7645-5106-X
- Holiday Decorating For Dummies
  0-7645-2570-0
- Home Improvement All-in-One
  For Dummies
  0-7645-5680-0

- Knitting For Dummies
  0-7645-5395-X
- Piano For Dummies
  0-7645-5105-1
- Puppies For Dummies
  0-7645-5255-4
- Scrapbooking For Dummies
  0-7645-7208-3
- Senior Dogs For Dummies
  0-7645-5818-8
- Singing For Dummies
  0-7645-2475-5
- 30-Minute Meals For Dummies
  0-7645-2589-1

# ERNET & DIGITAL MEDIA

0-7645-1664-7        0-7645-6924-4

**Also available:**
- 2005 Online Shopping Directory
  For Dummies
  0-7645-7495-7
- CD & DVD Recording For Dummies
  0-7645-5956-7
- eBay For Dummies
  0-7645-5654-1
- Fighting Spam For Dummies
  0-7645-5965-6
- Genealogy Online For Dummies
  0-7645-5964-8
- Google For Dummies
  0-7645-4420-9

- Home Recording For Musicians
  For Dummies
  0-7645-1634-5
- The Internet For Dummies
  0-7645-4173-0
- iPod & iTunes For Dummies
  0-7645-7772-7
- Preventing Identity Theft For Dummies
  0-7645-7336-5
- Pro Tools All-in-One Desk Reference
  For Dummies
  0-7645-5714-9
- Roxio Easy Media Creator For Dummies
  0-7645-7131-1

rate Canadian edition also available
rate U.K. edition also available

le wherever books are sold. For more information or to order direct: U.S. customers visit www.dummies.com or call 1-877-762-2974.
stomers visit www.wileyeurope.com or call 0800 243407. Canadian customers visit www.wiley.ca or call 1-800-567-4797.

 **WILEY**

## SPORTS, FITNESS, PARENTING, RELIGION & SPIRITUALITY

0-7645-5146-9

0-7645-5418-2

**Also available:**
- Adoption For Dummies
  0-7645-5488-3
- Basketball For Dummies
  0-7645-5248-1
- The Bible For Dummies
  0-7645-5296-1
- Buddhism For Dummies
  0-7645-5359-3
- Catholicism For Dummies
  0-7645-5391-7
- Hockey For Dummies
  0-7645-5228-7

- Judaism For Dummies
  0-7645-5299-6
- Martial Arts For Dummies
  0-7645-5358-5
- Pilates For Dummies
  0-7645-5397-6
- Religion For Dummies
  0-7645-5264-3
- Teaching Kids to Read For Dummi
  0-7645-4043-2
- Weight Training For Dummies
  0-7645-5168-X
- Yoga For Dummies
  0-7645-5117-5

## TRAVEL

0-7645-5438-7

0-7645-5453-0

**Also available:**
- Alaska For Dummies
  0-7645-1761-9
- Arizona For Dummies
  0-7645-6938-4
- Cancún and the Yucatán For Dummies
  0-7645-2437-2
- Cruise Vacations For Dummies
  0-7645-6941-4
- Europe For Dummies
  0-7645-5456-5
- Ireland For Dummies
  0-7645-5455-7

- Las Vegas For Dummies
  0-7645-5448-4
- London For Dummies
  0-7645-4277-X
- New York City For Dummies
  0-7645-6945-7
- Paris For Dummies
  0-7645-5494-8
- RV Vacations For Dummies
  0-7645-5443-3
- Walt Disney World & Orlando For Dum
  0-7645-6943-0

## GRAPHICS, DESIGN & WEB DEVELOPMENT

0-7645-4345-8

0-7645-5589-8

**Also available:**
- Adobe Acrobat 6 PDF For Dummies
  0-7645-3760-1
- Building a Web Site For Dummies
  0-7645-7144-3
- Dreamweaver MX 2004 For Dummies
  0-7645-4342-3
- FrontPage 2003 For Dummies
  0-7645-3882-9
- HTML 4 For Dummies
  0-7645-1995-6
- Illustrator CS For Dummies
  0-7645-4084-X

- Macromedia Flash MX 2004 For Dum
  0-7645-4358-X
- Photoshop 7 All-in-One Desk
  Reference For Dummies
  0-7645-1667-1
- Photoshop CS Timesaving Techniq
  For Dummies
  0-7645-6782-9
- PHP 5 For Dummies
  0-7645-4166-8
- PowerPoint 2003 For Dummies
  0-7645-3908-6
- QuarkXPress 6 For Dummies
  0-7645-2593-X

## NETWORKING, SECURITY, PROGRAMMING & DATABASES

0-7645-6852-3

0-7645-5784-X

**Also available:**
- A+ Certification For Dummies
  0-7645-4187-0
- Access 2003 All-in-One Desk
  Reference For Dummies
  0-7645-3988-4
- Beginning Programming For Dummies
  0-7645-4997-9
- C For Dummies
  0-7645-7068-4
- Firewalls For Dummies
  0-7645-4048-3
- Home Networking For Dummies
  0-7645-42796

- Network Security For Dummies
  0-7645-1679-5
- Networking For Dummies
  0-7645-1677-9
- TCP/IP For Dummies
  0-7645-1760-0
- VBA For Dummies
  0-7645-3989-2
- Wireless All In-One Desk Reference
  For Dummies
  0-7645-7496-5
- Wireless Home Networking For Dum
  0-7645-3910-8

# HEALTH & SELF-HELP

0-7645-6820-5 *†

0-7645-2566-2

**Also available:**
- Alzheimer's For Dummies
  0-7645-3899-3
- Asthma For Dummies
  0-7645-4233-8
- Controlling Cholesterol For Dummies
  0-7645-5440-9
- Depression For Dummies
  0-7645-3900-0
- Dieting For Dummies
  0-7645-4149-8
- Fertility For Dummies
  0-7645-2549-2
- Fibromyalgia For Dummies
  0-7645-5441-7
- Improving Your Memory For Dummies
  0-7645-5435-2
- Pregnancy For Dummies †
  0-7645-4483-7
- Quitting Smoking For Dummies
  0-7645-2629-4
- Relationships For Dummies
  0-7645-5384-4
- Thyroid For Dummies
  0-7645-5385-2

# EDUCATION, HISTORY, REFERENCE & TEST PREPARATION

0-7645-5194-9

0-7645-4186-2

**Also available:**
- Algebra For Dummies
  0-7645-5325-9
- British History For Dummies
  0-7645-7021-8
- Calculus For Dummies
  0-7645-2498-4
- English Grammar For Dummies
  0-7645-5322-4
- Forensics For Dummies
  0-7645-5580-4
- The GMAT For Dummies
  0-7645-5251-1
- Inglés Para Dummies
  0-7645-5427-1
- Italian For Dummies
  0-7645-5196-5
- Latin For Dummies
  0-7645-5431-X
- Lewis & Clark For Dummies
  0-7645-2545-X
- Research Papers For Dummies
  0-7645-5426-3
- The SAT I For Dummies
  0-7645-7193-1
- Science Fair Projects For Dummies
  0-7645-5460-3
- U.S. History For Dummies
  0-7645-5249-X

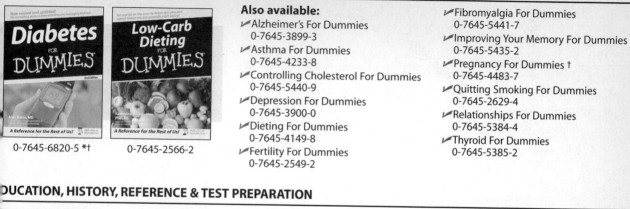

# Get smart @ dummies.com®

- **Find a full list of Dummies titles**
- **Look into loads of FREE on-site articles**
- **Sign up for FREE eTips e-mailed to you weekly**
- **See what other products carry the Dummies name**
- **Shop directly from the Dummies bookstore**
- **Enter to win new prizes every month!**

† Separate Canadian edition also available
‡ Separate U.K. edition also available

Available wherever books are sold. For more information or to order direct: U.S. customers visit www.dummies.com or call 1-877-762-2974.
U.K. customers visit www.wileyeurope.com or call 0800 243407. Canadian customers visit www.wiley.ca or call 1-800-567-4797.

# Wiley Publishing, Inc.
# End-User License Agreement

## 5. Limited Warranty.

**(a)** WPI warrants that the Software and Software Media are free from defects in materials and workmanship under normal use for a period of sixty (60) days from the date of purchase of this Book. If WPI receives notification within the warranty period of defects in materials or workmanship, WPI will replace the defective Software Media.

**(b)** WPI AND THE AUTHOR OF THE BOOK DISCLAIM ALL OTHER WARRANTIES, EXPRESS OR IMPLIED, INCLUDING WITHOUT LIMITATION IMPLIED WARRANTIES OF MERCHANTABIL-ITY AND FITNESS FOR A PARTICULAR PURPOSE, WITH RESPECT TO THE SOFTWARE, THE PROGRAMS, THE SOURCE CODE CONTAINED THEREIN, AND/OR THE TECHNIQUES DESCRIBED IN THIS BOOK. WPI DOES NOT WARRANT THAT THE FUNCTIONS CON-TAINED IN THE SOFTWARE WILL MEET YOUR REQUIREMENTS OR THAT THE OPERATION OF THE SOFTWARE WILL BE ERROR FREE.

**(c)** This limited warranty gives you specific legal rights, and you may have other rights that vary from jurisdiction to jurisdiction.

## 6. Remedies.

**(a)** WPI's entire liability and your exclusive remedy for defects in materials and workman-ship shall be limited to replacement of the Software Media, which may be returned to WPI with a copy of your receipt at the following address: Software Media Fulfillment Department, Attn.: *Cutting Edge PowerPoint Presentations For Dummies,* Wiley Publishing, Inc., 10475 Crosspoint Blvd., Indianapolis, IN 46256, or call 1-800-762-2974. Please allow four to six weeks for delivery. This Limited Warranty is void if failure of the Software Media has resulted from accident, abuse, or misapplication. Any replacement Software Media will be warranted for the remainder of the original warranty period or thirty (30) days, whichever is longer.

**(b)** In no event shall WPI or the author be liable for any damages whatsoever (including without limitation damages for loss of business profits, business interruption, loss of business information, or any other pecuniary loss) arising from the use of or inability to use the Book or the Software, even if WPI has been advised of the possibility of such damages.

**(c)** Because some jurisdictions do not allow the exclusion or limitation of liability for conse-quential or incidental damages, the above limitation or exclusion may not apply to you.

## 7. U.S. Government Restricted Rights. Use, duplication, or disclosure of the Software for or on behalf of the United States of America, its agencies and/or instrumentalities "U.S. Government" is subject to restrictions as stated in paragraph (c)(1)(ii) of the Rights in Technical Data and Computer Software clause of DFARS 252.227-7013, or subparagraphs (c) (1) and (2) of the Commercial Computer Software-Restricted Rights clause at FAR 52.227-19, and in similar clauses in the NASA FAR supplement, as applicable.

## 8. General. This Agreement constitutes the entire understanding of the parties and revokes and supersedes all prior agreements, oral or written, between them and may not be modified or amended except in a writing signed by both parties hereto that specifically refers to this Agreement. This Agreement shall take precedence over any other documents that may be in conflict herewith. If any one or more provisions contained in this Agreement are held by any court or tribunal to be invalid, illegal, or otherwise unenforceable, each and every other pro-vision shall remain in full force and effect.